The Handbook of Risk Management

For other titles in the Wiley Finance series
please see www.wiley.com/finance

The Handbook of Risk Management

Implementing a Post-Crisis Corporate Culture

Philippe Carrel

WILEY

A John Wiley and Sons, Ltd., Publication

This edition first published 2010
© 2010 John Wiley & Sons, Ltd

Registered office
John Wiley & Sons Ltd, The Atrium, Southern Gate, Chichester, West Sussex, PO19 8SQ, United Kingdom

For details of our global editorial offices, for customer services and for information about how to apply for permission to reuse the copyright material in this book please see our website at www.wiley.com.

The right of the author to be identified as the author of this work has been asserted in accordance with the Copyright, Designs and Patents Act 1988.

All rights reserved. No part of this publication may be reproduced, stored in a retrieval system, or transmitted, in any form or by any means, electronic, mechanical, photocopying, recording or otherwise, except as permitted by the UK Copyright, Designs and Patents Act 1988, without the prior permission of the publisher.

Wiley also publishes its books in a variety of electronic formats. Some content that appears in print may not be available in electronic books.

Designations used by companies to distinguish their products are often claimed as trademarks. All brand names and product names used in this book are trade names, service marks, trademarks or registered trademarks of their respective owners. The publisher is not associated with any product or vendor mentioned in this book. This publication is designed to provide accurate and authoritative information in regard to the subject matter covered. It is sold on the understanding that the publisher is not engaged in rendering professional services. If professional advice or other expert assistance is required, the services of a competent professional should be sought.

Library of Congress Cataloging-in-Publication Data

Carrel, Philippe.
　The handbook of risk management : implementing a post crisis corporate culture / Philippe Carrel.
　　p. cm.
　ISBN 978-0-470-68175-6
1. Risk management.　2. Corporate culture.　I. Title.
　HD61.C367 2010
　658.15′5–dc22   2009054371

A catalogue record for this book is available from the British Library.

ISBN 978-0-470-68175-6

Typeset in 11/13pt Times by Aptara Inc., New Delhi, India
Printed in Great Britain by TJ International Ltd, Padstow, Cornwall, UK

To Maurice

Contents

Preface xv

Acknowledgements xix

1 Introduction: Risk is People's Business 1
  1.1 The Essence of Capitalism 1
  1.2 The Move to Models; when Risk Ceased to be Managed 3
  1.3 The Decade of Risk Management 6
  1.4 Risk Intelligence Precedes Risk Management 9
  1.5 Risk Management and the Human Dimension of Capitalism 10
    1.5.1 Risk scales and balances 10
    1.5.2 A risk culture is corporate DNA 11

PART 1 DISTRIBUTING RISK EXPOSURE AND SENSITIVITY ACROSS THE ENTERPRISE 13

2 Identifying Risk Factors 17
  2.1 Specific Risk Factors 17
    2.1.1 The search for risk factors 18
    2.1.2 Root-risk factors 20
    2.1.3 Identifying valuation risk 24
    2.1.4 Identifying liquidity risk 26

2.2	Systematic Risk Factors	27
	2.2.1 Portfolios of external risks	28
	2.2.2 Systematic risk and factors correlation	29

3 Working with Risk Factors — 33
- 3.1 Approaching Risk Through Sensitivity and Scenarios — 34
- 3.2 Root-Risk Factors and Conduits of Sensitivity — 35
- 3.3 Back-Testing and Maintaining the Factors — 37

4 Working with Scenarios — 41
- 4.1 Scenario Definition — 43
- 4.2 High-Severity and Worst Case Scenarios — 43
- 4.3 Aggregating Firm-wide Risk Sensitivity — 45
- 4.4 Aggregating Scenarios — 47

5 From Aggregated Risks to Distributed Risks — 51
- 5.1 The Traditional Approach to Risk Management has Led to the Modelling of Exposure by Business Lines — 51
- 5.2 Distributing Risk by Risk Factors Leads to Creation of a Culture — 53
- 5.3 Distributed Risk Implies Data Analysis — 54

6 Creating an Adaptive Information Workflow — 57
- 6.1 Getting the System to Evolve — 59
- 6.2 Moving on to the Next Step — 61

PART 2 EMPOWERING BUSINESS AND RISK UNITS WITH RISK MANAGEMENT CAPABILITIES — 65

7 Allocating Risk Management Capabilities — 67
- 7.1 Business Managers are Risk Managers — 68
- 7.2 The Role of Executive Risk Committees — 71
- 7.3 The Role of Audit and Control Units — 73

8 Mitigation Strategies and Hedging Tactics — 75
- 8.1 Front-line Business Units — 75
- 8.2 Operational Units — 77
- 8.3 Management — 78
- 8.4 Risk Committees and Audit Controls — 80

9	**Risk Independence or Indifference to Risk?**	**83**
	9.1 Role of the Shareholders and Nonexecutive Directors	83
	9.2 Responsibility and Accountability	84
	9.3 Control and Report Hierarchy	85
10	**Risk-Weighted Performance**	**89**
	10.1 Principles of Risk-weighted Measurements	90
	10.1.1 Mark to time-weighted volatility	91
	10.1.2 Business resilience and countercyclical approaches	93
PART 3	**CREATING AN INFORMATION WORKFLOW FOR CONTINUOUS FEEDBACK AND PREVENTIVE DECISION MAKING**	**95**
11	**From Risk Appetite to Risk Policies**	**99**
	11.1 Risk: The New Bond	99
	11.2 Dynamic Two-way Information Workflow	100
	11.3 Preventive Rules for a Pre-Emptive Course of Action	101
	11.4 The Dynamic Assessments of Risk Factor Sensitivities	102
	11.4.1 Risk factor appropriateness tests	103
	11.5 Sensitivity Rules and Stress Tests	104
	11.5.1 Triggers	105
	11.5.2 Dynamic, swappable mitigation tactics	106
12	**Bottom-Up Activity Feedback**	**109**
	12.1 Keeping a Finger on the Pulse	109
	12.1.1 Continuous efficiency monitoring	110
	12.1.2 Test and result certification	110
	12.2 Aggregating Scenarios: The Actual Risk Appetite of the Firm	111
	12.3 Towards a Risk Information Bus for IT Purposes	112
13	**Enterprise-Wide Aggregation**	**115**
	13.1 Cross-asset Sensitivity Aggregation	115
	13.2 Cross-division Aggregation Potential Pitfalls	117

		13.2.1	Cross-market effects and correlations	118
		13.2.2	Of correlation and liquidity	118
		13.2.3	Model and valuation risks	119
		13.2.4	Technology risks	122

14 Top-Down Decisions and Feedback — 123
 14.1 Risk Dashboards — 123
 14.2 Pre-emptive Decision Frameworks — 124
 14.3 An Interactive and Adaptive Workflow — 126
 14.4 Hierarchy, Decisions, Overruling — 127

15 Deriving a Firm's Actual Observed Risk Appetite — 131
 15.1 Modelling Worst Case Scenarios — 132
  15.1.1 Aggregating figures — 133
  15.1.2 Aggregating qualitative assessments — 134
 15.2 Risk Policies Reconciliation — 135
  15.2.1 Quantitative: risk factors, sensitivity, scenarios — 136
  15.2.2 Qualitative: implied assumptions, distributions, correlations, market evolutions, back-testing — 138
  15.2.3 Solvency and liquidity management — 139
  15.2.4 Systematic risks — 141
  15.2.5 Regulatory risks — 144

PART 4 ALIGNING FUNDING STRATEGIES AND LIQUIDITY MANAGEMENT TACTICS WITH CORPORATE RISK POLICIES — 147

16 Liquidity, the Ultimate Operational Risk — 149
 16.1 Maintaining the Internal Balance — 149
 16.2 Internal Sources of Liquidity Risks — 150
 16.3 External Sources of Liquidity Risk — 152

17 Analysing and Measuring Liquidity Risks — 155
 17.1 Valuation-driven Liquidity Risks — 155
 17.2 Market Depth — 156
 17.3 Over-the-counter Markets — 157

18	**Funding Risk**		**159**
	18.1 Asset Liability Risks		159
	18.2 Systematic Sources of Liquidity Risks		160
	18.3 Concentration Risks		161
		18.3.1 Dynamic concentrations	163
		18.3.2 Concentration risk measurements	165
		18.3.3 Counterparty interdependence	166
		18.3.4 Regulatory-driven liquidity risk	167
19	**Managing and Mitigating Liquidity Risks**		**169**
	19.1 Laying Down the Foundations of a Corporate Strategy		170
		19.1.1 Chosen risk factors and appetite for risk	170
	19.2 Monitoring Concentrations		172
	19.3 Working with Risk Concentrations		172
		19.3.1 Reconciliations or risk concentrations and risk policies	173
		19.3.2 Managing concentrations	174
	19.4 ALM Analyses and Liquidity Management		175
		19.4.1 Margin and business risk analysis	176
		19.4.2 Sensitivity of duration gaps	178
		19.4.3 Convexity gaps	179
	19.5 Valuation Risks		181
		19.5.1 Market depth	182
		19.5.2 Counterparty-related liquidity risks	183
		19.5.3 Corporate governance	184
	19.6 Regulatory Risk		184
	19.7 Of Liquidity Risk and Correlation		186
	19.8 Funding Strategy is a Risk Profile		190
PART 5	**EXTERNAL COMMUNICATIONS, DISCLOSURE POLICIES AND TRANSPARENCY**		**193**
20	**External Communications**		**197**
	20.1 Risk, the New Media		198
	20.2 Disclosure Policies		199
		20.2.1 Communications directed at regulators and industry representatives	199

	20.2.2	Communications directed at shareholders and funding partners	207
	20.2.3	Communications directed at the public	210
	20.2.4	Public relations and disclosure policies	212

21 Enhancing Transparency — 215
21.1 Prices and Valuations Transparency — 215
21.2 Transparency of Internal Processes and Procedures — 218
21.3 Transparency of Corporate Governance Rules and External Communications — 221

22 Information Exchange for Risk Intelligence — 223
22.1 Proposal for a Global Credit and Collateral Exposure Surveillance Scheme — 223
22.2 Proposal for a Taxonomy of Path-dependent Derivatives and Retail Structured Products — 225
22.3 Risk Intelligence Ratings — 227
    22.3.1 Valuation risk ratings — 228
    22.3.2 Risk-based pricing frequency — 228

PART 6 THE REGULATORY UPHEAVAL OF THE 2010s — 231

23 The Great Unwind — 233
23.1 Regulatory Reshuffle — 233
    23.1.1 How risks have evolved — 234
    23.1.2 From risk regulation to regulatory risks — 237

24 Propositions for a Regulatory Upheaval — 243
24.1 Propositions Relating to Idiosyncratic Risks — 244
    24.1.1 Risk concentration benchmarks — 245
    24.1.2 Departure from the generalized assumption of normality — 246
    24.1.3 Benchmarks of risk exposure and liquidity concentrations — 247
24.2 Propositions Relating to Systematic Risks — 250
    24.2.1 Required Disclosure of Term Structures of Assets and Liabilities in Foreign Currencies — 251

	24.2.2	Dynamic capital adequacy requirements	251
	24.2.3	Preserving diversity	254
24.3	Propositions Relating to Systemic Risks		255
	24.3.1	Establish controls for cross-industry transactions and exposure netting	256
	24.3.2	Simulations involving multiple sectors and regulators	257

Index   **259**

Preface

A journey has begun that leads towards a new economic model where controls of risks rebalance the excesses of the continuous quest for growth and capital efficiency.

During twenty years of economic growth separating the fall of the Berlin wall and the failure of Lehman Brothers, the world has created unprecedented wealth while adding some 3 billion consumers to its economic map. Yet the structures of the financial industry and especially the core values driving its endeavours did not change as deeply. Existing models were merely scaled up and replicated, capital efficiency remained a sole value of corporate culture. Globalization is associated with standardization and uniformity as all regulators abide by the principle of convergence.

The awaking was brutal when the interbank money market ground to a complete standstill in late 2008, which caused national monetary authorities around the world to massively intervene, or seek the assistance of the International Monetary Fund. At that point, everyone would finally recognize that the system was dysfunctional, yet so many warning signals since 2006 had been ignored or dismissed. There is abundant literature on what went wrong, the paths that led to the crisis and the lessons that can be learnt. However, a model mismatch is much deeper a problem than a crisis.

A new model is naturally necessary, which will rebalance the search for capital efficiency with the management of the risk appetite individually expressed by each company's shareholders and funding entities. Diversity, as opposed to convergence, will finally reappear as the way for the finance industry to function again as an ecosystem, a critical condition for enabling an economy of a 6.5 billion population to function.

A handful of global banks featuring standardized balance sheets and capital ratios computed on market-based data are bound to fail at one point when the pressure of repetitive tail events – the severity of which is directly linked to the concentrations of wealth they themselves create during boom times – will grow too high. Their scalability is not unlimited. The lack of diversity in strategies and purposes creates inevitable concentrations that favour the formation and inflation of asset bubbles.

The diversity of risks is unlimited and exponentially multiplied by an unlimited diversity of ways in which those risks might impact and combine. Similar risk exposure does not necessarily translate into identical sensitivity, depending on which firm or system it impacts. The companies' specifics, their traditional funding sources, their privileged customer base, the nature of their assets, their history – in one word their culture – determines the way they should adapt to risks. Each one needs to be able to manage their own balance of value creation versus risk generation, in the context of the ecosystems they operate within. How could Asian banks, for example, financing local industrial developments develop an approach to credit ratings similar to giant retail operations in the UK, mortgage specialists in the US or investment banks of Wall Street? Even if it were at all sensible to do so, the external conditions of credit, liquidity supply, currency volatility and unknown factors that direct the way sensitivity materializes make the approach totally irrelevant.

There is room for regulations imposing guidelines and core principles, but at a higher level, with respect to the spirit in which risk mitigation should be carried out by each individual corporation, within the one or multiple ecosystems they belong to. The recent trend, which consisted of centrally modelling a profile for the entire industry by rigid definitions of business lines, risk classes and uniform methodologies, achieved the opposite of what it aimed for. It impeded firms to adapt to their environment, thus increasing their idiosyncratic risks. This is assuming that tail risks were only idiosyncratic in nature-enhanced systematic risks. The rigidity and complexities of entangled regulatory rules led systematic risks to externalize into systemic risk.

Regulators should not be required to say what should be done or how much is good enough. Even it were at all possible, it could only be achieved in the context of what is known at a given point in time, and thus, by definition, is unsuited to future developments. Instilling a culture for each and everyone to learn how to live with their own risks, adapt to the changing nature of risks and how to align them with their shareholders' and customers' expectations would be far more beneficial and adaptive.

Since the Glass–Steagall Act was repealed in 1999, many bridges were thrown between the worlds of securities and banking. Financial institutions were able to seek performance through inorganic and horizontal expansion, with the aim to become 'universal', grow value and conquer markets. Simultaneously, the demographics of consumers and savers, investors and funds deeply changed their needs and their behaviour. The quest for financial returns may be unchanged but the factors of risks willingly or unwillingly embarked through alternative investment strategies are entirely new to most. As a result, opaque levels of unwanted risks were transferred across continents, industries and indirectly allocated to investors supposedly averse to those types of risks. How could holders of European pension funds end up indirectly exposed to the US subprime real estate market through funds of funds, for example? A combination of uniform strategies and regulatory limitations incentivized the moves. Firms believed they needed what they thought was a 'low hanging fruit', while regulations compelled them to operate through securities.

Just like banks, all collective investment schemes, asset managers, private wealth management companies and hedge funds need a universal tool to adjust their risk exposure to the appetite of their clients, shareholders and whoever finances their operations. They need risk intelligence.

A financial ecosystem is not necessarily a sector in a country or a region. It is defined by risk profiles, factors of exposure and a community of partners and counterparties. Each financial ecosystem needs to re-learn how to independently adapt to the unpredictability of risk events in distribution and magnitude. Just as firms need to build some 'corporate DNA' whereby their anticipation of risks and sensitivity mitigation rules have become genetic information, so the financial ecosystem communities will also individually need to develop their own code of adaptation based on risk intelligence. This requires a whole culture of communications and transparency, an unlimited body of knowledge to be built, maintained and understood.

Supranational regulators and industry representatives are needed to foster the necessary culture to create an overall understanding of risk and adapt to it. The boundaries would be no longer ratios but ethics. Requirements would not be limited to some regulatory language but extended to multilateral dialogues for the authorities to assess idiosyncratic risks and compliance while creating risk intelligence to the benefit of the entire industry. The methods would not be limited to 'carrot and stick' but become productive exchanges of information. The rules of engagement and disclosure policies would be adaptive to the overall levels of risk and volatility faced by the system at different times.

This handbook proposes a methodology derived from countless discussions around the world with banks, asset management companies of all sizes, fund managers, regulators, central banks and governments that I have been given to meet through my assignments with Thomson Reuters. In the aftermaths of the 2007–2009 crisis, each of them faces new challenges and develops new ways to rebalance the creation of shareholder or commercial value with the generation of risk exposure. It is also based on a research of only the most recent approaches from scholars and thought leaders, in an effort to picture the looming aspects of post-crisis risk management.

This handbook gathers the spirit of their endeavours, as a set of key principles aiming to inspire the readers and their firms to start codifying their own culture as elements of corporate DNA embedding the core values of risk management.

Acknowledgements

I would like to extend special thanks to Lim (Asta) Yann Shinq, without whom this project would have remained a project, and to Thomson Reuters for providing me with the necessary exposure and trust to complete it as well as technical and data support.

1
Introduction: Risk is People's Business

1.1 THE ESSENCE OF CAPITALISM

Risk is the essence of free enterprise in liberal economies. The very act of incorporating a firm is an expression of risk appetite by which a number of partners will be holding liabilities to produce value and profit and meet a development objective. Meeting the revenue and profit objectives within the boundaries of the risk appetite is the mission of the executive management team. The Chief Executive Officer is the guardian of that bond between the shareholders and the board of executive directors.

The assets and human resources involved must therefore be utilized to maintain this balance between generating value and controlling risks. As such, one may argue that the discipline of managing risk has always existed. Since the 18th century's Industrial Revolution, firms have invested, created value, survived crisis, adapted to changing technology, competed against each other and weathered many crises and wars. Or have they? Few firms actually last more than 50 years. A minority may last more than 100 years. Others, on the other hand, will most likely cease to have a purpose as their shareholders lose their appetite for risk or operate in unsustainable conditions; some others might fail. In any case, these firms somehow lose the balance between generating value in reward for labour and capital and the risks involved. The very few that survive, expand and thrive usually evolve at a staggering pace, through organic and inorganic growth, continuously adapting and innovating from core business to new market niche, often transfiguring in each decade.

The transformation leading to survival is a demonstration of balance between risk and value management. Seldom a smooth transition, the history of corporations is fraught with crises, failures and restarts. More often than not, change is a painful implementation. It is the evolution of risks, the unexpected ones in particular, that seems to be pushing the boundaries of innovation by changing the conditions for survival.

Corporations and governments are forced to adapt as they face unstable and unsustainable situations – namely crises. Therefore they are periodically compelled to find new balances between risk and value generation, going from crisis to crisis. In other words, no approach to risk management, despite a brilliantly designed one, can be set in stone and dogmatically dictated to future generations of managers. Risk management is a continuous search of equilibrium, just as the balancing pole of a tightrope walker is always in movement. Managing risks requires bringing into question the very hypothesis it relies on, time and again.

In the finance industry, risk management is of even greater importance since the core business is about managing others' money – others being the depositors of a bank, the investors of a fund or clients of an asset management service. It is also about managing others' risks – corporates, retail customers or funds that operate on margin. So there is a double balance between value and risk generation to be maintained when operating in the finance industry – the balance of any corporation between risks and the value extracted from growth and operations and the balance between customers' risks and customers' support.

As the link that holds all business sectors, households, corporations, governments and institutions together, the finance sector plays a central role in every economy. Since the late 1960s, no business, administration or institution would run any operation by funding any part of its activities in cash. Hence the finance industry plays a far more critical role, akin to a heart pumping blood throughout an economy. The modern theories of efficiency in management have led absolutely every agent of a modern economy to operate 'on margin'. Banks lend to corporates to invest, corporates in turn lend to each other to produce, whereas customers and retailers use credit for all they consume. Credit and financial activity is absolutely everywhere, in everything we touch, drive, produce and consume. Since the late 1980s, the fall of the Berlin Wall and the emergence of new economies, the model has become global. As a result, one can say that the whole world economy runs 'on margin', as a gigantic hedge fund. Therefore the balance of risks and value generation is even more crucially necessary for the finance industry. Losing it immediately impacts on other parts of the economy as any imbalance spills over its externalities to other sectors.

1.2 THE MOVE TO MODELS; WHEN RISK CEASED TO BE MANAGED

The above reasoning leads to an obvious conclusion that risks somehow existed ever since the very notion of investing for generating some kind of return was born. One can therefore state that from the agriculture of the Romans to the Industrial Revolution, the techniques of financial risk management have slowly evolved and inherited their progress from the growing sophistication of financial instruments, starting with the currencies of the kings and letters of credit they would issue, where the very first forms of securitization appeared in the 17th century.

Yet the term of risk management as an art or a science (at the very least as a discipline) appeared in the late 1990s, when an end-of-day report at JP Morgan that was produced at 4:15 pm became the '4:15 pm report' – a statistical assessment of potential losses in the future based on the volatility and the covariance of assets in a portfolio. Value-at-risk (VaR) was born. JP Morgan later spun off the service into a start-up that became Riskmetrics and further developed risk management software and services. Other methodologies appeared and risk management was better publicized as a new profession when in 1996 a book by Professor Philippe Jorion, *Value-at-Risk*, presented several methodologies to compute VaR and a building block methodology to implement those calculations across the enterprise. Many other publications and variations appeared immediately after but it is a fair assessment to recognize the role of JP Morgan, RiskMetrics and Professor Philippe Jorion in the formal establishment and development of risk management techniques.

Ironically, risks ceased to be managed on the very instance risk management attempted to become a form of science. In fact, from that moment onwards, the finance industry merely managed data and models, and progressively detached the management of risks from the risk management functions.

VaR then proceeded to spread around the world like wildfire. Large banks embarked in education programmes for their clients, lectured the emerging markets and presented the very use of VaR as a management tool as though it was a label of quality. There were few dissenting voices claiming that overreliance on VaR presents a false sense of confidence to the industry as it was, after all, a modelled prediction of exposure and by no means a protection against risks. A few duels over the Web and white papers distinctly opposing Philippe Jorion, and Nassim Taleb, a long-time specialist of financial derivatives, unfortunately reached only a niche of the financial industry interested in this very specific issue and failed to alert a broader audience such as the regulators.

In addition, the cry from the failure of Long-Term Capital Management (LTCM) could have been heard as a warning against model risk and dependence on modelled exposure, but it was interpreted differently. The emerging market meltdown that followed was instead seen as a lack of risk management techniques, which prompted the regulators to recommend a more formal approach.

This led to the Basel Committee for Banking Supervision (BCBS) consultation of the industry in the late 1990s to set up guidance rules for each central bank to enforce itself to some extent. As the consultations were essentially focused on large banks, which at that time seemed to have all the answers, they were quickly directed to quantitative analysis, VaR-based capital allocations and the building blocks approach. The language of Basel 1 and Basel 2 formally associated risk management sophistication with predictive modelling of market and credit exposure. The roadmap, transitional arrangements to implement risk management frameworks, would typically consist of laying out some foundation followed by refining the approach over time. Be it for market, credit or operational risks, for capital allocation, securitization or liquidity management, fine tuning in risk management was always implicitly associated with more sophisticated statistical analysis and modelling.

The generalization of VaR as a management tool and the fact that the regulators formally endorsed the methodology as the best approach to measure risk exposure and sensitivity would have two major consequences on the finance industry. First, risk management became essentially associated with modelling and statistical analysis. Second, risk management was inappropriately associated with regulatory compliance. In other words, the balance of risk and value generation, which had always been the discretionary practice of each enterprise as they adapted to changing conditions, was now handed over to mathematical models guided by standards defined by regulators. Risk management was thus not only detached from the business activities of the enterprise but was entirely removed from it.

Hordes of business and technology consultants roamed the planet with a two-pronged value proposition: First, model-based risk management dashboards are to be implemented to maintain a competitive edge in derivatives, control the costs of trading operations and monitor credit exposure. Second, banks can actually reduce the cost of the approach by optimizing their risk-based regulatory economic capital. The complexity of implementing statistical modelling and the magnitude of projects for creating straight-through processes throughout the enterprise remained a blessing for consulting firms, quantitative analysts and IT departments, but further isolated the practice of risk management into ivory towers of science and computing technology, further away from business reality and even from the executive managers.

A third consequence would eventually impact the entire world economy. The regulators embraced the methodology of statistical analysis as a main standard for computing net exposure, and hence risks and mitigations, as well as the capital structure ratio of financial institutions. This led to a worldwide standardization of capital ratios and in unprecedented uniformity of risk mitigation tactics and diversification strategies. For example, by recognizing credit mitigation tools to net out counterparty exposure, the regulators indirectly incentivized the use of credit derivatives. In a deregulated fast pace global economy driven by a relentless search for growth and capital efficiency, banks soon found themselves compelled to use credit derivatives.

When a rigid and uniform set of rules defines the conditions for doing business, it also shows the way by which those rules can be circumvented. In this case, the modelled approach to risk-weighted economic capital, resulted in a massive undercapitalization of the industry since banks were allowed to literally clean up their balance sheets of unwanted credit quality by mean of securitization and off-balance sheet schemes. More capital available would further inflate the lending capabilities, which would result in an even poorer credit quality standard, further fuelling the speculative bubbles and ballooning securitization.

Evidently, the chaos of the 2008–2009 crisis did not wait for the subprime crisis of 2007. It results from a long process in which statistical analysis progressively replaced human judgement, while electronic processing replaced informed decision. Financial institutions gradually lost sight of their internal balance of risk and value generation in respect of corporate policies desired by the shareholders. Externally, a culture of uniformity and convergence progressively replaced the corporate diversity that kept markets in balance. With financial institutions increasingly embracing similar strategies and tactics for business purposes and adopting standardized rigid financial structures, and the world economy operating like a leveraged hedge fund, it was only a matter of time before the entire structure lost its own balance and brought risk management into question.

1.3 THE DECADE OF RISK MANAGEMENT

Risk management brings balance sheets into perspective. Performance and especially overachievements can be perceived negatively. When investment banking divisions, for example, benefited from the exceptional volatility of all markets at the beginning of 2009, they were requested in many firms to bring transparency to their results or they would risk being considered potentially hazardous to their groups.

As the management of risks validates the performance of a firm, it becomes a strategic driver within firms, therefore deserving a new level of consideration. The role of the risk managers is changing accordingly since they now hold the keys of enterprise value. Functions that create value and are essential for firms to grow have a massive impact on corporate hierarchies, on the relative importance of the C-level executives sitting on the boards and on how Chief Executive Officers (CEOs) are selected. In the 1960s, for example, firms could grow through industrial development and technical innovation as the post-war world was accelerating its modernization. Engineers who could invent new products to create wealth and growth were a driving force of corporate strategies and their views would drive strategies. The companies that thrived in this new world were the innovative powerhouses of the automobile and electronic industries. Instilling a culture of innovation within their core structures, they organized their entire operation around the process of inventing, manufacturing and distributing. Then in the 1970s, the consumers' markets of the developed world saturated and it became more critical to sell products than to produce them. It became the decade of marketing, advertising and publicity. Marketing divisions became powerful influencers. The cultural changes led to the appointment of chief officers for 'marketing and innovation' in large organizations who owed their success to their capability to convey their messages before shipping their products. The CEOs of the 1970s were likely to be picked from among them.

In the 1980s, the developed markets were saturated with both products and communications. To maintain growth, firms needed to become international. Firms started to systematically export their products and relocate their productions; the critical size for firms to become multinationals was dramatically reduced. Chief Financial Officers (CFOs) then replaced the engineers and the marketers as leading influencers of corporate strategy. It was their turn to hold the keys of the true value behind the balance sheet. This trend accelerated so much in the 1990s, with the emergence of the new economies of Asia, Central Europe and Latin America, the NAFTA agreement, the fall of the Berlin Wall and the entry of China to the World Trade Organization (WTO), that firms were no longer challenged to meet the requests of local and international clients but to develop strategies to cover the world. A decade of merger and acquisitions (M&As) followed, where the power shifted from pure finance to financial engineering. Firms would no longer wish to be present in every country. Translating, converting, adapting and communicating their offers would take too much time and effort. Growth and capital efficiency would rather result from mergers, acquisitions and – less publicized – 'unmergers' and division sales. The new generations of CEOs dreamt of becoming one of those visionary heroes who built empires like one manages a portfolio, buying and selling financial, technical and human resources based on return and capital efficiency. Shareholder value was the main focus, as long as it was achieved and rewarded appropriately, the amount achieved did not matter. This is where the disconnect between C-level board executives and the rest of the operations actually happened, leading to the compensation mismatch that later created public outrage. By merely recognizing performance through capital efficiency, the fate of CEOs, senior executives and whoever is incentivized with tools relating to shareholder value is no longer directly linked to the technical, commercial or human achievements of the company.

The early 2000s did not change much from the philosophy of the previous decade apart from, following the repeal of the Glass–Steagall Act in 1999, the fact that the spheres of banking and securities were bridged to create even faster development, higher leverage and unheard of returns on capital.

Clearly, then, the 2010s will be the decade of risk managers. New CEOs of ailing financial groups are increasingly being selected based on their risk management skills and experience, a trend that no doubt is expected to continue. In 2008 and 2009, the worst crisis since the Great Depression highlighted the urgency of restoring the lost balance, which made risk management the top priority of all regulators and most governments. Yet a stronger dose of a medicine that failed – or even made things worse – is unlikely to durably cure the patient. Making the rules even more rigid would not fix their vulnerability. Fixing methodologies for market or credit risk assessments can only achieve immediate objectives. Once growth and innovation have resumed, any regulatory-based approach, assumingly perfectly created, would necessarily be misaligned with new types of exposure, or industry structures from which growth will result. Supplementary capital requirements, mandatory liquidity buffers, new reports and special rules for the 'too big to fail' may, as a combination, have a dramatic and unpredictable impact on the corporate strategies and, even if they eventually turn positive, would be short lived.

Change needs to penetrate the industry deeper in order to restore the lost balances and reconnect the management of exposure and mitigations with business operations. Realigning the interest of the shareholders with those of the staff involved in business operations at every level of the hierarchy takes more than restructuring of a company or rolling-out a preconfigured methodology from a consulting firm. It consists of repurposing all resources – financial, technical, commercial and human – that inevitably lead to readjusting the perceived value of capital versus labour. How does the availability of capital at risk enable the creation of a working environment for human resources to contribute to increasing the value of such capital? The former and the latter clearly fulfil each others' purposes. The key is to find to which extent they do so and define the rules of engagement. This is not the role of any regulator or policy maker. Neither is it a paradigm shift but it is, more importantly, a distinct cultural change.

The culture of free enterprise as a whole must better integrate the values of managing risks by balancing the quest for capital efficiency using the judgement of the human beings who are assigned to deliver it. It must happen through the right people, instead of relying on models or regulations. The following five chapters propose a methodology progressively to involve each level of a corporate hierarchy in the identification, assessment and mitigation of risks. It does not preclude the use of models and known methodologies but repurpose their use. The proposed methodology elevates risk management to the level of a corporate culture by which corporations will make sure that they are best suited to adapt to the ever-changing environment. Harmonious developments based on such organic adaptation and diversity will in turn foster the conditions of financial stability among nations and regions throughout the world. The last chapter focuses on industry and regulatory issues and proposes changes at this level as well.

1.4 RISK INTELLIGENCE PRECEDES RISK MANAGEMENT

When risk is managed as a corporate culture and brought as a core value to the forefront of corporate strategies, then the current systemic crisis will be over. Whether it is the cause or a consequence of the crisis, the financial system as we knew it will continue to disintegrate. The regulatory structures are far too misaligned with the realities of the global economy. The risk management techniques – not limited to but mainly inspired by regulatory requirements – are poorly adapted to the complexities of modern financial instruments. Funding strategies and liquidity management techniques are not sustainable under the current business conditions.

For these reasons, the new system order that will eventually restore confidence shall necessarily be based on the management of risks. Making risk management a corporate culture means bringing risk awareness to the very heart of each centre of profit and each centre of cost. As we will demonstrate and propose in the following chapters, it requires a risk-based information workflow throughout the enterprise, the backbone of the new corporate culture. For corporations to adapt naturally to their ever-changing external business conditions and internal challenges, their approach to balancing risks and performance must be adaptive, as a piece of 'corporate DNA' (the deoxyribonucleic acid that contains and distributes genetic information in living organisms).

Several levels of information layers will be necessary to establish the necessary exchanges. First, the information workflow ensures that the brain and the organs are perfectly in sync and react together to information about internal and external conditions. We later refer to cause and effect reflexes. Second, the system must be able to store critical information and build its own body of knowledge. The following chapters will propose in detail a step-by-step methodology to create and maintain those flows.

Moreover, the culture of risk management and the risk-based information flow must pervade the financial sector, as well as national and regional economies. The above types of information flow are again necessary: first, the creation of cause-and-effect processes in order to take action and prevent risk from becoming losses as early as possible and, second, creating and maintaining a body of knowledge in which action taken, risk events, gaps and failures can become lessons for the entire system to use for adapting. The final step is to redistribute the knowledge and information under formats that can be read and understood by all.

New or revamped regulations should therefore promote reactivity and agility rather than imposing uniform tactics and standard internal structures that may not necessarily meet corporate cultures and the shareholders' objectives. The regulators and the industry representatives need to embark in constructive cooperative programmes to define the key principles of the workflow.

The build-up of a body of knowledge, which would help to define the overall business conditions and detect asset concentrations of 'bubbles', for example, is a key element of the adaptation process. Statistics, monographs, databanks and generally all information that would let the members of a sector understand in which type of 'regime' they operate, with alert triggers and emergency support available, are tools used in other industries when they collectively face adverse business conditions with potential effects reaching beyond the sector they operate within.

1.5 RISK MANAGEMENT AND THE HUMAN DIMENSION OF CAPITALISM

The task of rebalancing the values of capital and labour within the financial sector and then within the economy is certainly daunting, but the human approach to the balance of risk and returns that we propose to re-establish through the methodology hereafter can be used as a key. Once understood and implemented as a culture, the management of risks is precisely the hinge between delivering performance and maintaining sustainable business conditions to achieve corporate or systemic goals. In other words, the inner notions of managing risks are the missing links between capital and labour if those who are tasked with delivering performance use judgement, skills and experience to remain within the boundaries of the risk appetite expressed by the providers of capital.

1.5.1 Risk scales and balances

Capital is provided by the shareholders for corporations to deliver a return. To this extent, we can say that the conditions of obtaining capital define the performance objectives. The cost of capital, for example, drives return expectations. Yet the performance objectives are pondered by the risks that corporations have to expose themselves to. The external business conditions, the regulatory and legal requirements or the volatility of the markets require an appetite for risk that the shareholders may or may not have, depending on their corporate culture. Whenever the risk appetite of the shareholders matches the risk management capabilities of the executive team, an agreement is found and a bond is established. It is only and exclusively in the context of a specific corporate culture that the bond exists between the executive management team and the shareholders. Thus if risk management is part of the corporate culture shared by all staff within a firm, all participants within a system, then the core values used to manage the corporate risks are the very limitations of capital objectives. If the values are truly shared and rooted in the corporate culture, then the more human intervention in the management of risk, the more accurate will be the balance between the value of human labour and capital efficiency. Following the excessive independence of executive management boards in the 1990s and early 2000s, which resulted in a disconnect notably illustrated by the compensation mismatches, the corporate world will now evolve towards finding a new balance between the perceived value of labour and capital remuneration. This balance will solely rely on the adequacy of risk management principles individually applied to each specific corporate culture.

1.5.2 A risk culture is corporate DNA

A corporate culture is generally defined as a set of core values shared by a community, defined and abided by through common principles. A corporate culture of risk management is much more than that. Because risks are never still and keep changing in nature and magnitude, risk management principles need to be more than just defined and even more than just kept alive. They need to adapt.

As previously discussed, managing risks as a corporate culture relies on exchanges of information and on the existence of cause and effect reflexes. It also requires the continuous accrual of countless tiny pieces of information into a body of knowledge, a memory databank that progressively assimilates patterns and uses them to readjust the information flows and the cause and effect reflexes. In time it creates a self-adaptive culture that becomes 'corporate DNA' influencing all decisions and perceptions shared by the providers of resources, capital, liquidity and labour.

A DNA process not only creates a culture but also keeps it alive. Precisely the main role of DNA is not only to store information but also to code it so that it becomes instructions used to build other components.

Data become genetic information brought over to the operating organisms in units, which are able to spell out their genetic instructions. This is achieved through a genetic code that the organisms are able to read and understand.

The risk management culture of each specific firm replicates this process. First, it needs to gather sensitivity from risk factors by establishing sensors in order to read information arising from the outside and the inside, in order to understand how they impact each other. Following this, it must analyse whether the sensitivity to the hazards fits the instincts and desire for survival of the shareholders (risk appetite). To what extent the existing cause and effect reflexes (or lack of) are fit or unfit for the designated purpose is the risk management assessment continuously accrued as a body of knowledge containing risk intelligence. For these data to become genetic information they must be analysed and understood. A scenario-based approach simulating the potential effects of shocks on the risk factors estimates the boundaries of exposure that can meet the expectations defined by the risk appetite. Those boundaries (exposure and sensitivity limits) must now be codified in such a way that the organisms (units) can read them and use them as instructions. Their feedback will in turn increment the corporate memory, which becomes risk management intelligence.

Our proposed methodology for the definition and implementation of a corporate culture based on risk management will therefore consist of the five following steps (Parts 1 to 5):

1. Distributing risk exposure and sensitivity across the enterprise
2. Empowering business units with risk management capabilities
3. Creating an information workflow for continuous feedback and preventive decision making
4. Aligning funding strategies and liquidity management tactics with corporate risk policies
5. Enabling external communications, disclosure policies and transparency

Part 6 then follows, which suggests ways regulators can abide by the same principles in order to establish an adaptive risk management culture among the financial sector participants.

Part 1
Distributing Risk Exposure and Sensitivity Across the Enterprise[1]

Executive Summary

This part describes the first critical step towards implementing a corporate culture focused on risks: distributing all risk exposure by risk factors to all groups or individuals of a company that are responsible for it, instead of cumulating them on business lines.

To distribute risks, one first needs to identify the factors and conduits that lead to the root-risks. Then one can assess the exposure of groups and subgroups of individuals to those factors. Once the exposure is understood and acknowledged by all, each business unit can estimate the sensitivity of the exposure based on a baseline scenario, a high-severity scenario and a catastrophic one. In return, risk managers will be in a position to collect and aggregate risks as understood and estimated by the agents conducting day-to-day business activities – the actual generators of risks. This is a major departure from the previous approach, where computing risks out of exposure merely relied on models. This new scenario-based approach fosters a collective participatory environment, which is key to establishing a culture.

Distributing the exposure to the respective individuals through risk factors that they define and understand is the initial step to raise awareness. Further engagement would require business unit managers to assess the sensitivity and quantify risks. Eventually, 'risk-conscious' behaviour should pervade throughout the enterprise into all areas such as company expenditures, product quality or customer satisfaction.

---

[1] This part leverages and develops some ideas from a White Paper by Philippe Carrel, 'Implementing risk management as a corporate culture: from cumulated risk to distributed risks', made public by Thomson Reuters in May 2009. Some of the graphics have been extracted.

Information systems must be designed to create an adaptive and dynamic workflow of risk-based information. The architecture must be mapped on such workflow, thus integrating the multiple and ever-changing sources of information, distributing exposure and collecting feedback as a nervous system enables body movements. The resulting risk information workflow, or 'Risk Bus', is critical to implement the successive steps towards establishing a corporate culture, empowering the units so that they are in control and fully accountable for their risk mitigation.

The key to truly control risks is to take action where and when risk arise and prevent rather than cure. To achieve this, risks must be contained within predefined limits, either through hedging or sensitivity caps.

This, however, is more of an art than a mathematical science, for sure hedges and stable limits are difficult to determine or achieve. The responsibility of designing, implementing, monitoring and adjusting the hedges must therefore be allocated to responsible and accountable units. To achieve this, it is necessary to empower people with the corresponding accountability for the risk they take, and rewarding them appropriately for maintaining exposure within the defined boundaries. Human intervention at this stage would be critical to the success of risk management. Risk exposure and sensitivities do not merely rest on amounts and figures. In other words, risk is a changing geometry, an adaptive complex system that reacts differently in time to yet identical factors.

To truly manage its risk, a firm must make the largest number of people responsible and accountable for it. However, people can only feel responsible for what they understand and would only take action on what they can see. Hence, the cause-and-effect relationship between risks measured as exposure, sensitivity and maximum loss, and the action they take must be clear and obvious. Value-at-risk limits, for example, imposed by the mid-office departments to front office desks, have failed to produce the desired effect. Most traders would find them theoretical, hypothetical and, more importantly, belonging to another culture.

Leverage effects must be well accepted. This means that the trade managers or unit directors must feel 'comfortable' with their leverage, avoiding the sensation of piloting a car too fast for one's skills. So the total amount of responsibility for risks must first be understood and accepted firm-wide, and then distributed to each of the responsible actors. Whenever the relation between business operations and risk management is no longer linear, or is blurred by excessive complexity, further distribution of risks would be needed.

Identifying risks factors that people can comprehend and quantify as their 'comfort level within those risks is the very first step to implementing a culture of risk management. To move to the next level of risk management, the distribution of risks by risk factors as well as deriving action from risk information are absolute prerequisites, as opposed to simply estimating potential losses based on historical observations.

The traditional approach to risk management consists of cumulating exposure by business lines, which has been suggested by the risk managers and regulators who wanted to break the silo structures inherited from the rapid inorganic growth of the roaring 2000s. The diversity of business lines, however, meant that assessment of risks was akin to comparing apples with oranges, which led to model-based theoretical approaches. An example was the 2007–2008 crisis, which later revealed that the operational risk of cross-division modelling was even worse than the credit and market exposure it initially wanted to hedge when credit risks transferred from banks to asset management divisions ended up in an equity market crash.

In the post 2007–2008 crisis era, managing risk departed from implementing strategies in a uniform manner, where estimating exposure extended beyond modelling it. Undoubtedly, mitigating and managing risk must become a corporate culture, a set of values and attitudes shared by all operating units within a firm. Risk is people's business.

A long journey to raise risk as a core value of the corporate culture has begun. Among the changes that are necessary to implement a corporate culture based on risk, and as a starting point to involving people at all levels of the hierarchy, business managers should be required to assess the exposure they generate through the operations they conduct. The total exposure should therefore be distributed by risk factors on to the various business units, which will also be required to estimate the risk sensitivity and maximum losses.

2
Identifying Risk Factors

Two types of factors typically expose a firm to risks: the specific factors that derive from its very existence, history, culture and main customers, and the systematic risk factors associated with the sector, country or economic environment the firm operates within. Although less commonly highlighted, a third type of risk factors – systemic – have in recent months been a major source of concern. While systemic risks won't be directly manageable by a firm individually, their fast evolution and potentially devastating impact requires special attention.

2.1 SPECIFIC RISK FACTORS

Banks have typically been created out of cash pools initially used to fund cash generating activities or investments. Whether it was to fund the gold rush of the 19th century, the Irish merchants sailing to America, infrastructure developments in the European colonies of Asia and Africa, or the local farmers, each bank has a history where its business culture and customer base is strongly rooted. These roots are much more important to the risk culture of each institution than one might have thought. Even in our modern, globalized and somewhat normalized business environment, the cultural heritage of financial institutions – including the global ones – plays a great role in everyday decisions as it is the only remaining conveyor of shareholders' views. In a family owned business, it continues greatly to influence strategies, especially the association with risks. It is the 'DNA' of the bank. The same is true for some asset management firms and many insurance companies as well. All collective investment schemes were created from pools of investors with a precise risk and return project in mind.

The impact such 'DNA' has on risk exposure is massive. A bank that has established its roots by funding local agribusiness industries, for example, would typically derive a substantial part of its funding from local retail deposits and would generally hold collateral sensitive to local business conditions. A bank initially created to fund a handful of massive industrial projects or public investments would have been funded through bond issuance and convertibles and hold either government bonds or utilities assets as collateral. Both banks are exposed to the same risk factor, say interest rate, yet have very different sensitivity to it and world-apart risk mitigation strategies.

Standard Chartered Bank, for example, still derives 90 % of its profit from Asia, Africa and the Middle East. Not only does the privileged access of these markets define the factors of risk the firm is exposed to, but it generates further opportunities to expand and support the globalization, with subcustody services, for example.

Rooted in agriculture, the cooperative Rabobank prides itself on its origins and continues to develop in countries where it can remain close to a strong rural base.

Crédit Agricole (CA) was also created as a network of local syndicated pools of credit, designed to lead the French farmers of the late 19th century that were traditionally credit averse. Now one of the largest financial institutions in the world, CA is strong with 58 million retail customers.

By contrast, JP Morgan Investment Bank serves 8000 customers worldwide.[1] Engineering huge deals with major corporations such as Microsoft or Renault is obviously a springboard for innovation in structured securities and credit derivatives, for example.

2.1.1 The search for risk factors

Although the endless diversity and changing nature of the factors of idiosyncratic risks may seem daunting at first, the search and identification of the true underlying sources of risks is an essential awareness-raising preliminary exercise because it involves all business units to focus their attention on risks. This is a critical step towards creating a culture of risk management as, perhaps for the first time, risk becomes everyone's problem and no longer the responsibility of an independent risk department. Moreover, mitigating those risks greatly depends on how the assessment of exposure sensitivity is carried out and how the hedging tools are used. Involving all people from all operating units in risk identification, sensitivity assessments and valuations is a critical step towards instilling a sentiment of responsibility and accountability.

---

[1] Mario Draghi, Governor of the Bank of Italy and Chairman of the Financial Stability Board at the IOSCO Annual Conference, Tel Aviv, June 2009.

Transparency will eventually arise from the consensus created through this process.

To highlight their specific risk factors, each bank should go through an introspective search of their traditional sources of exposure:

(a) Traditional funding sources (retail, wholesale, interbank market, securities issuance)
(b) Traditional type of assets (type of loans, securities, holdings)
(c) Traditional type of collateral
(d) Predominant client segments
(e) Predominant geopolitical and legal environment.

The key risk factors are derived from the above characteristics. Commercial banking activities, for example, traditionally expose a firm to private, individual or corporate counterparties. Structural risk factors associated with commercial banking would involve the competitiveness of offered rates, costs of operations, costs of collateral management, the transparency of collateral values, inflation rates and reputational risks. Trading activities might reflect more market and counterparty related factors, such as the volatility of underlying prices, unpredicted correlations, counterparty defaults or IT blackout.

Brokerage activities and execution, on the other hand, would most likely emphasize operational risks. A major brokerage company, for instance, would in all likelihood identify the fact that most risk factors are associated with issues from the following categories: legal, reputational, resources, processes and IT. Heads of businesses are gathered periodically to discuss and agree on five key risk factors in each of the categories, making a total of 25 operational risk factors to be monitored. With large divisions, subfactors are also defined by various risk managers, provided these factors eventually aggregate under the umbrella of the 25 macro-risks. The process is illustrated by Figure 2.1.

A business manager in derivatives, as shown in the following example, would highlight relevant areas of operational failures, mismanagement of orders, failures of executions, etc. The manager then freely subdivides each of those five key risk factors into subfactors. The purpose of thinner granularity is not analytical but may be relevant in improving mitigation or facilitating the quantification of risks under scenarios. For example, the replacement cost of failed executions can be a measure of severity for failed executions, within the 'process' category of the trade executions.

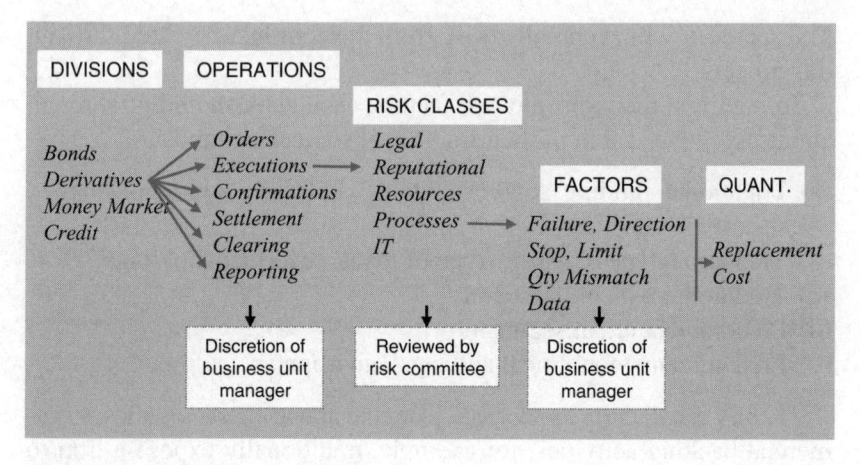

```
DIVISIONS      OPERATIONS
                            RISK CLASSES
               Orders       Legal
Bonds          Executions   Reputational
Derivatives    Confirmations  Resources       FACTORS         QUANT.
Money Market   Settlement   Processes    Failure, Direction
Credit         Clearing     IT           Stop, Limit          Replacement
               Reporting                 Qty Mismatch         Cost
                                         Data
         ↓                      ↓                    ↓
   Discretion of          Reviewed by         Discretion of
   business unit          risk committee      business unit
   manager                                    manager
```

Figure 2.1 Risk factor identification process

2.1.2 Root-risk factors

The purpose of identifying risk factors is to distribute the exposure to those factors to business unit managers so that they eventually become responsible for the risk they generate through the operations they control. As risks will later be managed through hypothetical scenarios and mitigated with instruments of reverse sensitivity, it is critical to find the true source of sensitivity for each factor and to keep them up to date.

For example, a corporate loan department can assess their client's credit risk through the variables impacting their activity. In a manufacturing sector, it could be the cost of raw materials, economic growth, interest rates and external competition. Each industry is linked to factors as typically highlighted in analysts' research: airlines would be associated with energy costs and economic growth, the automobile industry would be linked to base metal and interest rates, and the retail industry would be tied to inflation and credit, media or chemicals.

Each trading desk, each loan department, each investment bank know their business inside out. They are most qualified to pinpoint the factors of sensitivity that truly affect their clients or their business and to estimate to what extent they might end up creating unexpected losses for the firm. Traders open up their screens every morning and immediately check the key underlying prices, volatility, rates and news that might be important throughout the day. Likewise, each division of each bank and each manager of each portfolio, anyone in charge of a P/L and responsible for their risk, must know where to look in terms of the sensitivities or market signs that would let them foresee potential changes.

2.1.2.1 The changing nature of risk factors

The difficulty or challenge lies in the evolving nature of the root-risk factors. These factors are not set in stone and may disappear and reappear in time. At the same time, their importance and 'weight' as an overall source of sensitivity may diminish or strengthen with business conditions and shifting perceptions. For example, to stress test the risks of running a mortgage loan business unit, one may closely look at the changes in unemployment rates within the region. Two years ago, a key factor would have been the progression of property prices, which would lead to more or less speculation and business activity. Obviously it was the 2007–2008 crisis that changed the focus and perception, and the correlations. But when did it exactly happen? How soon was it possible to sense the perception shift and start considering different risk factors?

It requires the permanent attention of all people in charge to monitor the factors, the changes, the sensitivities and impact and how they might develop into triggers of catastrophic scenarios. No amount of modelling, gurus or external consultants could do that and, even if they could, it would necessarily be achieved in the context of what it is possible to know at a given time. Yet we have seen that many factors depend on perceptions, assumed correlations and even the mathematical links with the underlying exposure, which can dramatically change over time. In some cases, today's hedges may turn to additional exposure tomorrow. Models or professionals rolling out a predefined methodology based on preconfigured models would necessarily miss the dynamics of risk exposure over time.

Fortunately, even though perception shifts and changes in correlations may happen suddenly, it does not occur too often. In addition, people's perceptions are often guided by herd instincts. When leaders of the pack change direction, the herd follows and suddenly risk factors and correlations would have changed too. Over the years the pace of information may have accelerated but the behavioural process remains unchanged.

What follows is a new interpretation of the efficient market hypothesis (EMH).

2.1.2.2 Selective market efficiency

Markets still reflect all information that is possible to know or acquire at a given time, but such reflection may not be encapsulated by the closing prices and the price return. In the 21st century, market data need to be looked at in perspective. Under the EMH, the day-to-day return on a security depends on the fundamental value derived from a set of news and information, which is totally unpredictable. In mathematical terms the market is kept on a continuous stochastic equilibrium expressed by

$$E(r_{i,t+1}, \Omega) + \varepsilon_{i,t+1} = r_{it}$$

the expected return on security i over period $t + 1$, conditional on Ω, the set of information available at the beginning of the period t and $\varepsilon_{i,t+1}$, a prediction error.

However, the world of information has changed dramatically since the days of Markowitz and William Sharpe. With the blessings of technology and the Internet, news is now available in real-time, as well as prices and bid/ask spreads. In all respects, the accelerated pace of information and decision stresses the principle but does not make it obsolete.

More notably, a much more fundamental change is the fact that the set of information available at a given time regarding a given security is no longer composed of independent variables, but of tightly interrelated and autoregressive components. Expected returns on securities are directly linked to credit spreads as well as credit news, for example. In turn, these credit spreads depend on probabilities of default estimated from variables including equity prices. Hence, when credit news point towards a given direction, a compounding effect results, leading to acceleration in the value depreciation process.

Higher volatility on a given security progressively reaches the rest of the market for several reasons. First, as for most widely used models, higher volatility of equity prices mathematically increases the probability of default, which further impacts credit spreads and so on. Second, high volatility is pervasive due to the role and use of indices. When one or several securities increase the volatility of key indices, then the effect of portfolio compliance and rebalancing techniques lead to a general increase in market volatility. Finally, media tends to crystallize the focus on particular topics or aspects of information. As a paradox, the recent multiplication of media and communication networks does not widen the spectrum of available information and certainly does not make it better. The extent and speed to which media can possibly convey news from one sphere to another continues to grow at an accelerating pace with communication technology. Virtual communities and networks have already developed to the point where the public itself is the media. The result of this is the creation of massive white noise, which leads to self-avoidance of news outside a number of streams that each individual needs to select based on personal interests and focus. In other words, an uncontrolled rapid spread of information kills information.

2.1.2.3 *What truly moves markets*

As one can see, the universe of available information at a period t is far from a random walk. Within that universe, the weight given to different types of information keeps changing and drives the risk factors. What truly moves prices, emotions and perceptions – and hence liquidity – are the changing colours, the sudden shifts of focus on which news makers and media emphasize.

According to EMH and 'classics' the expected prediction error is conditional on the previous period's prediction errors,[2] given by

$$E(\varepsilon_{i,t+1}, \Omega) = \rho_i E(\varepsilon_{it}^2, \Omega) + E(\varepsilon_{it} e_{i,t+1}, \Omega)$$

If one were to rewrite this today in a more forward looking approach, one may argue that the expected prediction error is instead conditional on weights given to specific domains within the universe of all available information. Contrary to a common belief, those weights and domains do not drive liquidity. In fact, they are driven by it. Evident from 2003 to 2006, the global market experienced excessive liquidity with billions pouring in each month from oil-producing countries, as well as China, India and rapid emerging countries. During that period, the key challenge was to find investment opportunities for liquidity instead of trying to allocate funds to a variety of instruments. It created the infamous 'Greenspan conundrum', which led the Fed to lose control of the long end of the yield curve. Understandably, investors were focused on news and information relating to high yield, inflation and commodity prices. Every single dollar added to the price of a barrel of oil would impact on the foreign exchange rates and depress equity prices. By 2007, liquidity became scarce, and the focus shifted to credit risk. When the credit crunch almost grounded the system to a halt, the perceived corporate credit risk sent yields to unheard-of levels. In 2009, with steeper energy prices driving equities to higher levels, crude oil above US$60 provided a relief for anxious equity holders, whereas only 3 years ago, prices remotely above US$50 would have been perceived as an apocalyptic scenario.

---

[2] David Blake, *Financial Market Analysis*, McGraw-Hill International Editions, 1990.

The traditional approach to market efficiency

FACT → INFORMATION → VALUE DRIVEN INVESTMENT → IMPACT ON MKT LIQUIDITY

The new rules of market efficiency

LIQUIDITY → LIQUIDITY DRIVEN INVESTMENT → IMPACT ON MKT PRICES → INFORMATION

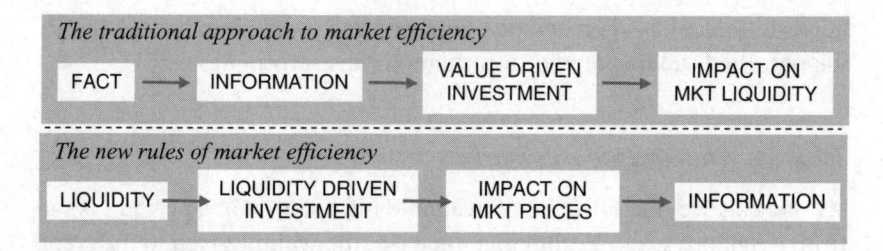

Figure 2.2 The new market efficiency is liquidity-driven

Under these conditions, any attempt to predict the evolution of a risk factor, and the variables driving it, necessarily involves a thorough understanding of the dynamics of liquidity in each sector and how they relate to the creation and divulgation of information. In the 21st century, market efficiency is thus effectively liquidity-driven instead of value-driven (see Figure 2.2).

The bias that liquidity-driven market focus and emotions have on the aggregated value of asset and liabilities is critical to assessing risk. Indeed, the exercise of assessing and mitigating risk is essentially an estimation of the forward value of assets, liabilities, collateral, hedges and the liquidity conditions of the market. In short, managing market and credit risks is to manage valuation risks.

2.1.3 Identifying valuation risk

If specific risks are operational in nature, then they can be addressed as such. Leaving aside operational risks such as frauds or embezzlements, most market and credit risks boil down to valuation issues. Most company failures that took place in 2007, for instance, started with mispricing of assets such as structured products, mortgage-backed securities, collateralized debt obligations (CDOs) and other derivatives. They were severely affected from a combination of model risk, data management risk and pricing process operational risks that we identify as valuation risk.

The assessment of valuation risks is essential to the identification of the specific risk factors each division is exposed to. Valuation risks point out the main areas of uncertainty and potential failures in risk mitigation. The level of precision with which the exposure and the sensitivity of a risk factor will be measured is directly linked to the valuation risks.

Combining issues associated with the acquisition and management of data, processing it through pricing models, warehousing, historizing and redistributing the output, as well as portfolio estimations and reconciliation, valuation risk is by far the most important area of operational risks impacting all buy-side and sell-side firms in their daily business. Being complex and nonlinear in nature, valuation risks are not hedgeable with a simple course of action. They can, however, be predictable. The quality and integrity of data, the nature and compatibility of models in use, the adequacy of their underlying assumptions with the scenarios in use are just some of the questions raised when considering the potential impact of valuation risks. Stress testing a portfolio for extreme market movements, for example using models calibrated for normal distributions while assuming that some of the variables would remain unchanged, would make no sense at all.

Measuring the credit exposure to a particular counterparty depends on the valuations of the position held with them, on the value of collateral they pledge, on an assessment of their balance sheet and on their own operational ability to maintain sufficient collateral. Each of those also depends on the horizon at which the liquidation of the investment is foreseeable. A firm's credit risk therefore depends on its counterparties' market risk, on their operational aptitudes and on the transparency of the entire information flow. Under these conditions, there is little value in running several thousands of Monte Carlo paths with regards to the level of interest rates, price of collateral and other variables to measure the level of exposure moving forward.

The true value at risk of a position at a given time depends on the price volatility moving forward to an investment time horizon, on the uncertainty of the related valuations within such timeframe, on the adequacy and integrity of hedges (if any) during this period and on the reliability of information to calculate all these elements. Thus

$$PVaR_{i,t} = \sigma_{i,t} + \delta_{i,t+n} + (i - hi)_{t+n} + \varepsilon_{i,t}$$

where $\sigma_{i,t}$ is the volatility of the price of an instrument i at time t, $\delta_{i,t+n}$ is the price slippage at the investment horizon and $(i - hi)_{t+n}$ is the degree of hedge protection at the investment horizon. The error coefficient $\varepsilon_{i,t}$ expresses a degree of uncertainty related to obtaining all the necessary information.

We have seen that the very notion of the risk factor immediately raises a side issue of valuation risk. In the aftermath of the 2007–2008 crisis, valuation related failures were also perceived as drivers of reputational risks, which can directly impact funding costs, customers' confidence and shareholder value. The importance of valuation risk itself depends on the market's emotions. In times of high emotions, a perceived uncertainty of exposure and lack of accuracy in valuations can lead to a run on bank deposits or investments.

2.1.4 Identifying liquidity risk

If valuation risk is the source of all potential mismanagement of market and credit exposure, then liquidity risk is the ultimate operational risk they translate into (see Figure 2.3). Liquidity issues derive from the mishandling of risks at the investment horizon. They relate to a variety of operations including funding, portfolio and collateral management, counterparties, failed settlements and other operational issues. It is the failure to anticipate the potential impact of future adverse developments across the risk factors that exposes the firms to liquidity risks. Such failure can result from valuation issues, sudden and unforeseen changes in external business conditions or from failures to properly identify the true variables of risk, the root-risk factors.

As such, liquidity risk is not another standalone risk that needs to be managed alongside market and credit risk. The general perception is

FUNDING	ASSETS	COLLATERAL	GEO/POL/LEGAL
Retail	Private loans	Cash	Geo-political risk
Wholesale	Corp loans	Securities	Legal framework
Interbank	Project	Sub-Investment	Regulatory risks
Issuance	Merchant	Private RE	Covenants
	Investments	Commercial RE	Guarantees
	Securities	Investments	
	Structuring	Commodities	
	Trading	Guarantees	

→ VALUATION RISKS ↓ LIQUIDITY RISKS ←

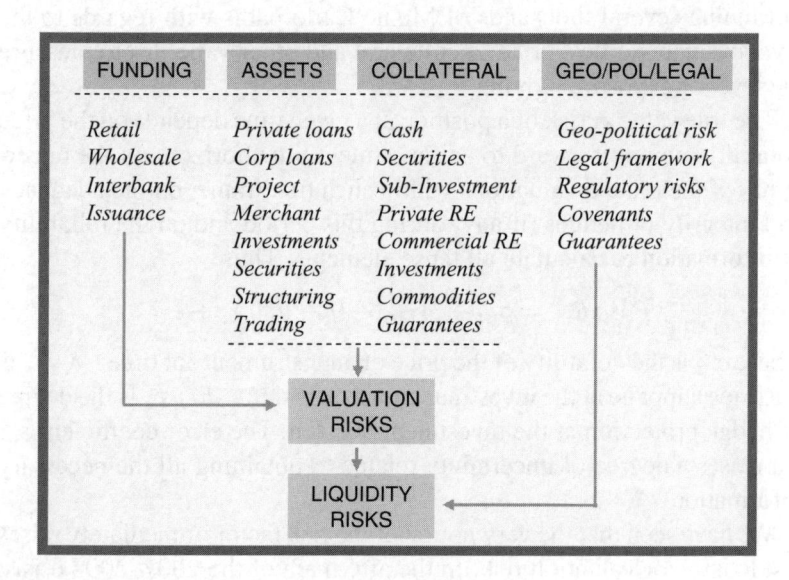

Figure 2.3 The true nature of idiosyncratic risks

of a 'poor parent' type of risk that was neglected until 2007 and now needs to be added to the long list of models and capital requirement computations that are not only flawed but could unwittingly lead to a false sentiment of security.

Liquidity risks generally become obvious only when it is too late, when available funding becomes scarce or when a market has dried up to the point where liquidating positions is no longer possible. To further complicate the situation, liquidity swiftly seeks liquidity, so that 'liquidity holes' deepen as investors try to liquidate some investments through fire sales in order to fund other positions.

In this respect, liquidity holes are not as unpredictable as they may appear to be. It is where liquidity is at the highest at a given point in time that such holes are most likely to appear again in the future when investors run in panic.

Liquidity risk should have a critical impact on the choice of risk factors and the identification of root risks. We will see that when firms work with risk factors, some factors that may appear to be of secondary importance or perceived as negligible sources of risks can turn lethal when valuation risks or liquidity risks multiply their impact exponentially.

Risk factors are the essential sources of risk a firm is truly exposed to. The exposure measured in sensitivity to those factors represents only one dimension. Valuation and liquidity risks are the second and third dimensions of exposure as they express the volatility of sensitivity. Since the same issues may apply to other firms and to entire sectors, areas of high valuation risks are good indicators of areas of systematic risks.

2.2 SYSTEMATIC RISK FACTORS

If we assume that most firms have or should have appropriate risk control procedures in place to manage their individual market and credit risk exposure as part of their routine business operations, what remains is their natural exposure to issues impacting their respective sector. A commercial bank can collateralize loans to mitigate credit risks, diversify its regional exposure with a portfolio of asset-backed securities (ABS) and hedge interest rates with futures or swaps. The bank, however, still remains exposed to an economic slowdown. Separately, an industrial firm can integrate operations vertically in order to control its costs of supplies and distribution prices; it can hedge its exposure to foreign currencies and cost of funding; it can diversify geographically to be less dependent on the economy of individual countries; yet it will remain exposed to the customers' needs for its products or to the development of new technologies.

In the above illustrations, monitoring the systematic exposure of the firms would require scanning the risk factors which, combined altogether, would define what an economic slowdown or a technological shift would consist of. In a modern, global, diversified and deregulated economy, systematic risk can be defined as the sum of risks arising from overall external business conditions and legal and regulatory issues, which may impact on a firm's balance sheet without being directly linked to the way it conducts its business operations.

This begs the same question with specific risk factors. Which systematic risk should be considered and how does one measure them?

2.2.1 Portfolios of external risks

Systematic risk has been traditionally defined as the nondiversifiable risk since the concept was initially derived from the capital asset pricing model (CAPM) portfolio theory. The concept of mitigating risks through diversification to a portfolio of exposure relies on assumptions such as the Brownian motion of variables and implicit correlation effects. Considering a firm's assets as a portfolio of exposures that can net each other out either naturally with or without hedging tools, its systematic risk is defined as the remaining exposure to the overall activity and characteristics of its business sector, legal framework or system it operates within. As with any hedged portfolio, the exposure is naturally kept in balance by market volatility and rates of return. The equilibrium is indicated by

$$\gamma = \frac{\overline{r_m - r_i}}{\sigma_m^2}$$

where r_m is the expected return of a market, r_i the riskless rates of the market at time i and σ_m^2 the volatility of the market.

What results is that higher volatility must reflect higher expected returns relative to the level of riskless interest rates. Otherwise, the value of assets needs to be corrected. Higher volatility in asset value and higher cost of funds therefore increases the systematic risks.

Firms facing the systematic risks of the sector, region or system they operate need to identify the true nature of systematic exposure and timely address it with appropriate risk mitigation techniques. To achieve this, risk analysts need to unfold key risk factors of systematic into component factors.

As an example, in order to monitor the impact of adverse external economic conditions of a particular sector, one would need a set of measurable variables defining such conditions, such as inflation rate, interest rates, energy prices and so on. Some of the variables can be negatively correlated so that their respective impacts would tend to net each other out. Some others can be positively correlated so that their respective impact might actually add up.

2.2.2 Systematic risk and factors correlation

If systematic risk is defined as the nondiversifiable exposure to risk factors, then this risk relies on expected correlations or noncorrelations between those factors. Continuously monitoring those variables is necessary to identify and measure the systematic risks. Their dependence on each other can help in understanding how perception shifts reverse correlations and lead to better anticipation of the systematic risks. Correlation matrices will illustrate such dynamics and provide the essential tool for monitoring fundamental changes within a market or a sector.

No variable is more volatile and less predictable than a correlation factor. Trying to define rules based on linear functions involving correlations is a pointless task. This also applies to the attempt in predicting correlations, since they derive from irrational associations of perceptions inspired from complex human behaviour. What is most useful, however, is to monitor the changes in correlation. Since correlations mirror people's understandings and rules at a given time, their changes and reversals will allow the analyst to know that the herd is currently changing its course. A typical example is the correlation between gold and platinum. Gold has a triple status as a commodity, a safe investment or a reserve currency. In times where tension about the economy and fears about rampant inflation are very low, gold typically behaves as a commodity. The levels of offer and demand would drive its value, with the usual seasonality rules in full play. In this period, platinum trades at a premium over gold (20 to 25 %), with the correlation between both precious metals positive and very high (0.8 to 0.95). In times of uncertainty and high emotion on the markets, as we have seen in late 2008, gold loses its status as a commodity to become a safe play against inflation, monetary erosion and all other systemic concerns. At that stage, the premium of platinum over gold is much lower and correlation is very low. Should gold regain its status of reserve currency, due to a major confidence crisis on sovereign debt for example, gold would soar to unprecedented levels, leaving platinum at a deep discount. The correlation between the two precious metals would most certainly reverse as gold would rise with the level of uncertainty and economic mayhem, leaving most commodities, including platinum, with very poor prospects.

Monitoring correlations is by no mean an attempt to predict the future. It is about watching the market sentiment evolving and trying to identify perception changes in real-time. What is perceived as a hedge today might double or treble the exposure of a portfolio tomorrow. It is the true nature of markets to be made of complex, nonlinear and autoregressive distributions. It may sound as a paradox that tail events that are not necessarily related to the past do influence the future, and the phenomenon due to the long memory process of market price and return distributions will be analysed later in this book.

Typical correlation matrices are simple tables crossing factors and correlations, as exhibited in Figure 2.4. Those correlations point out the systematic risk factors firms are exposed to. Their results and the

Macro-Factor: External Economic Conditions (ECO1)

GDP Growth	STIR	Inflation	Energy
Impact bus. volumes, May impact Inflation, Energy prices, Short Rates	*Impact bus.volumes May impact inflation ...*	*Impact STIR, Energy ...*	*Impacts Inflation May impact STIR ...*

Expected/Observed Correlations

ECO1	Growth	Inflation	STIR	Energy	...
Growth		-0.4	-0.4	0.7	
Inflation	0.8		0.5	0.8	
STIR	-0.4				
Energy					
...					

Figure 2.4 Unfolding the factors of systematic risks

conclusions they lead to are not only totally unpredictable but they are also dependent on the parameters set-up. Samples computing the last 250 days, for example, can return very different or even opposite results compared to samples computed using 100 weeks or 36 months. Thus the choice of methodology is less important than the relative movements between the parameters, the changes in correlation and the frequency of those changes. The chart in Figure 2.4 demonstrates a case of monitoring correlation changes across a number of variables known to have an effect on the risk factors selected.

3
Working with Risk Factors

Once the key idiosyncratic and systematic risk factors have been identified and acknowledged by the risk executives, they must be distributed to each business and risk unit in the form of macro-factors, which they will further refine within the context of their own activities. There is no generic rule of granularity applicable to all. Risk factors must be further broken down into subfactors or root-factors until sensitivity can be understood and risk is 'manageable'. The goal is eventually to establish risk targets and sensitivity limits that would enable a swift response to risk as a course of action based on risk. As a key step towards establishing a culture of risk management, this is perhaps the only way to make people responsible and accountable for the risk they generate through their daily business activities.

Although creating a corporate culture involving all people is desirable, it would be overtly ambitious to expect all business units, front line or back office, and even the management teams, to define their own factors and conduits of sensitivity. Even if they could, the sum of all factors would not be manageable and would lead to a fragmented approach to risks. Instead, the appropriate approach is based on building a consolidated view of risk factors and sensitivities across the enterprise, as a mosaic composition.

Establishing an iterative process will therefore allow the respective business divisions to participate in the build-up of a risk management framework involving their own concerns and their own contributions. The process is summarized in Figure 3.1.

As a distinct departure from the traditional approach where the risk committee or risk department independently assess risk and allocate discretionary targets, the respective committees or departments now play a critical role in coaching and supervising. Creating a culture requires responsibility and accountability to be distributed. In most firms, this will involve a massive undertaking of education.

The role of the auditors will also be different in the proposed new framework. Since an iterative process involves discussions, this may lead to disagreements or even friction, which might end up to be

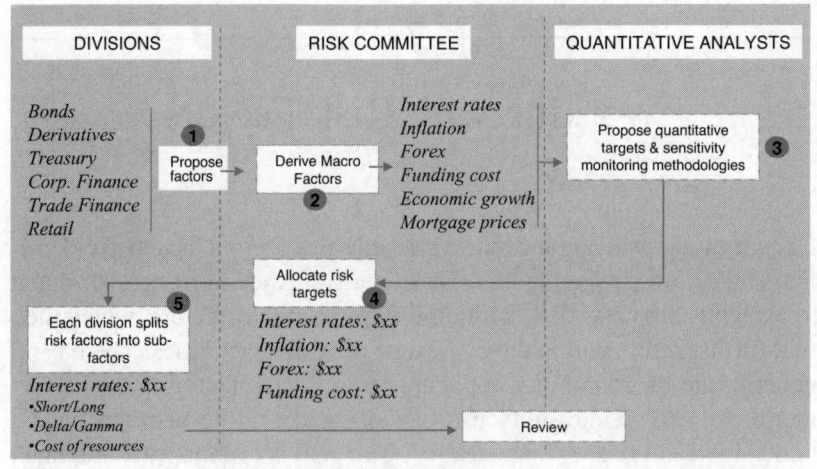

Figure 3.1 Risk factor distribution process

DIVISIONS: Bonds, Derivatives, Treasury, Corp. Finance, Trade Finance, Retail

RISK COMMITTEE: Interest rates, Inflation, Forex, Funding cost, Economic growth, Mortgage prices

QUANTITATIVE ANALYSTS: Propose quantitative targets & sensitivity monitoring methodologies

1. Propose factors
2. Derive Macro Factors
3. (Propose quantitative targets & sensitivity monitoring methodologies)
4. Allocate risk targets — Interest rates: $xx, Inflation: $xx, Forex: $xx, Funding cost: $xx
5. Each division splits risk factors into sub-factors — Interest rates: $xx • Short/Long • Delta/Gamma • Cost of resources
— Review

(1) Each business division or group identified as a 'risk generating unit' proposes their own factors, based on their experience and business activity. For example, interest rates or forex volatility do not impact a trading desk of a back office in similar ways but remain risk factors to both.

(2) The Risk Committee aggregates all factors into macro-factors, say Interest Rates

(3) The Risk Committee and the quantitative analysts agree on methodologies to allocate targets and monitor risk sensitivity limits. For example with interest rates, bpv limits, credit dv1 limits, collateral haircut, etc. Models, data sources and valuation processes are selected at this stage.

(4) The Risk Committee proposes quantitative targets by risk factors to the units

(5) Business units refine macro-risk factors into factors they can monitor and sensitivity they can hedge. For example, the factor interest rates can be divided into dv1, credit dv1, gamma and vega by a bond trading desk. A back office department can translate it into a number of failed executions due to higher volatility. Each department assess their own sub-factors of sensitivity and review with the targets with the Risk Committee

counterproductive unless they are immediately channelled back into the discussion. Auditors will adopt a new role of refereeing whenever discussions with respect to factor definition, scenario building, quantitative assessments and limit monitoring need to be balanced.

3.1 APPROACHING RISK THROUGH SENSITIVITY AND SCENARIOS

Multiple layers of derivatives, complex legal frameworks and the innovative structures of some hybrid products have sometimes hidden or blurred the true origins of risks, impeding or corrupting the measurements of sensitivity. Each business centre, each centre of operation and each business manager should be able to identify the structural and cyclical risk factors they are exposed to, as well as the means to evaluate such exposure. The level of granularity required depends on the complexity of the risks involved. The more complex, the thinner it should be, until risks become clear, measurable and 'hedgeable' by the group or the manager who owns them.

For example, a fixed income trading desk exposed to fluctuations of interest rates may have to break exposure down to long, mid-curve and short end, rates volatility, basis risk, cross-currency basis, liquidity at various tenors, geopolitical factors and so on until it senses where sensitivity truly originates from. Meanwhile, the back-office department of the firm can estimate that being exposed to interest rate levels and volatility translates into higher volumes and greater diversity of products, increased frequency of exception to manage and longer settlement times, for example. At that stage, both the trading desk and the back-office department are able to estimate the costs of scenarios regarding interest rates, through sensitivity measures. Both units consider an identical risk factor – interest rates – but the approach, the impact and estimated severity are entirely different. Similarly, the mortgage loan or the securitization departments would develop their own individual approaches to that same issue – interest rates – breaking down the macro-scenario into relevant sets of risk factors of which they can sense the variables.

Once all units are able to quantify their own sensitivities to each of the subsequent aspects of the macro-scenario, the Executive Risk Committee or Risk Management Department is able to add it all up into a total cost of the macro-scenario. Eventually all are required to produce simple figures for each factor or subfactor they define:

- $ exposure,
- $ sensitivity under a baseline scenario,
- $ sensitivity under a high severity scenario,
- $ maximum loss under a worst case scenario.

Figure 3.2 illustrates the main workflow of risk factor distribution, macro-scenario interpretation, sensitivity estimates and risk aggregation, for one example of a macro-factor: interest rates.

3.2 ROOT-RISK FACTORS AND CONDUITS OF SENSITIVITY

As explained earlier, an essential aspect of assessing the exposure is to identify the conduits of sensitivity that turn variable shifts into risk. Those conduits depend on the root-risk factors. Should a fund manager purely base his or her assessments on equity prices or involve the factors

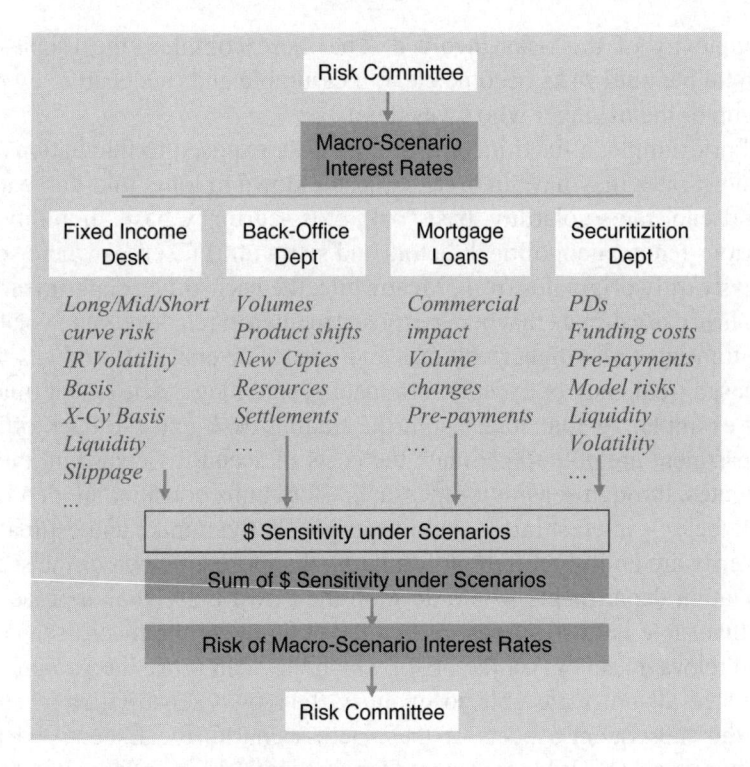

```
                    Risk Committee
                          │
                          ▼
                  Macro-Scenario
                  Interest Rates
   ┌──────────────┬──────────────┬──────────────┐
 Fixed Income   Back-Office    Mortgage      Securitizition
    Desk           Dept          Loans           Dept

 Long/Mid/Short  Volumes       Commercial     PDs
 curve risk      Product shifts impact        Funding costs
 IR Volatility   New Ctpies    Volume         Pre-payments
 Basis           Resources     changes        Model risks
 X-Cy Basis      Settlements   Pre-payments   Liquidity
 Liquidity       ...           ...            Volatility
 Slippage                                     ...
 ...
   └──────────────┴──────────────┴──────────────┘
                          ▼
              $ Sensitivity under Scenarios
           Sum of $ Sensitivity under Scenarios
                          ▼
           Risk of Macro-Scenario Interest Rates
                          ▼
                    Risk Committee
```

Figure 3.2 Sensitivity distribution workflow

that may impact those equities? Should a fixed income trader monitor interest rate movements or watch the underlying macro-economic factors? Once the position is hedged, could exposure further arise from volatility or correlation changes? In other words, to what depth should a risk manager drill down and unveil the underlying (asset) of the underlying? The answer is: As deep as necessary to identify the variables that truly trigger price changes and validate the root-risks, which are the true factors of sensitivity.

As part of the process of subdividing macro-factors into smaller, more refined factors that one can fully comprehend and manage, the question of root-risk will inevitably be raised. Identical risk factors may have different 'root-risks' depending on the exposure and business activities considered. A fund manager may require low latency equity prices, and consider the information as an essential tool to monitor and assess the exposure to a given firm. Meanwhile, a private wealth manager exposed to the same equity would require market consensus, credit spreads and measures of the company's indebtedness as key indicators of sensitivity. Both managers are considering a similar exposure to a similar equity but have identified different variables as root-risk factors of sensitivity.

Differences may arise from the nature of businesses as in the above example, or from timeframes, skills and experience of the managers. In other words, these nuances are derived from the corporate culture of the firm. A credit officer lending funds to a mining company, for example, may identify ore prices as a root-risk factor, while another officer lending similar funds in similar circumstances might feel more comfortable with balance sheet ratios.

Risk Managers and Risk Committees would require a thorough understanding of the preferences and of the culture and experience behind them in order to refine the firm's risk policies. Each respective member's contribution to achieve a fine balance between diversity and standardization forms part of each firms' risk management culture. Undeniably, there has been a trend in recent years to be assertive and prescriptive in risk measurement methodology. This has led to a culture of uniformity and standardization throughout the industry, which rendered the financial institutions helpless when tail events occurred and multiplied. On a larger scale, it created systemic risk. In haste to implement a scientific approach to risk, the firms and the regulators have forgotten the first rule of risk management: diversity always mitigates risks while uniformity always increases risks.

3.3 BACK-TESTING AND MAINTAINING THE FACTORS

Not only do root-risk variables depend on the internal culture and preferences of the managers, they may also be influenced by external perceptions resulting from market developments – almost like fashion! To trade corporate bonds in the 1980s, for example, dealers would focus on corporate data, balance sheet ratios and interest rates. After a crash sparked off by US data released on Monday 19 October 1987 triggered massive rates cuts, corporate bond traders cultivated a habit of monitoring and anticipating on data employment, CPI, housing starts, confidence index and macro-economic variables to trade those same bonds. Following Enron and Worldcom in 2001, counterparty risk, default probabilities and credit spreads became key variables to monitor. Corporate bonds desks turned to credit trading. As Parmalat demonstrated in 2003, credit spreads should never be monitored or traded without consideration for equity prices, leaving a huge arbitrage window open for 48 hours. In more recent times, credit spreads have lost some of their significance due to government bias to credit risk and financial institutions' calls for real-time updates on risk issues and default probabilities.

Clearly, the variables to monitor in order to assess the sensitivity of exposures continuously change with external market conditions, market perceptions, traders' emotions, regulators and government influence. Those who live and breathe with the markets, who witness the importance of perceptions as they change, are best suited to identify the relevance of the variables. Remote analysts, detached from the pressure and the white noise of the markets, are better poised to assess the fundamental reasons for the volatility of the variables. The firm's ability to identify, measure and properly mitigate its exposure to risk therefore relies on an efficient flow of information between those groups, and on its agility to adapt to the changing nature of the variables or root-risks. Failure to adapt timely to the root-risk factors of sensitivity can have devastating consequences in times of high volatility and changing correlations. Corporate failures and bankruptcies resulting from unknown exposure or wrong-way hedges either occur from operational failures from the firm's blindness to perception shifts, which typically materialize as correlation changes.

It will appear that there are no universal solutions, advisable levels of granularity, nor an exhaustive monitoring list of variables that would match predefined types of risk profiles. Only a sensible interpretation of the corporate policies can define, under the guidance of professional risk managers, what the appropriate sensors and monitors of risks should be. Back-testing the relevance of those factors, subfactors and root-factors

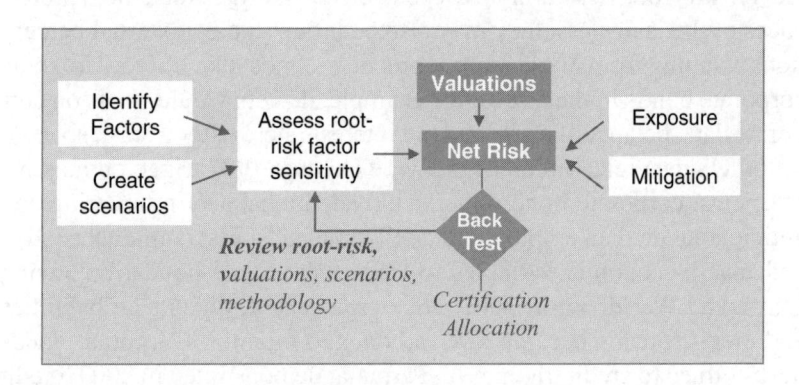

Figure 3.3 Back-testing root-risk and risk factors

is necessary to establish a channel of continuous feedback, leading to updates or modification in the sources of information and the interpretation. Figure 3.3 illustrates this process.

Embedding this permanent concern and continuous search for improvement within the core principles of a firm's corporate culture is the only way to truly protect it from risk. In a nutshell, only a culture embracing risk as a core component of strategy can produce a framework that is well adapted to the ever-changing structures of the firm, the volatility of the business conditions and the unpredictable perception shifts that continuously re-model exposure to risks.

4
Working with Scenarios

Once the risk factors and the root-risks have been identified, it is necessary to consider valuation scenarios to translate exposure into sensitivity. The ultimate goal is to bring each business or risk unit into a position dynamically to manage 'risk targets' as sets of exposure and sensitivity limits. These limits will be used to control the exposure, coach the mitigation efforts and reward appropriately each unit's effort to comply with the policies. In this case, not only is risk measured but also managed.

One key aspect of post-crisis risk management is the need for more transparency. From 2008 onwards, no board would comfortably face shareholders without a plain figures description of the risk taken and a well-articulated strategy to be deployed under a worst case scenario. This is perfectly illustrated by the bank stress-testing required by the US Administration in early 2009: simple figures under a worst case scenario are expected to answer basic questions of business sustainability.

Claiming high transparency across the multiple types of risks faced by a large business organization requires departing from probabilistic, model-based approaches. Transparency is not about finding the sharpest figures. It is about being able to explain the figures, their components, the choice of models and back-engineer processes if needed. The main difference is that the exposure is no longer modelled but estimated by those who are best suited to understand it and empowered to hedge it. Once the exposure is distributed by risk factors and sensitivity has been linked to the root-risk factors, the persons or groups accountable for risks will be the owners of at least three categories of scenarios: baseline, high severity and catastrophic.

Under baseline scenarios the owners will be requested to measure or validate the sensitivity to the risk factors they have helped to identify. Under a high-severity scenario, the owners are requested to consider the factors under adverse conditions and estimate the impact on their risk exposure and especially whether they remain within limits. Catastrophic scenarios are obviously meant to describe tail risks. The difficult exercise of assessing losses under extreme conditions is the key to identifying appropriate mitigation tools and methodologies. This step is therefore a cornerstone of a risk-based corporate culture since the business owners are invited to think as risk managers. The purpose is not to turn each and every one into a quant (quantitative analyst). Each person is simply required to provide an estimation of sensitivity under the various scenarios he or she has defined and maintained. Within the boundaries agreed with the Risk Committee and the Audit, each business unit is in charge of using the methodology they feel is most appropriate to estimate the risks they create and the sensitivity of their exposure. Some might want to leave it to quantitative analysis while others might prefer internal gatherings and empirical assessments. As long as they meet the firm's established guidelines for methodology and transparency requirements, allowing for this diversity is a way to make key managers accountable, to ensure transparency and to make sure the risk practice evolves in time with the business practices and the external conditions. All these constitute the main characteristics of a culture (see Figure 4.1).

Modelling can be used in parallel for benchmarking or back-testing but should no longer be considered as a unique risk assessment methodology. This is especially so with tail risks, where models have performed rather poorly in recent months.

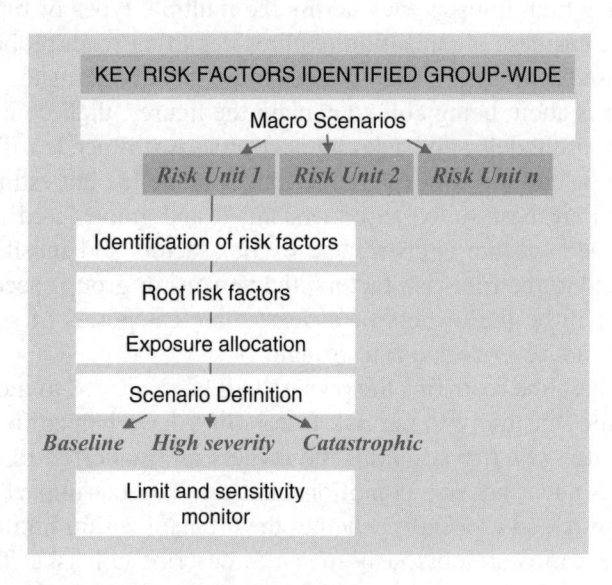

Figure 4.1 From macro-scenario to risk limits

4.1 SCENARIO DEFINITION

As we had seen with the risk factors, the Risk Committee, the management and the Audit define macro-scenarios that they distribute to the risk units. Requiring all business and risk units to define their own scenarios in isolation would lead to the processing of enormous quantities of information, based on unrelated assumptions, and would quickly become counterproductive. The Risk Management Department or Risk Executive Committee must therefore prepare macro-scenarios outlining the main variables and 'state-of-the-world' types of approach, and then hand them over to the risk units for them to refine the approach further. Against this backdrop, each risk unit creates as many scenarios as they wish as long as they remain within the three categories (baseline, high severity and catastrophic) and within the macro-scenario. Once they have the granularity they require, they can shock the factors and root-factors accordingly. The resulting sensitivity is measured and reported back to the Risk Committee who can aggregate it. Figure 4.2 exhibits a table of sample macro-scenarios for two categories of risk factors, market data and counterparty data.

For each 'state-of-the-world' type of macro-scenario, business units can break down risk factors into root-risk factors or further refine the factors' granularity as well as the impact of the scenario. Using the above scenario, a foreign exchange trading unit, for example, can pick one of the key factors (GBPEUR) and, using the methodology defined for identifying factors, refine the scenario as shown in Figure 4.3.

The appropriate level of granularity is the one that will allow the risk owner to sense the factors of sensitivity properly and be responsible for the mitigation of those risks. Choices can be influenced but should not be dictated; while risk managers can propose and suggest options, the risk owner remains the sole decision maker as to which risk should be mitigated with what tool.

4.2 HIGH-SEVERITY AND WORST CASE SCENARIOS

Stress-test owners define their own scenarios and maintain them as well. No scenario, not even baseline, should be set in stone. No stress scenario should be driven by auditors or by managers not directly involved in the business. Certainly members of a Risk Committee or auditors can educate and coach their respective teams, have an influence on choices,

44 The Handbook of Risk Management

Macro-Scenario 1: High Inflation			
Risk Factors	Baseline	Severity 1	Catastrophic
Markets EUR	+100pts	+2k pts	+7k pts
JPY	−500 pts	−3k pts	−5k pts
GBP/EUR	−100 pts	−1.5k pts	−5k pts
Eur3mVol	+/− 1%	×2	×4
Gold	$900	$1.5	×5
Oil	$50	$150	×5
OilVol	+10%	×2	×5
$3m Dep%	0	0	3
$10y %	2.5	3.5	7
$30y%	2	4.5	10
Equ Defensive	+10%	+15%	−35%
Equ Cyclical	+5%	−20%	−50%
Counterparties			
Spread Client Group1	+50 pts	+250 pts	D
Collateral Group1	−10%	−50%	0
Guarantees	75%	30%	0
Spread Client Group2	+100 pts	>250 pts	D
Collateral Group2	−5%	−50%	0
Guarantees	y	n	0

Figure 4.2 Macro-scenarios

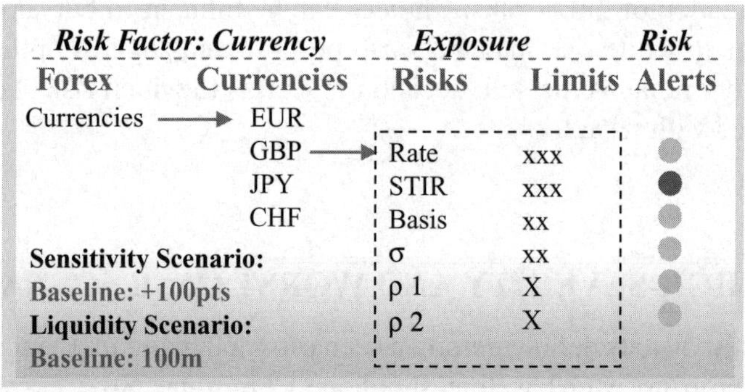

Risk Factor: Currency		Exposure		Risk
Forex	Currencies	Risks	Limits	Alerts
Currencies ⟶	EUR			
	GBP ⟶	Rate	xxx	●
	JPY	STIR	xxx	●
	CHF	Basis	xx	●
Sensitivity Scenario:		σ	xx	●
Baseline: +100pts		ρ 1	X	●
Liquidity Scenario:		ρ 2	X	●
Baseline: 100m				

Figure 4.3 Refining the scenario

but a correct assessment of what constitutes a worst case scenario requires hands-on experience and a continuous presence on the market. A 'worst case' is obviously a very subjective notion and the external definition of it requires a thorough knowledge of the environment. Yet it is not so much the number of 'sigmas' that matters most in this case but rather the impact the scenario might have on clients' credit, their business or their product. Estimating those impacts requires being involved on a day-to-day basis with customers and products, or with funding partners.

The assessment of risk sensitivity under scenarios is a key part of the risk culture, as it necessarily raises awareness across department and constitutes an indispensable step towards making people responsible and accountable for their own risks. This is not limited to front-line operations. Back-office, IT department, administration and even management need to define their own worst case scenarios and estimate the costs (or sometimes gains) under a baseline, a high-severity and a catastrophic scenario at least.

As with baseline scenarios, high-severity and catastrophic scenarios can be built upon state-of-the-world outlooks defined by the Executive Risk Committee or by the Risk Management department. Each department can estimate a worst case development of the factors and root-risk factors involved. Measuring the potential impact of scenarios is a first step towards refined and adaptive mitigation.

For example, a scenario might suggest that the credit spreads of large clients could rise above 500 basis points, with impact on net positions. A traditional approach would consist of estimating the probability of such an event happening and then of allocating risk-weight capital accordingly. In the approach suggested here, business managers are invited to think of mitigation tactics they would roll out in the event the scenario happens, regardless of probabilities. Involving and empowering the risk/business owners also allows for a refined approach. In this example, the business managers could be invited to think of the potential impact of the clients' credit deterioration on volumes traded, on the funding costs and on resource utilization.

4.3 AGGREGATING FIRM-WIDE RISK SENSITIVITY

Once the obtained sensitivity figures are reported back to the Risk Committee, they can be aggregated together according to category and

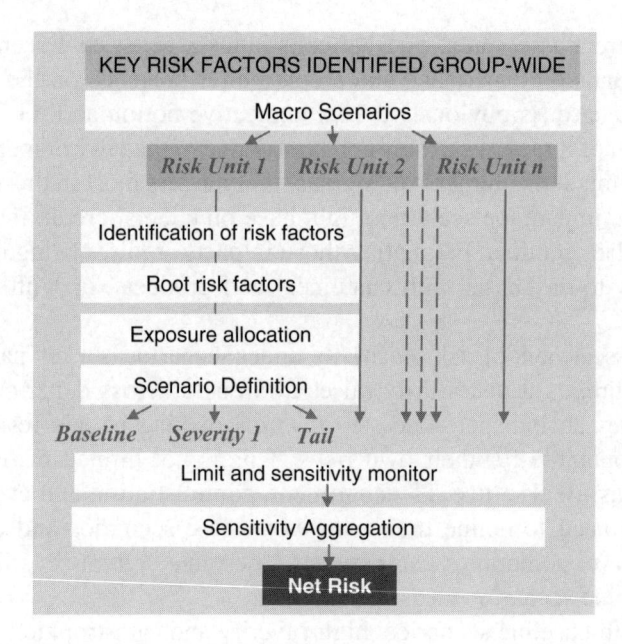

```
                KEY RISK FACTORS IDENTIFIED GROUP-WIDE
                          Macro Scenarios
                  Risk Unit 1   Risk Unit 2   Risk Unit n
                Identification of risk factors
                     Root risk factors
                    Exposure allocation
                    Scenario Definition
              Baseline   Severity 1   Tail
                  Limit and sensitivity monitor
                    Sensitivity Aggregation
                              Net Risk
```

Figure 4.4   From macro-scenario to aggregated risk

factor, and fed back into the broader frame of the key categories of the macro-factors and macro-scenarios. The resulting snapshot would show the firm's risk sensitivity under baseline, high-severity and catastrophic scenarios.

Figure 4.4 adds aggregations as a final step compared to the workflow described earlier in Figure 4.1.

Clearly this is a departure from computing value-at-risk (VaR) in isolation from the business units. The purpose of highlighting this distinction is not to compare a methodology against another one, nor to determine whether modelling VaR is better in describing risk than scenario-based aggregations of sensitivity (SBAS). The proposed methodology involves the business units, with the managers eventually responsible for loading up risks that we want to make them accountable for. No methodology, be it magically blessed with absolute forecasting precision, can therefore be understood, respected and continuously adapted unless it involves the people running the business.

Typically, VaR models are set to offset the redundant effects of shocking multiple factors. Results are usually consolidated in classes such as equity, interest rates, forex, commodities and a risk overlap resulting from correlations. For example, the VaR of strongly correlated equities and commodities would be readjusted so that the impact on commodity prices is not accounted for after equity prices have been already simulated. The proposed methodology does not involve this type of calculation, predominantly designed to compensate for the natural deficiencies of VaR methodologies. It instead focuses on real variations of sensitivities.

Some notable points arise. First, no correlation measured from past data is a valid element to be projected forward or used for risk hedging purposes. Second, if the scenario-based aggregation of sensitivity (SBAS) leads several units to hedge sensitivity potentially arising from a single risk factor, it actually reflects a leveraged exposure (multiple deltas) to this particular factor. Finally, as reiterated in the previous paragraphs, the purpose of the methodology is not to be scientifically accurate but to involve all people and to guide them until they feel comfortable with risk factor sensitivity and mitigation tools. In some cases, the individuals may choose to use quantitative analyses and VaR systems if that is what they are most comfortable with. As long as they are given the responsibility to account for the results and its corresponding transparency, and so long as it helps these individuals remain within their risk limits, then the goal of implementing a risk management culture throughout the company is reached.

4.4 AGGREGATING SCENARIOS

Another key benefit of distributing the tasks of scenario building for stress testing to the business units is that it gives the Risk Committee the possibility to reaggregate high severity and catastrophic scenarios defined by all field players across the firm. This brings major benefits, along with concepts entirely new to the world of risk management.

First, the estimate of what the sum of catastrophic scenarios would really cost to the entire organization shows the true value at risk of the firm. This is because the sum of sensitivities and maximum losses derived from very different types of activities is the aggregated view from the business managers who carry out the business themselves. We will see in later chapters how we maintain the integrity and reliability of their input. The Risk Committee no longer needs lengthy disclaimers estimating the possible deficiencies of the models in use or about the compatibility of underlying assumptions. The estimates no longer replicate the reality, for the results show the reality.

Under normal circumstances, people do not imagine scenarios they cannot cope with. Even when pushed to build catastrophic scenarios they are likely to refer to their own experience as a baseline. There is nothing wrong with business managers thinking within their own box, since this is precisely what they are required to do. The Risk Committee, on the other hand, is able to aggregate the mosaic with views from each 'box of thinking'. They will be able to estimate the usual sensitivity, extreme sensitivity and maximum losses of the firm, as seen by their own respective actors. Hence, they will be able to reconcile the views of the company with its own strategy. No company can deliver to plans while its own teams believe it will not pan out.

The aggregated view of the risk scenarios paints an overall picture of the actual risk appetite expressed by the firm through its day-to-day operations. Indeed, the sum of catastrophic scenario definitions arising from all units is an empirical description of what they collectively consider to be a worst case. This information is invaluable as it enables units to benchmark their own risk appetite against the rest of the company, allowing them to align their own risk aversion to the corporate risk policies. Further, it allows the Risk Committee to use these benchmarks to point out the hot spots of risk within the company – who is risk averse against who is overtly daring.

The collective expression of what constitutes high severity and catastrophe describes the actual risk appetite of a firm, simply because it describes its understanding of tail risks. Thus, the Risk Managers or the Executive Risk Committee can reconcile that actual risk profile of the firm against the risk appetite initially expressed by the shareholders through the risk policies. Equally important, this approach enables true transparency, unparalleled information feedback from and to the management, and a dynamic adjustment of risk policies if necessary.

A culture of risk management is now being established. It must firmly rest on a culture of transparency, which brings before the firm's management and shareholders the real value at risk, estimated by the very actors within the firm. The accuracy of the figure is less important than the fact that it emanates from the firm's components.

Figure 4.5 exhibits the process by which the risk appetite initially expressed by the shareholders and by the company's main creditors is translated into quantitative risk targets by the Executive Management. Once the exposure and sensitivity limits are in place, the risk managers collect all feedback to report the risk estimations from the operating managers responsible for their mitigation. The aggregated

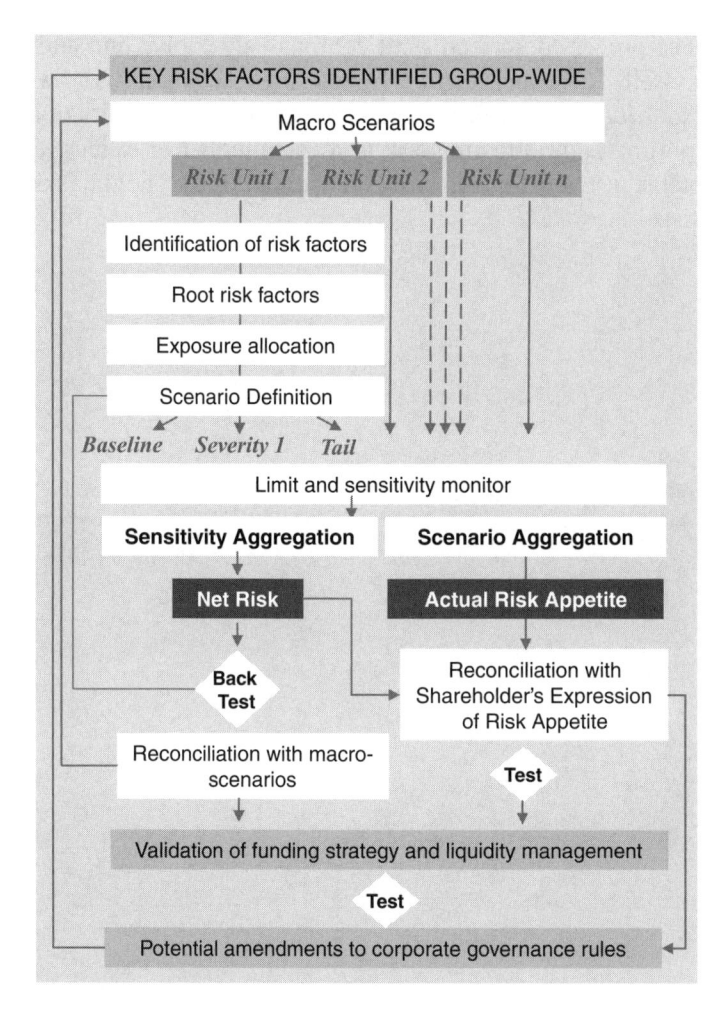

Figure 4.5 The real-life approach to value-at-risk

baseline, high-severity and catastrophic scenarios also provide invaluable feedback on the actual risk appetite the firm demonstrates through its business operations.

The final reconciliations with the shareholders' appetite for risk as described by the risk policies will be discussed in later chapters. They are critically important because it is at this stage that the firm becomes proactively responsive to risks, to the perception of risks and to the various assessments made by people responsible for delivering the firm's strategy. It is important to note that a state of perfection will never exist. The process described shall continuously evolve and attempt to perfect itself. Risk, as a culture rooted in every action, is now being managed. Moreover, the process has spread the responsibility of assessing, reporting and mitigating risk to a vast number of executives held accountable instead of laying the responsibility on the shoulders of a few specialists.

5

From Aggregated Risks to Distributed Risks

Traditional approaches to risk management, largely inspired by regulatory requirements such as Basel 2,[1] have led to enterprise-wide views where risk exposure was aggregated by business line. Such an internal control structure was essential to understanding how the risk profile of a diversified company would evolve over time and adjust capital allocations accordingly. By doing so, the focus was always on large exposure and concentrations of risks on business sectors, instead of risk factors.

5.1 THE TRADITIONAL APPROACH TO RISK MANAGEMENT HAS LED TO THE MODELLING OF EXPOSURE BY BUSINESS LINES

According to the Basel Accord, paragraph 752 on Pillar 2, 'In all instances, the capital level at an individual bank should be determined according to the bank's risk profile and adequacy of its risk management process and internal controls. External factors such as business cycle effects and the macroeconomic environment should also be considered.' This is a sound and simple principle intended dynamically to manage capital adequacy ratios. However, the first and the second Basel Accord documents consistently worked at dividing business activities by sectors, business lines, zones and so on, while considering only three main factors of risk – market, credit risk and operational risk – in Basel 2, thus leaving it to the banks' discretion to define for themselves their own factors of exposure within these three categories.

Focusing on concentrations while the firm was considered to be a collection of individual business lines has led to a dependence on modelling. The exposure to interest rates risks, for example, cannot be measured in

---

[1] *Core Principles for Effective Banking Supervision*, Basel Committee on Banking Supervision, September 1997, and *Core Principles Methodology*, Basel Committee on Banking Supervision, October 1999.

the same way at a trading desk as at a mortgage lending or securitization division. Therefore it would take a theoretical approach to model the impact of interest rates on credit risk across business silos. Since credit or market risk concentrations across the multiple activities of a business line are highly dependent on correlated risk factors – which as discussed earlier are extremely volatile and totally unpredictable in times of high market emotions – all attempts to 'break the silos' while aggregating risk exposure on business lines made risk assessments more theoretical, impractical and subject to model risk. In other words, value-at-risk (VaR) might be convenient in adding up apples and oranges but the resulting picture is not a basket of fruit. Furthermore, the complexity of modelling risk across those activities has contributed to the isolation of risk management from the business divisions in an eclectic, sometimes exclusive, world of quantitative analysis.

Figure 5.1 attempts to describe the main workflow of a traditional approach to risk management, through aggregation by business lines.

In this framework, risks are first aggregated by business division. Within the business division, the exposure is redistributed by 'asset classes'. Under Basel 2, the definition of an asset class amounts to product types of business activities, such as project finance, corporate finance and commodities finance. Rules are further specified for retail exposure as opposed to equity or wholesale banking, just to name a few. Clearly, the spirit of IRB (credit risk) or AMA (operational risk) is to derive a risk-weighted exposure for each business line, so that capital can be allocated according to such a 'risk profile'. Although the approach requires mining the possible sources of risk exposure to

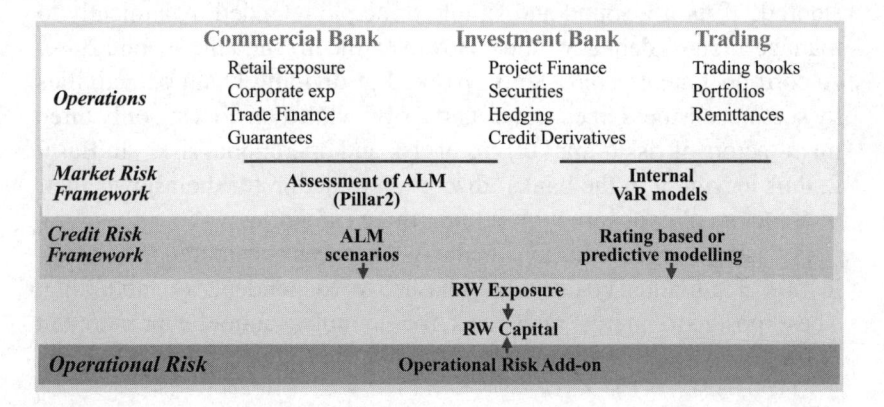

	Commercial Bank	Investment Bank	Trading
Operations	Retail exposure Corporate exp Trade Finance Guarantees	Project Finance Securities Hedging Credit Derivatives	Trading books Portfolios Remittances
Market Risk Framework	Assessment of ALM (Pillar2)		Internal VaR models
Credit Risk Framework	ALM scenarios		Rating based or predictive modelling
		RW Exposure ↓ RW Capital ↑	
Operational Risk		Operational Risk Add-on	

Figure 5.1 Traditional risk framework

qualify and quantify them, the philosophy clearly remains to measure the efficiency of capital rather than controlling the net exposure to loss events that might occur.

To a large extent, risk managers, in their haste to model all sorts of exposure and predict risk-weighted exposure moving forward, have detached the assessments of risks from the day-to-day reality of bearing the exposure. Traders end up, for instance, with VaR limits, computed overnight by mid-office risk management departments. In most cases these traders have little idea of how their trade tickets will impact the marginal VaR and what will come the next morning as a limit utilization figure. If requesting someone to be respectful of some figures that seem totally remote from their world, then it would be even harder asking this individual to be accountable for it. To address this, some sophisticated dealing rooms have implemented intra-day VaR proxies, which help traders grasp an idea of what will be the final impact after overnight computation. The true benefits of such complexity, however, remain questionable. Traders may now see the marginal impact of new tickets, but the philosophy of the whole process remains misaligned with their typical approach of sensitivity. A similar outcome would apply to mortgage loan or project finance departments. VaR can be useful for measurement of risk to measure, benchmark or compare capital efficiency, but it is by no means a risk 'management' tool. Such a tool should be designed so that it enables immediate action based on the measurements.

5.2 DISTRIBUTING RISK BY RISK FACTORS LEADS TO CREATION OF A CULTURE

The proposed distribution of risk by risk factor, on the contrary, leads to discussions, where all managers responsible for business activities, or P/L, get a chance to assess sensitivities on their own terms, with the tools of their choice and with the granularity that they feel appropriate.

As explained above, once a macro-factor, say foreign exchange, is distributed to the business divisions, each of them will derive microfactors from it. A trading desk, for example, may turn the macro-factor 'foreign exchange' into G7 currency movements, volatility, interest rate changes, interest rate volatility, emerging market currency spread, and so on. Following this, the desk may estimate the sensitivity to each of those factors under the scenarios. Simultaneously, a back-office department may derive 'foreign exchange' into micro-factors such as settlement in non-CLS currencies, traded volumes, volatility of interest rates – just to name a few. Project finance may translate 'foreign exchange' into funding rates in specific currencies and their impact on customers' collateral, and so on. In fact, 'foreign exchange risk' means different things to each business centre of the firm. Requesting each respective entity to estimate their losses or gains under various scenarios is an empirical way to measure the perceived sensitivity of the whole firm to foreign exchange movements. Modelling is unable to look at the risk from the different perspectives that the people in charge can do. Neither can regulators propose or impose a uniform methodology to assess the exposure to a given risk factor because it is peculiar to each company and even to each division within a company.

Certainly this approach renders discussion. Risk managers tasked with educating each department to dissect their risk exposure, refine risk factors and scenarios, assess and report sensitivities and estimate worst cases need to open frequent in-depth dialogue with the business units. Gone are the days of strictly 'ivory tower' quantitative analyses. Even though making people accountable for risks involves educating them to understand sensitivity and propose mitigation tactics, and will necessitate discussions regarding the choices of factors, scenarios and the methods to measure the sensitivity to those factors under those scenarios, so that risk limits can be derived, it is undoubtedly an important step towards establishing a culture of transparency and self-assessments of risks.

5.3 DISTRIBUTED RISK IMPLIES DATA ANALYSIS

Once the iterative process of choosing risk factors and defining scenarios is carried out, the next question that follows is finding the appropriate sources of data and information and defining the channels to convey it. Again, the aim of this mining and mapping process is twofold: obtaining the information as well as optimizing the workflow. Too often, the independence between risk management and operations has led to set multiple information channels, which over time may end up redundant, inefficient and a source of discrepancies.

Figure 5.2 is an example of intra-day monitoring of risks for a foreign exchange trading department. It sets P/L and sensitivity limits to the very variable chosen by the risk managers and business managers together. The report combines real-time data ticking from trading and processing systems, imports from databases such as customer relation management

Risk factors	Subfactors	Limit (Target)	Baseline Sensitivity ($)	Severity 1 Max loss	Catastrophic Max loss
Currency pairs	Delta	limit + utilization	P/L change	P/L change	P/L change
	Vega	from positions			
	Rho	by currency			
	Basis	by pair			
Options	Delta	delta limit +util.			
	Gamma				
	Vega	from options			
	Rho				
	Cx effect	valuation spread	Δ / scenario		
Counterparty	Default	PD x position	PD/sce x position		
	Spread	L/S exposure	P/L from spread		
	Credit	Ctpy limit			
	Collateral	Haircut	$ Δ / scenario		
Settlement	CLS				
	Others	Settlement limit			
Back-office	Exception	Nb failed trades	scenario impact		
	Misallocation	Nb trades			
Operations	Wrong-side trade	Nb trades	est cost/benefit		
	Missed stop	$ limit	est from claims		
Liquidity	Price slippage	Diff at execution			
	Collateral	Diff in value			
	Spot funding	$ rollover			
	Fwd funding	$ carry			
	Delta hedge	$Bkrs/Margins			

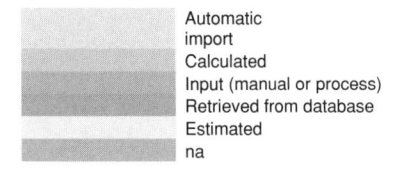

Automatic import
Calculated
Input (manual or process)
Retrieved from database
Estimated
na

Figure 5.2 Sample intra-day risk report of a foreign exchange trading unit

(CRM) or external services, calculations or pure estimations such as the impact of catastrophic scenarios or of intangible variables.

The first column features limits and utilization ratios. They range from the total position exposure to overall counterparty and settlement limits, the number of back-office misallocations or a quantified price slippage estimation. The other columns are the estimated changes in limit utilization under the respective scenarios. Take, for example, the change in P/L or in sensitivity due to the impact of the scenario. What was calculated is the difference before and after the scenario impact, which may require live links to the systems used for modelling, pricing and interpolation.

Clearly, the proportion of estimated versus calculated figures increases with the level of severity of the scenarios. This is a very important step towards establishing a corporate culture of risk management. Each risk and business unit is required to go through their own definition of high-severity and catastrophic scenarios and to estimate the potential costs of the failures that might result. This clearly requires the coaching and support of the risk managers to facilitate the necessary discussions and orient them in such a way that the output can be directly productive. As such, it is a very important awareness raising exercise, expected to create new bonds between the risk management and the operating units.

6
Creating an Adaptive Information Workflow

Allowing for an information workflow as described above to take place requires the a culture of risk management that allows for risk-based decision making. The culture needs to evolve, in order to put systems in place to provide the workflow and the quality of information. It is therefore critical to design an IT architecture that keeps adapting and refining as the culture gets deeper into the company's core strategic values and evolves with the external business conditions – bearing in mind that information should come first, followed by technology. It must be emphasized that with the focus on risk concentrations and transparency, the technology must adapt accordingly to the information flow and the culture – not the other way around.

There are three key challenges for the IT infrastructure to facilitate the risk information workflow.

First, the risk factors and exposure calculations that derive from multiple systems are used in different divisions with very different processing methods, also named silo processing. For example, for a macro-risk factor 'interest rates', a risk unit may be driven to combine data coming from bond trading systems, from OTC derivatives desks, from mortgage loan departments, collateral repository, yield curves calculators, volatility surfaces and more. To use a biological analogy, this is akin to laying out a nervous system.

Second, the retrieval of relevant information to enrich data sets is required. A price, for example, can be directly fed into a chart, but the sensitivity of the exposure must be computed. Since the exposure may arise from multiple sources and corresponding data from several systems, computing the sensitivity of exposure from all sources under a single scenario is a real challenge in terms of valuation risks, compatibility and integrity of methods. Multiple systems for data enrichment and financial libraries must be in sync with the scenario builders to obtain that timely information on exposure, sensitivity and maximum

58 The Handbook of Risk Management

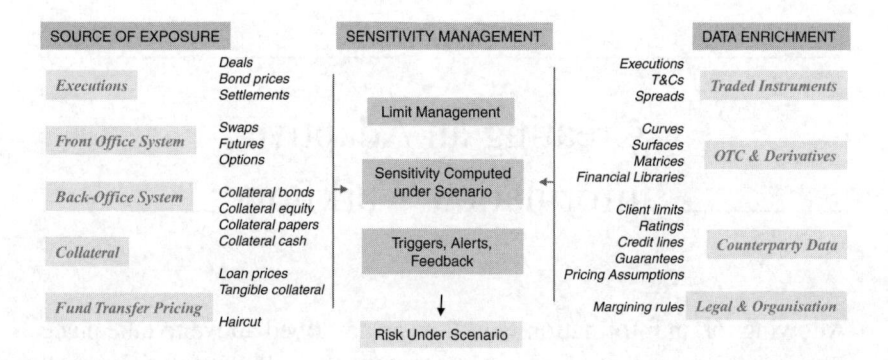

SOURCE OF EXPOSURE		SENSITIVITY MANAGEMENT	DATA ENRICHMENT	
Executions	Deals Bond prices Settlements		Executions T&Cs Spreads	*Traded Instruments*
Front Office System	Swaps Futures Options	Limit Management	Curves Surfaces Matrices Financial Libraries	*OTC & Derivatives*
Back-Office System	Collateral bonds Collateral equity Collateral papers	Sensitivity Computed under Scenario	Client limits Ratings	
Collateral	Collateral cash	Triggers, Alerts, Feedback	Credit lines Guarantees Pricing Assumptions	*Counterparty Data*
Fund Transfer Pricing	Loan prices Tangible collateral Haircut	↓ Risk Under Scenario	Margining rules	*Legal & Organisation*

Figure 6.1 Macro-risk factor: interest rates

loss. Going back to the biological analogy, this is like plugging system components into one another.

Third, when risk policies are translated into quantified risk targets managed by the units, triggers and alerts should be set up to react to the unwanted or excessive exposure that might arise from either business operations or changing market conditions. Such information needs to reach the decision makers so that they can make timely and informed decisions. It is only at this point that the 'nervous system' will kick-start and be well alive.

Figure 6.1 exhibits the typical workflow for a single risk factor, interest rates. The workflow is designed to distribute and monitor risk exposure by factors, identify root risk factors, manage scenario-based sensitivity and eventually reaggregate all scenarios into a live picture of the firm's risk appetite. This architecture allows the firm to retrieve exposure from multiple sources, to process or enrich data centrally and to compute the sensitivity and exposure limit utilization ratios. At the same time, it conveys information across the firm, back and forth, between business units and risk managers.

The information system is also the main repository of the scenarios. It allows for the definition of multifactor scenarios. A repository is necessary to draw information from and proceed with the scenario aggregation so that the risk managers can reconcile the risk appetite demonstrated through business activities (see Part 3) with the initial risk policies and macro-scenarios defined in concordance with the shareholders.

Whether the initial breakdown and final aggregation should be in a single or in multiple systems is a technical choice that IT departments can make depending on their size, legacy, skills and preferences. A single system may simplify processes but can complicate controls. On the other hand, multiple systems may produce more complexity but are potentially more flexible and with room to evolve.

To successfully implement a culture of risk management precisely requires the departure from all technocratic approaches where the information flow would depend on the systems. Preferences or distribution of powers should be de-emphasized. What is absolutely essential is that the users' needs in terms of information should supersede all technological aspects or the system itself will face difficulties to evolve.

6.1 GETTING THE SYSTEM TO EVOLVE

Financial institutions, like any other corporations, evolve organically with new instruments and services, innovations, new target markets and inorganic growth through mergers and acquisitions. Undeniably, this impacts on the factors of risks the company is exposed to.

In the old frameworks, where exposure was aggregated by business lines that were then modelled for market, credit and operational risk calculations, a new business meant a new silo. It would inevitably result in more technical integration and more modelling complexity. If the new factors overlapped old ones or made them redundant, it would take a whole audit on models to spot the issue, amend the processes, back-test the results, check potential failures, and so on. In the new framework, a new business is a series of additional risk factors. They are immediately allocated to the business managers generating the new exposure. If factors are overlapping or redundant, the business managers will make sense of it themselves through their overall sensitivity assessments.

To make this clearer, we will compare both methodologies through the example of a bank treasury department who wish to add interest rates option business to the existing money market derivatives trading books. The banks will now trade deals in swaptions, caps, floors, collars and bond OTC options.

In a traditional framework, adding interest rate options to the treasury management, activities would commence with the need for the IT department to provide back-office processing systems and possibly pre-trade analytical tools (pricers, deal capture, etc). The IT department either purchases a new system on top of legacy or extends the remit of a modular system they might have already implemented. Either way, additional source data come as a new feed, post-trade data are exported to ledger, to accounting systems and to whatever produces activity reports. Simultaneously, the risk managers update their own systems. It starts with plugging the legacy into the new sources in order to account for the new instruments in their reports. The additional risk factors arising from the new activity need be modelled within VaR calculations. Here starts the real complexity. The VaR methodology splits the exposure by risk drivers (rates, equity, fx, commodities) and extracts the individual risk from each factor out of correlation or covariance matrices. As a result, adding a new instrument may not lead to the review of the entire methodology. The matrices need to be reopened each time, which raises other questions with respect to data integrity among financial instruments and the individual liquidity of their respective markets that lead to the correlation measured.

The exercise is not only tedious and costly. It piles up assumptions and models on top of each other, which only relies on correlation assumptions built empirically as houses of cards. Model risk is at its maximum and no Monte Carlo simulation will factor the possibility that the models misprice the exposure or the hedges. More importantly, the process does not involve those who generate the exposure, hedge it and manage it on a day-to-day basis.

Through the new approach, where exposure from the risk factors is distributed to the operational units responsible for it, the new macro-risk factor, say interest rate options, is split into micro-factors, such as interest rates, volatility, delta/gamma, model risk and settlements allocated to the business desk. The desk manager in charge of dealing those instruments along with the previous ones is then also tasked with sensitivity assessments under scenarios that are believed to be plausible according to the specialists who trade them. The vega, delta and gamma limits they obtain add up to the existing ones. Therefore, if the exposure is mispriced due to the inappropriateness of the models, it will show immediately in the Greeks and can be adjusted instantly. Mid-office managers can still compute Monte Carlo simulations in the background for the purpose of back-testing and benchmarking, but no longer to define risk limits, control exposure nor allocate capital.

The whole process is not only faster and pragmatically efficient, it most importantly involves the actual players, raises their awareness and lets them live with the concerns of the risk they generate. If they reach a point of overleverage, they will feel it and be uncomfortably aware of it, thereby enrooting the culture even deeper.

The IT infrastructure deals with the additional complexity through an open architecture, allowing it to manage hundreds of feeds that run periodically. Information needs to be temporarily stored in buffer zones while enriched data are being conveyed or computed. Going back to our fixed income derivatives example, the system may retrieve bond prices used as collateral. While bonds can be priced in real-time, the collateral information may be retrieved from a back-office system, use margining information (haircut) from another system, and so on. For the final exposure and hedge sensitivity calculation to take place, all data are stored in a temporary repository where scenario-based curves and credit matrices are interpolated and rule-based processes on margins and haircuts can be carried out.

The new approach of distributed exposure by risk factor simplifies this process. Since the operating desks manage the haircut exposure, they become responsible for the risk sensitivity as part of pre-trade analytics. Measures of risk are no longer someone else's problem. The operating units are frequently aware of the deteriorating liquidity of a market or price slippage before anyone else. If they do not want to be in discrepancy with the back-office reports due next day because of valuation issues, they might ring alerts immediately as soon as information on their screens notifies them of a credit event on one of the issuers, as an example. Moving forward, the back-office departments could even be inspired from this practice to upgrade their own process and use the availability of credit events as real-time data within their systems, for example.

6.2 MOVING ON TO THE NEXT STEP

This chapter has described and commented on the first critical step towards implementing a corporate culture of risk management. It consists of distributing all risk exposure by risk factors to all groups or individuals of a company that are responsible for it, instead of cumulating it on business lines.

To distribute risks, the management team and the risk management division first need to identify the macro risk factors that might impact on the operations or the balance sheet of the firm. It is necessary to work through conduits that lead to the root-risks in order to pick the actual variable that is the original source of volatility. The macro-factors are then submitted to all who can assess the exposure of groups, subgroups of individuals to those factors and to their components, the micro-factors. Once the exposure is understood and acknowledged by all, each unit can estimate the sensitivity of their exposure under a baseline scenario, a high-severity scenario and a catastrophic one, or more scenarios within these categories.

Following this process, risk managers are in a position to sum up all the estimated risks associated with each factor and aggregate all scenarios as an expression of the firm's actual appetite for risk.

Notably, the main benefit of this methodology, which is also its challenge, is to involve the largest possible population in the identification, mitigation and reporting of risks. The mission of the risk management department therefore evolves to fostering a culture of risk management. This indicates that there will need to be coaching and education involved until all units can identify, quantify and mitigate risks. This may require insights of business operations, back-office procedures, quantitative analysis, management, administration and production.

Another distinct benefit is the simplified pragmatic approach that our methodology brings to the critical issue of valuation risk. Considerable efforts can be made by a firm to minimize the risks of mispricing, late valuations, data integrity, model risk and all other operational issues that can impact on the value of assets, liabilities and collateral. Yet a share of those risks, which are quite unpredictable and difficult to measure, will remain. The delegation of sensitivity assessment and scenario building to the very actors who manipulate financial instruments days in days out, speak to counterparties continuously and see that markets moving in real-time will not fix the issue of valuations, but it gives the firm an opportunity to react in a timely manner, adjust figures or even methodologies as the market evolves.

The methodology builds on the core principles of risk management. Tail risk is a reality, unpredictable, rare, but repetitive when it does happen. Standardization and uniformity always concentrate risk. Only diversity mitigates them by spreading exposure out. External, systematic and systemic risks and their impact on idiosyncratic risks need to be taken into consideration. The scenarios should clearly describe this relation.

The methodology recommended is not rigidly set. On the contrary, it is designed to evolve with the changing market conditions, legal and regulatory frameworks, and internal changes such as staff turnover, etc. It is designed to adapt the firm's operations to those external conditions in the context of the mission statement from the shareholders. The reconciliation with the shareholder's risk appetite eventually comes from the aggregation of risk sensitivity and scenario, a process that will be subsequently described in detail in Part 3, which is dedicated to creating a risk-focused information workflow across the enterprise.

Part 2
Empowering Business and Risk Units with Risk Management Capabilities

Executive Summary

This Part deals with one of the main dogmas of traditional risk management methodology, which requires a total separation of front-line and back-office operations with risk management. Although the rationale for a 'Chinese Wall' preventing accumulations of power to lead to abuses is intuitively sensible, it has over time contributed to disconnect business operations and risk management. The proposed methodology fosters an environment of responsibility and accountability, ensuring that risk can no longer be 'someone else's problem'. The corporate DNA we want to establish as a key strategic driver requires common goals and a common language in order to decipher instructions.

The Part clarifies the role of business unit managers with respect to their responsibility for the risks they generate through the business operations they control. It repurposes the role of the risk department, audit and controls, providers of methodology, coaches and referees, and, most importantly, the respective roles of the executive management team (CEO, CFO and CRO) as well as the responsibility of the shareholders. The distribution and empowering of the key business leaders with risk management capabilities require a tight control to maintain the alignment between the exposure and sensitivity they generate with the appetite of the shareholders. Such appetite must therefore be clearly defined and communicated, it must remain reasonably stable and, most importantly, the right values must be rewarded. It is difficult in reality to make someone responsible for risks if the only performance recognized is the return on capital and the growth of margins.

In this Part we therefore propose a new methodology to approach risk-weighted performance, significantly departing from the current ones. The major change is that it recognizes notions of sensitivity and volatility in position accounting methods. Independently from the achieved returns, the timeframe of an investment should logically influence the mark-to-market frequency and methodology. There have been interesting proposals to mark positions to market as a function of the costs and availability of funding, or ones that depend on the investors' holding timeframe. These attempts to integrate a notion of liquidity in position valuations are very valid but clearly impractical on a large scale.

We suggest a mark-to-volatility approach in which the frequency of mark-to-value would depend on market volatility, itself containing factors of time, liquidity, transparency of information and leverage to risk factors.

This new definition of market efficiency recognizes the fact that there is some effectiveness in the way the financial markets respond to changes in information but the response is not necessarily in sole closing prices as imagined by Markowitz and Sharpe. The figure that seems to encapsulate all information available and unevenly disclosed to the market participant is increasingly the implied volatility of those prices.

The second step following the allocation of risk and sensitivity targets to all business and risk units is to empower them with the following: the capability to mitigate, control their risk and task them with reporting the efficiency of their mitigation and compliance with risk limits.

For a firm to claim that risk management has become a core value of their corporate culture, it needs the head of units in charge to feel not only responsible but accountable for the risk they generate and for its mitigation as well. This is because people will not feel accountable for issues they do not comprehend. For this reason, Part 1 was dedicated to allocating the responsibility of identifying and measuring risk to the business unit, coached by the risk managers and under the control of the audit department. The next logical step is to ensure that each unit that receives a risk management target gets a chance to mitigate such risks with tools and methodology it fully understands and wholeheartedly likes to use.

This subsequently leads to new challenges in terms of providing data for a consistent use of hedging and risk mitigation methodologies.

7
Allocating Risk Management Capabilities

Allocating risk mitigation responsibilities and tasking the respective managers accordingly is an important first step. In the past, risk committees driven by the risk management department would report exposure and risks to an executive risk committee who might enforce rules to maintain risks within the desired boundaries. Eventually the risk mitigation action would be carried out by the business unit. Whether it is for a trading desk to unwind some positions, the back-office to call for additional margin or for a loan department to adjust their collateral policies, the executive committee would direct the course of action, but rarely implement it themselves. This invariably leads to time consuming processes, discussions and potentially frictions or conflicts.

In addition to these inefficiencies, there are three major drawbacks attached to the traditional methodology.

First, the time spent between the moment a risk alert is triggered, a limit is overridden and an action is taken can be considerable. Let us take the example of one credit event hitting the news. Typically, not all banks or asset managers learn of the news simultaneously. The time zone differences, the varying network efficiency and internal processes means that some managers will receive the information first. A typical reaction during the short period of time when a firm knows of an important piece of information before everyone else is aware of it is to unwind positions as quickly as possible. The firm may be directly exposed to the defaulting counterparty through a credit line, but the exposure can also come from securities, bonds or equities, held in portfolio.

The total time it will take to translate the information (credit event) into a decision (unwind) and into a confirmed trade ticket is critical. In the meantime, price, spreads, volatility, correlations, liquidity and many other variables have ample time to turn unfavourably for the firm. In times of high market tension, the time it takes to turn the confirmed trade tickets into cleared and settled transactions can dramatically impact the firm's funding costs and reputational risks, if the market believes (rightly or wrongly) it is overly exposed.

Second, there is considerable operational risk in detaching the decision from the front line. Going back to the example of a diversified firm like a bank, with an unexpected exposure to a defaulting issuer, all trading limits should immediately be frozen as the event is known on the market so that the firm does not unnecessarily load unwanted exposure, which may come unexpectedly if orders left in electronic equity books get filled within minutes as prices fall sharply. In some cases, the different desks within the very same firm have been arbitraged against one another by external counterparties. During the days preceding the default of the Italian company Parmalat, for instance, an arbitrage window between CDS trading desks and equity desks was left open for 48 hours at many firms. Indeed, CDS spreads were already severely affected by the growing rumours. Meanwhile equity desks and more critically equity options desks were still trading within the normal range. Needless to say all 'buy stop' and 'limit sell' orders at equity desks were rapidly filled so that unaware firms found themselves with huge long positions in Parmalat. Following the costly incident, the market learned how to arbitrage equity volatility with default probabilities.

The key issue stems from one of the fundamental principles of traditional risk frameworks. It states that business operations and risk management should be totally independent, with respect to lines of reporting, valuations and accounting methodologies and even in the choice of their data sources. All entities would have worked very hard at establishing 'Chinese Walls' between front-office, back-office and risk management operations. In reality, rules can become so rigid that they become predictable. It is then only a matter of time before a rogue trader, a computer geek or some white collar criminal outsmarts the systems and uses its rigidity against itself.

7.1 BUSINESS MANAGERS ARE RISK MANAGERS

The next step after making business managers aware and responsible for risks and sensitivity is to make them accountable for it. The notion of accountability is essential to creating a culture that is to go far beyond the notions of practice, code of conduct or even a discipline of risk management. If no one can feel responsible for things they do not understand, then no one would feel accountable for things they cannot control. For this reason, the tasks related to the mitigation of risks must be allocated to those who we want to make accountable for it. What needs to be avoided is the feeling that risk is the problem of someone else. The only way to achieve the right mindset is to consider that each business manager is a risk manager. Not only the front-line operation units, but the back-office, the senior management, legal and administration departments, production units, IT, and even contractors, everyone who generates risk exposure of any sort on behalf of a firm, should be given risk targets and made accountable for mitigation. How can this be achieved? How can we unwind the most 'set-in-stone' precept of risk management that front-office, back-office and mid-office must be fully independent of their valuations, risk assessments and decision making or else the firm runs the risk of creating entire generations of rogue traders or simply lead honest managers into complacency?

We must first acknowledge that the precept led to disastrous situations and that the lessons learnt from risk management failures such as Barings, Long-Term Capital Management (LTCM) and, more recently, Société Générale do not seem to impede new crises. The concept of running separate calculations using individual data sets and methodologies, and then interpreting risk results and reconciling front-office and back-office, is actually harmless. The menace is when this principle leads the mid-office or risk managers to be solely accountable for risks and business operations, yet to feel either detached or isolated from it. There is nothing wrong in having dual calculations if those whose actions generate risks are also accountable for the assessments and for the calculations leading to such mitigation. There is nothing wrong with having an independent risk management coaching the effort, providing with resources, education and back-testing the results for performance appraisals. Certainly there will be times for discussion and the need of arbitration that we recommend the audit department to be responsible for. Those discussions are necessary and essential to instilling a culture of risk management.

Eventually there must be a single manager or managing group responsible for compliance to risk targets. It is absolutely critical for firms to develop the kind of agility and responsiveness that are needed in the face of fast-moving, volatile markets where tail risks can develop unexpectedly. If risk managers are left with the reconciliation of front-office and back-office P/L, for example, and need to find the source of discrepancies before they can interview both parties and express a view on the source of the issues, it may take weeks before anyone can unravel whether there is a failure in models, methodology or

70   The Handbook of Risk Management

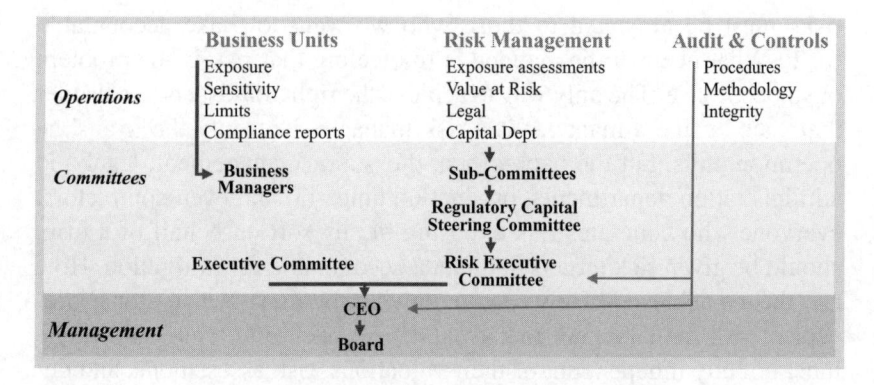

	Business Units	Risk Management	Audit & Controls
Operations	Exposure Sensitivity Limits Compliance reports	Exposure assessments Value at Risk Legal Capital Dept	Procedures Methodology Integrity
Committees	Business Managers	Sub-Committees ↓ Regulatory Capital Steering Committee	
	Executive Committee	Risk Executive Committee	
Management		CEO ↓ Board	

Figure 7.1 Conventional risk reporting and escalation procedures

perhaps an organizational issue. Meanwhile, markets have had time to change, reverse or dry out – which can be costly to the firm. More importantly, the approach does not really keep the sources of risk exposure under pressure and it certainly does not make them feel accountable beyond their normal workload. For the firm to be responsive, business managers must be given the power to control and mitigate their risks themselves. The risk management department would be accountable for the methodology and for the transparency of the process rather than the end result. The audit department could serve as a referee as well as a coach on procedures, ethics and corporate governance issues while the legal department would be involved in producing assessments at each step of the process. Figures 7.1 and 7.2 illustrate the necessary changes to be made when allocating risk management capabilities and responsibilities.

	Business Units	Audit & Controls
Operations	Operations Risk Management Exposure Mitigation Sensitivity Risk scenarios Net exposure /scenarios Limits Compliance to risk policies	Procedures Methodology Integrity
Risk Committee *Management*	Risk Executive Committee ↓ CEO ↓ Board	Compliance Referral *Risk Policies*

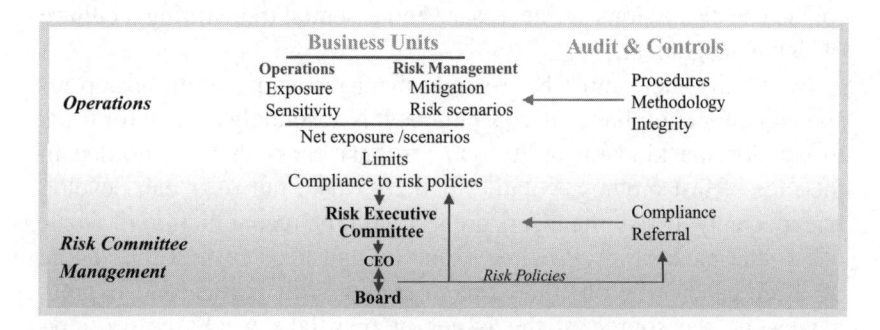

Figure 7.2 New age risk control and reporting framework

7.2 THE ROLE OF EXECUTIVE RISK COMMITTEES

The knowledge, experience and expertise of risk managers, risk committees and executive risk committees, combined with their resources and IT infrastructure offer important value to the methodology and integrity of the risk calculation processes and results that business managers are now responsible and accountable for. The role these committees play now leans towards the upper end of the curve . The taste of the 2008–2009 crisis has been instructive for risk management. The widespread notion, thereafter, was that the neglect on managing risk was fatal and risk managers should secure extended powers from the board to fulfil their obligations and potentially enforce some of their decisions. It was clear the failure did not lie in the process, nor the methods, models or calculations. It was the failure *of* the process. Risk management frameworks that consisted of computing extremely sophisticated assessments on a daily basis, sometimes using intra-day and low-latency market feed, mainly led to printed reports. Typically, those reports were checked and recomputed by risk committees who then aggregated enterprise wide exposure, essentially for regulatory capital calculation and periodic high-level reporting to the management. In hindsight, the process produced impressively accurate results but was futile in helping firms to be agile in the face of risk.

Moving forward, risk managers, risk departments and Chief Risk Officers (CROs) as well as executive risk committees should be tasked with developing the agility, responsiveness and precision of the firm to handle properly any risk factors that might affect it. To achieve this, it will be necessary to participate in the identification of risk factors, the build-up of risk scenarios, computation and valuations of assets, liabilities and collateral, risk mitigation, transparency and integrity throughout the process. The processes currently set in place are suitable, but the purposes and the utilization of end results are fundamentally different.

What about the risks involved in the process? In the past, business managers have been detached from tasks involving risk analysis in order to avoid being misguided by erroneous results without a chance to seek a second opinion or fooled by the duality of functions that could produce biased results potentially leading to extreme situations, such as embezzlements or disastrous losses. Yet the most efficient systems can only be designed in the context of knowledge or information that can be learned at that given point in time. Companies constantly evolve, grow, diversify and merge, just as personnel continue to change as staff turnover takes place. If a risk management framework is arguably perfect today, it cannot account for business operations and personnel that are yet to be in existence at the time when the framework is designed. Hence, if the system does not support the evolution of the risk management culture as the business continues to grow with personnel change, then the days are numbered before a rogue trader who understands the loopholes in the rigidity of the system makes use of the system for inappropriate purposes. Every system, every set of rules that is rigidly deployed and implemented becomes predictable, hence making it vulnerable. Nick Leeson at the former Barings Bank and Jerome Kerviel at Socgen were able to carry out activities without the awareness of their respective risk management departments because they knew their respective bank systems inside out. Bernard Madoff, who infamously ran a multibillion dollar Ponzi scheme, knew everything about the controls he might face and how to escape regulators' scrutiny. These detailed insights allowed him to hide his fraud scheme for years.

The rigidity in the risk procedures, the predictability (or lack) of audit controls, create loopholes. With the new approach in risk management, an unscrupulous manager tempted to abuse the system for personal benefit, embezzlement or any other unauthorized purposes would be in the same functioning position as in the old approach. However, in the new approach, the unscrupulous manager could never be sure of the controls independently carried out to reproduce and back-test the produced results. Moreover, as previously explained in Part 1, the manager is now tasked with reporting not only the P/L and exposure but also factors such as sensitivity, scenarios, maximum potential losses and risk limit utilization by risk factors. If a manager conceals fake deals, the exposure will not match the sensitivity. If positions are opened and then closed intra-day so they do not appear in exposure, then the sensitivity figures and statistics will reflect unusual shifts and movements. Alternatively, if an unusual amount of transactions are cancelled or amended, there will be alerts.

Most importantly, through the depth of risk analyses required the business manager will now have gain skills. This is the point when executive risk committees and risk managers have progressed to a new level of independence.

7.3 THE ROLE OF AUDIT AND CONTROL UNITS

Discussions are inevitable, if not necessary, to the process of establishing a corporate culture. Similar to product quality workshops or customer satisfaction seminars, which many corporations frequently conduct, everyone needs to sit down and think about the individual share of risk management they can bring to the firm. Such discussions should not be left to their own devices, and would be productive only if they are guided and oriented in a purposeful manner. In the proposed framework, the risk managers will initiate the discussions, lead business units to define their own monitoring mechanisms, negotiate the targets with the units and establish the information workflow to monitor exposure, sensitivity and maximum losses at all times. Active involvement of the CEO and the executive management team in the process will be highly beneficial. However, as they are unlikely to devote enough time and attention to the issues, the role would be best filled by the audit department.

If operating units are tasked with risk management and risk managers are responsible for the methodology and processes, then the audit department will fit in the role of refereeing between both of these two independent groups. The referee's role would focus on upholding the integrity and consistency of methodologies applied throughout the enterprise rather than pure arbitration. For all purposes, the audit and control department should be supported by the legal department, as many of the options and choices could have legal repercussions.

The integrity, consistency and compatibility of risk management methods are critical to reflect properly the corporate risk policies. Auditing risk methodologies is not about deciding what is good and bad. The main purpose of the risk committee is to translate the risk policies into risk targets, hedging tactics, reporting methodologies and compliance strategies that reflect the true appetite for risk that the shareholders have expressed. They must be coherent, compatible and focused to allow room for agility and decision making. For example, some private banks with a recent audit of their methodologies may have discovered that the risk measurement methods used for their fund management business starkly differed from those used for bond trading. In other words, there would consistently be a difference in the sensitivity measured at the customer portfolio level to the ones traders believe they have passed on to their customers. The discrepancies may have come from data feed, pricing methods, valuation frequency or, more worryingly, from some unknown mark-up practices. Auditing the consistency of the methods used not only helps to ensure that the difference is acceptable but that it is fully understood, controlled and documented – in a nutshell, 'transparent'.

Every mitigation strategy is based on purposes. Oil producers sell their production forward and engineer their hedges in very different ways from a hedge fund, even though the resulting course of action remains a forward sale in both cases. The former may choose long maturity rolling contracts to minimize basis risk while the latter may privilege liquidity. Auditing methodologies are about determining whether a strategy or a set of tactics is appropriate to the purpose and whether it suits corporate values.

In some cases, arbitration between business units and risk managers will be required and, interestingly, a desired side effect from raising awareness and a sentiment of responsibility. We expect people to become passionate about risk and should therefore brace themselves for friction in opinions. The audit department, following the reviews of methodologies and appropriateness, is in a perfect position to rule on conflicts. Let us assume an example where business managers and the risk department would disagree on sensitivity limits. If there is a P/L target, there should be an activity volume target. If there is a business volume, then there is corresponding sensitivity. A disagreement on sensitivity may either come from differences in expected business volume, scenario, sensitivity calculations or data mismanagement, where discussion on business volumes can be settled by the parties themselves. However, the philosophy and assumptions underneath the scenario and calculations should correspond to established methodologies. Curve-fitting methods, for example, or interest rate option models may be different depending on the risk profile of the company. Data sources may be different but they should not be misaligned. The methodology debate on the sources that should prevail, their accompanying rationale and corresponding case should be well mediated by the audit department.

While the risk management department is ultimately responsible for the taxonomy of financial instruments, selections of financial libraries, project management procedures and scenario building methodologies, the accountability for the integrity in which those rules are applied and the consistency with the risk policies lies with the audit and control department.

8
Mitigation Strategies and Hedging Tactics

Once the roles and responsibilities have been well allocated, then the hedging instruments and risk mitigation tools can be distributed. The relative independence that has been engineered to make the various business units more responsible and especially accountable for the risk they generate should not be followed by uncontrolled hedging strategies leading to an unmanageable number of risk mitigation tactics or hedging instruments. On the contrary, the level of awareness and expertise in risk sensitivities should have distinctly improved so that the people in charge have a more pragmatic grasp on risk management tools and their efficiency.

Equally important, the risk management department needs to set up boundaries and controls to make sure that the whole undertaking continuously guides towards more agility and responsiveness, instead of opacity or unwanted exposure.

8.1 FRONT-LINE BUSINESS UNITS

The first example of risk mitigation and hedging strategy that naturally springs to mind is the case of trading rooms, using derivatives to control and fine-tune their risk exposure. Let us take the example of a fixed income desk and go through the iterative process.

First, the risk committee considers macro-risk factors, such as levels of interest rates, inflation, defaults, etc. The desk turns those macro-factors into components of risk. Interest rate risk, for example, becomes short end, long end, curve steepening, flattening, interest rates volatility, basis risk and cross-currency basis. The desk sends these back to the risk management for approval. Once approved, the managers work out the key variable to monitor (root-risk), believed to be the key driver of sensitivity of each micro-factor. Going back to our example, the liquidity of short money market instruments can be monitored though the spreads between Eonia (euro overnight index average) and Libor

(London interbank offered rate). Now that the risk management and the business units have agreed on a variable to monitor the liquidity risk of short end instruments, they can precisely compute the exposure to the variable and what it is likely to become through scenario roll-out. Once this is achieved, the desk can set precise and transparent risk targets under each scenario.

The next step is for the desk to identify risk mitigation tools and propose them to the risk managers. A discussion takes place on the appropriateness and accuracy of the hedging tools, perhaps Eonia swaps and Libor future options. The risk management department can at this point deploy all their quantitative analytical tools to run simulations, stress tests and calibrations. When the set of hedging tools is finally approved, the desk receives the authorization to use those tools for the defined purposes and within limits associated with the maximum acceptable exposure.

If we compare this iterative process with what is commonly achieved today, the end exposure and tools I use may not be very different, but the transparency, the internal dialogues and the overall level of engagement from each side are distinctly different. In traditional risk management frameworks, the hedging tools are generally picked by the position managers who use them the way they want as long as they remain within the defined limits. The risk management team then computes independently the value-at-risk and stress scenarios and hands over the results to the executive risk committee, which may or may not be willing to discuss the appropriateness and the efficiency of the hedges. If a discussion follows, it often leads to swift opposition to the pragmatism and experience of the traders and preference to accept the theoretical assessments carried out essentially through quantitative analytics by the risk managers. Regardless of the direction of the discussion, it rarely ends up in consensus building, and nor does it promote a culture of disclosure and transparency. In any case, the process does not enhance agility and is unlikely timely to detect inefficiencies in hedging.

Another issue is that hedges may need to change over time. The same hedging tool may lose its efficiency as the markets change and evolve. Counterparty risks and market liquidity continuously change the way they provide exposure for use in hedging purposes. With the new approach proposed, each hedging tool is directly linked to a hedging purpose itself attached to a variable and a target. If the hedging instruments lose some of their efficiency and if the hedges tend to slip, then it will immediately appear on the limit utilization figures. Since

Mitigation Strategies and Hedging Tactics 77

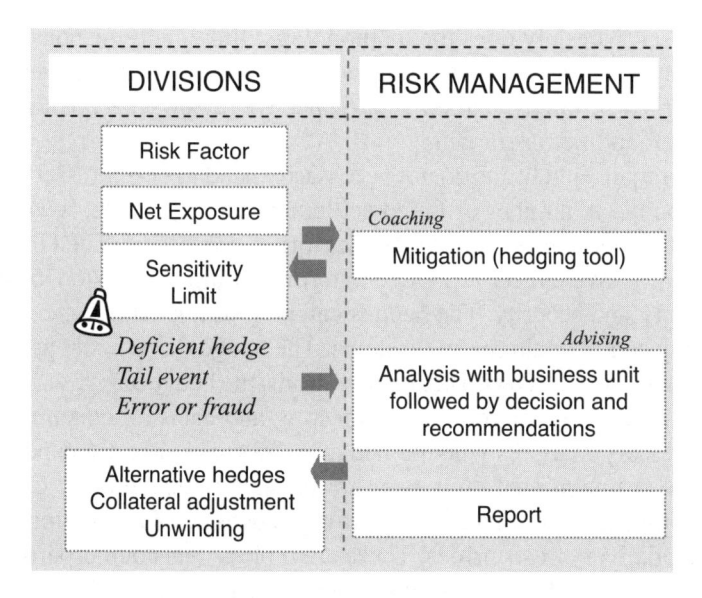

```
┌─────────────────────────────┬──────────────────────────────┐
│         DIVISIONS           │      RISK MANAGEMENT         │
├─────────────────────────────┼──────────────────────────────┤
│     Risk Factor             │                              │
│                             │   Coaching                   │
│     Net Exposure       ──►  │   Mitigation (hedging tool)  │
│     Sensitivity        ◄──  │                              │
│     Limit                   │                              │
│  ⚠                          │              Advising        │
│  Deficient hedge            │   Analysis with business unit│
│  Tail event            ──►  │   followed by decision and   │
│  Error or fraud             │   recommendations            │
│                             │                              │
│  Alternative hedges    ◄──  │                              │
│  Collateral adjustment      │   Report                     │
│  Unwinding                  │                              │
└─────────────────────────────┴──────────────────────────────┘
```

Figure 8.1 Dynamic sensitivity control and hedging

the choice of the hedging tool initially resulted from a discussion between the business units and the risk management, it will be easy to resume discussion, analyse the issue and look for alternative solutions. The whole process is now dynamic and reacts to changes more quickly (see Figure 8.1).

8.2 OPERATIONAL UNITS

Not all operational units are trading desks and the measurement of hedging efficiency may not always be a quantitative ratio. It remains that every operational unit that exposes the firm to risk factors should be allocated risk targets and similarly agrees with the risk management on mitigation methodologies.

Take the example of a back-office department, where financial products sometimes generate long life cycles. Floating rates need to be reset, payments processed, collateral adjusted, etc. The macro-risk factor 'interest rates' may have been cut into micro-factors such as delayed payments, currency changes and collateral adjustments. The chosen variables for monitoring root risks could be the rate volatility or the numbers of early terminations. The hedges could be additional resources or the purchase of electronic settlement tools implemented with the largest customers. Not only does the methodology allow more responsiveness and more pragmatic ways to address issues, it also helps to unveil operational risks through the internal introspective reviews that are necessary to implement the risk targets.

Risk targets and limits do not necessarily need to be expressed in dollar amounts. A number of failed settlements, for example, would be a good expression of sensitivity for back-office processing. The IT departments may have targets expressed in terms of output precision, business continuity and security. The hedges can be multiple data sources, a hot recovery centre or alternative systems. The hedges have a cost just as futures contracts do. As with hedged positions, the hedge may lose or maintain its efficiency. Therefore stress testing and catastrophe simulations are necessary to assess whether hedges perform as they are expected.

Risks at operational units may not be strictly operational. Counterparties may, for example, fail to provide necessary information or default on delivery of securities. These are no less than counterparty risks, which can be evaluated in terms of what the failures would cost to the company, risk concentrations and potential repercussions on other departments. The mitigations would be alternative sources, diversification and avoiding concentrations of risk on a small number of counterparties. Again, questions need to be raised, and preferably answered, to assess those risks and design mitigation plans, which are key to enhancing transparency through a productive involvement and participation of all parties. The process would then be identical to front-line operations, whereby each risk unit receives sensitivity targets and limits and remains responsible for the follow-up and reporting of the efficiency of mitigation techniques.

8.3 MANAGEMENT

Clearly the firm's mid-management and senior management teams are also risk generators. For example, a product strategy, a marketing campaign or a financial plan are direct generators of market, credit and operational exposure. There will be two types of risk targets at management level: those that are allocated to front-line and operating units and those that would only result from the management decisions. These are not to be confused with the risks of the business units under their control. For example, by making the decision to invest in a new market, a retail banking department exposes the bank to new market, credit and operational risks that have been distributed to the units and assigned for mitigation as described above. In addition, the decision itself exposes the firm to reputational risks, legal risks and additional operational risks related to the management of the project itself. The new activity has an impact on the economic and regulatory capital, therefore creating a cost of funding. More importantly, the same type of scenarios as described in Part 1 must be carried out. Going back to the current example, if a banking group decides to invest in retail banking in China and by doing so partners up with a local bank, there will be a number of catastrophe scenarios to be considered. The scenarios would involve the country risk, asset and liability exposure due to the project itself, legal risks, currency risks and, if the firm is sophisticated enough, even the cost of opportunity.

At the mid-management level, the sensitivity assessment and the selection of mitigation tactics may be almost identical to the process described above. We can anticipate, however, that the task of extracting the sensitivity of investment decisions, highlighting risks and discussing mitigation strategies with the senior managers or even the board members who control the company may be more delicate. It is at this stage, as we reach the role of the CEO and board members, that having created a culture of risk management is absolutely critical to truly managing risks. Unless the CEO and the senior executive team have committed to high levels of transparency and integrity in risk management, the endeavour may reach an end. The commitment of the senior management team to risks is absolutely fundamental to the success of risk management culture. It must be accompanied with a sincere willingness of indentifying, assessing and reporting all forms of exposure in a most transparent way, even if this leads to self-criticisms. Is it at all possible? If a firm has committed to 'corporate culture projects' in the past, such as product quality, resource diversity or even customer satisfaction, then it has already demonstrated that it was able to be self-critical and to develop its own code of ethics, code of conduct and compliance rules. Certainly the level and the implications of self-criticism with respect to the risks involved by management decisions is a notch higher than what is required for product quality, but this is where success truly lies in terms of establishing a culture of risk management. It starts with a culture of transparency.

8.4 RISK COMMITTEES AND AUDIT CONTROLS

The executive risk committee is as usual tasked with triggering the appropriate introspective reviews of the management decisions in order to translate them into risk factors and sensitivity targets through scenarios. This is certainly a most difficult role, to be carried out independently if the managers themselves are not involved in it. Evaluating the risks involved with investment projects such as mergers and acquisitions, for example, requires insights and most likely confidential information related to the project itself. For all these reasons, risk management must be represented as a function of the board, and independent from finance or audit and controls.

A recent trend from the onset of the crisis of 2008–2009 is to 'reinforce' the role of the CROs. In reality, these were either PR tactics designed to reassure shareholders and customers or to alleviate part of the risk responsibility suddenly felt by the top managers. Overloading the CROs with all aspects of risk would not make the firm any safer or more efficient as it actually places one more concentration on a single person or department, ironically creating additional operational risks.

What is next proposed here goes far beyond the reinforcement of the role and budgets of existing risk departments. For a senior risk manager, say the CRO, in order to have sufficient independence and the clout to point out risks at management level and report them transparently, the CRO must sit independently at the board and only report to the CEO. Even then, the risk that the judgements of the CRO could be influenced or biased remains. The personality and management style of the CEO will be critical, and these are considerations that should not be abandoned to random chances or luck.

How then, can a CEO be questioned on risk policies, contingencies and mitigation? Managers with strong personality, or poor ethics, can willingly or unwillingly influence a board. In some cases, the CEO is also a key shareholder. So how can listed companies at least be assured that someone watches over the interests of the shareholders with regards to risk management practices and integrity with a management style that truly matches their expectations? Ideally, the shareholders should do that themselves, but in most cases they could be underequipped and not readily available. A set of regulatory reports may not always be transparent enough and the problem of depth and frequency of information feedback remains to be addressed.

We propose the appointment of nonexecutive directors specialized in risk management to represent the shareholders before the executive management team. The purposes are to balance the power of the CEO in terms of risk management, add independent unbiased views to the internal ones and ensure best practice and adequacy of the risk management framework with the policies defined and accepted by the shareholders. Quarterly reports to the shareholders with quantified targets, limits and utilization, along with scenarios and stress tests, should be presented by the nonexecutive directors to the shareholders. The reports would describe the adequacy of the risk management style, strategy and tactics in place within the context of the risk policy expressed by the shareholders. The process will be the baseline control of the adequacy of the firm's declared appetite for risk with the actual appetite demonstrated in the field.

9
Risk Independence or Indifference to Risk?

Why is the appointment of external auditors to provide an unbiased and professional audit of risk methodologies at management level not recommended? This is because it may not always be completely unbiased and could sometimes even be excessively formal.

While the entire profession of external auditors should not be criticized due to isolated cases of abuses that could happen in any industry, there cannot be a guarantee of no conflict of interest when external professionals are appointed to appraise the very people who appoint them to do so. Moreover, while the competency of external auditors is dependable, their professionalism and high level of expertise may focus their analysis on methodology. Any sort of concentration always adds to risks, even if it is the uniformity of the methodology and risk management practices itself. Even the best consultants and external auditors would in all fairness roll out a preformatted methodology to analyse and report internal practices according to an exhaustive list of criteria. To a highly experienced senior executive being appraised, the criteria may over time become 'predictable' and thus vulnerable.

If external auditors are to be appointed due to the complexity of the size of the task to be carried out, however, it should be done and controlled by the nonexecutive directors accountable solely to the shareholders. Combining the external views of nonexecutive directors with the expertise of external auditors may be a more balanced approach, better representing the interests of the shareholders and maintaining independence.

9.1 ROLE OF THE SHAREHOLDERS AND NONEXECUTIVE DIRECTORS

Certainly the proposed role of the shareholders in controlling the risks of the firm is much greater than the reality of what is commonly taking place. This recommended level of involvement is an indispensable part of the cultural shift. Too often in the past, the presumed independence of risk services has only resulted in a total indifference to risks.

Risk exposures were professionally aggregated and measured with extreme care by highly qualified professionals but they were only used to draft reports. Those reports merely fed higher-level enterprise risk exposure reports. Those were seldom analysed or discussed in depth by the top management. These reports would make their way to the shareholders at general meetings, together with many other issues on the agenda. The main purpose of the risk reports was essentially to give the measure of risk-weighted capital efficiency, or risk-adjusted return on capital (RAROC). Widely considered as a top achievement of risk management, a company providing enterprise-wide RAROC figures to the market or shareholders would be considered very advanced in this respective field indeed.

Yet, for all the complexity and sophistication that RAROC involves, it does not manage the risks as it does not involve a certain course of actions to be directly triggered by the measures under given circumstances. To make matters worse, this type of risk management sophistication created a false sense of safety among shareholders, who believed that their executive management teams were perfectly in control.

The new culture propose here does not consist of replacing an old methodology with a presumably better one that we would invent today in the context of what we know or should have known yesterday. It is about creating a culture of responsibility and accountability of risks, and making sure it has the potential to evolve in the future depending on sets of events and circumstances that we cannot anticipate today.

9.2 RESPONSIBILITY AND ACCOUNTABILITY

To be fair, there is little interest in blaming any of the main corporate groups, management, audit or shareholders, with regards to the deficiencies of risk management procedures and poor achievements of the past. The culture was entirely geared towards capital efficiency and everyone did a great job in this respect. However, if the goal is now to replace this culture with a new one based on risk management, then it will require a culture of transparency and a culture of responsibility and accountability to be defined, and implemented, throughout the industry.

In the past, executive directors had very few opportunities to be truly involved in risk management. Each business decision, each project or investment is usually accompanied with a description of project risks and contingencies, often with mitigation recommendations. While those risks would be thoroughly inspected by the decision makers, the risk management department would carry out an entirely different course of action in an ivory tower devoted to quantitative analysis. This disconnect, supposedly independence, was in reality a show of indifference to risks.

Risk managers were indifferent to risks that they could not quantify. Executive managers were indifferent to risks because they could not sense any linear function between their business decisions and the measurement of risk exposure and sensitivity that would follow. Regulators were indifferent to risks because they did not investigate or question risk management frameworks and methodologies as they were overly focused on capital ratio reports.

Instilling a new culture of responsibility and accountability to risks would therefore require each group to make sure that there is clear communication among the three groups and that an efficient exchange of information makes the whole system agile and proactive to adjust business strategies to the desired risk exposure. This implies that the executive team communicates the details of their projects and operations to the risk management teams, not merely the related financial aspects. In return, the risk management team needs to find simple ways to measure and communicate the exposure and sensitivities that the projects and strategies would generate. The simplicity of their language and measurement should depend on the awareness of the audience being communicated to. As internal service providers, risk managers need to adapt to the culture of those they advise, instead of the other way around. Last, but not least, the regulators should encourage this cultural diversity in risk-weighting companies' activities and exposure instead of rewarding uniformity in tactics and methodology.

9.3 CONTROL AND REPORT HIERARCHY

What should be the control and report hierarchy in the new approach? There shall be two types of workflow: (1) the quantitative workflow, which consists of the risk targets, limits and limit utilization, scenario building and reports; (2) the qualitative workflow, which assesses the appropriateness of the scenarios, the suitability and consistency of the methodologies in use, the integrity and transparency of reporting, as well as the audit and feedback. The dual workflow is described in Figure 9.1.

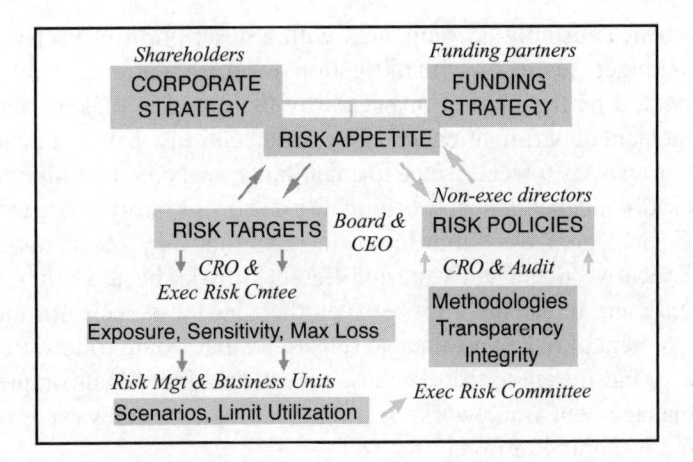

```
                    Shareholders              Funding partners
                    CORPORATE                 FUNDING
                    STRATEGY                  STRATEGY
                              RISK APPETITE
                             ↙  ↙
                                      ↘ Non-exec directors
                    RISK TARGETS  Board &  RISK POLICIES
                                   CEO
                       ↓ CRO &  ↓           ↑ CRO & Audit  ↑
                       Exec Risk Cmtee
                                            Methodologies
                    Exposure, Sensitivity, Max Loss   Transparency
                              ↓       ↓     Integrity
                       Risk Mgt & Business Units
                                              Exec Risk Committee
                       Scenarios, Limit Utilization ↗
```

Figure 9.1 Risk reporting hierarchy and role distribution

Initially, the very existence of the firm is due to an expression of risk appetite, from its founders, shareholders and whoever funds it – banks, funds, private equity, venture capital, etc. Under the responsibility of the CEO, the board supported by the risk manager translates the risk appetite into risk policies. Within risk policies there are quantitative and qualitative elements. The quantitative, as explained in Part 1, should not be more complex than a selection of macro-risk factors, the exposure to risks, the sensitivity under macro-scenarios, the maximum loss and, finally, the capital efficiency. The qualitative aspects of risk policies are about the policies themselves and, especially in the case of large or public companies, the social role of the firm and the social implications of the risk it takes.

As described in Figure 9.1, the risk policies are turned into quantitative risk targets and risk limits distributed as explained in Part 1. Then the scenarios that have been used, especially the adverse and extreme ones, are aggregated back into a macro-scenario that represents the actual appetite for risk demonstrated by the activities of the firm throughout its day-to-day operations and its results. It is at that stage that the qualitative aspects start to become important.

The executive committee and the risk management group, in their reaggregation of scenarios, first have the opportunity to examine the quantitative aspects of the methodology closely. The data, for a start, should be reviewed with respect to its integrity, consistency of use, reliability and cleanliness. All aspects of valuation risks as discussed in Part 1 are to be audited and reported: the models, their compatibility with one another, their suitability with respect to the data and the scenarios in use, and all other aspects of operational risks related to valuations of assets, liabilities and collateral. The important aspect at this stage is no longer to discuss the appropriateness of the methods, but rather to review their consistency across the various department and groups and appraise the coherence of the methodologies as a whole.

Besides methodology, an audit of transparency is essential. In many aspects, creating a culture of risk management is creating a culture of transparency. The methodology review described above is by no means an easy task. In fact, it should be considered tedious enough so that the workload will be appropriately distributed as an everyday task to be carried out by all persons involved in risk management, audit or enrolled in one of the committees. Only when this process has become routine, transparency can start to improve. The different aspects of transparency will be reviewed in detail in Part 3, dedicated to the information workflow. At this stage, let us just note that besides the need of data and valuation transparency, a massive effort needs to be carried out across the enterprise with respect to the transparency of methodologies and disclosure. This, as previously discussed, is the role of the audit and risk management departments and, moving into the senior level, endorsed and supported by the nonexecutive risk directors. Finally, regulators should also endeavour to foster a culture of transparency within the financial sectors, such as banking, asset management, brokerage, custody and executions. A regulatory framework purely based on a 'stick and carrot' approach will never be able to evolve dynamically as the market changes and will continue to challenge the participants to circumvent the rules rather than abiding wholeheartedly to their spirit.

The ultimate report of transparency and methodology is achieved as a consensus by all decision makers within the company, involving executive and nonexecutive directors, the risks specialists and representatives of the shareholders. It is about the social implications and potential externalities that risks taken by the firm may have. As a starting point before ruling on this complex subject, the regulators should first develop awareness of the issue and try to initiate discussions about it. The process could start with a simple report from every large public company explaining their own views of the potential external effects that their losses or failures could have under the scenarios that they consider to be catastrophic. This will certainly help the regulators to focus their attention on areas they might not have thought of before, and may also provide valuable insights into the approach of large firms to tail events.

10
Risk-Weighted Performance

If capital efficiency is no longer a sole aspect to measure and appraise how the balance of risks and returns plays for each firm, then the measurement of performance should be enriched as well. Traditional risk management practices strongly implied that as the degree of expertise and risk management sophistication expand across the enterprise, the measurement of risk-weighted returns would become increasingly quantitative, until it reaches the ultimate point where the entirety it is possible to know about a particular firm could be encapsulated into one final figure: the risk-adjusted return on capital (RAROC). The next frontier, following full Basel compliance, would have been to measure a risk-adjusted return on risk-adjusted capital (RARORAC). The goal of achieving RAROC enterprise-wide is no longer the ultimate achievement of a risk manager. Simply, the previously essential quantitative and technocratic approach of risks by models is no longer acceptable to the shareholders or the boards. Hopefully regulators will also come to this conclusion sooner rather than later.

What then should be the new principles for measuring risk-weighted performance? We suggest adaptation to the new expectations and new goals defined for the risk management framework. Beyond capital efficiency, the new culture of risk management is expected to maintain the alignment with the risk appetite through compliance with the risk policies – this will involve all aspects of asset and liability management (ALM) and balance sheet structure management, transparency of valuations, procedures and communications, and operational efficiency, making the firm overall more agile, especially with respect to tail events and the ability to deliver regulatory compliance. Above all, the risk management framework is expected to foster a culture that will support its own evolution as the firm grows, diversifies, merges and as the business environment changes.

10.1 PRINCIPLES OF RISK-WEIGHTED MEASUREMENTS

An essential performance criterion for a risk management system is to ensure business resilience. In our model, resilience is achieved less by capital allocation than by dynamic adjustments to the sensitivity of risk factors under various conditions of severity. Therefore the notion of risk weight should not only reflect exposure but also sensitivity.

Under the Basel 2 framework, the baseline risk-weighted assets for credit exposure (foundation or advanced methodologies) is a function of probability of default. In other words, a theoretical credit model determines the overall exposure for a fixed maturity and fixed loan given default (LGD). The risk-weighted capital is then computed as

$$\frac{\text{Capital}}{\text{Credit risk-weighted assets} + [12.5 \times (\text{market capital charge} + \text{operations capital charge})]}$$

The market capital charge is also in essence based on modelled exposure and the operational capital charge is based on gross income by business lines, multiplied by some fixed industry indices or calculated from overly complex methodologies. Overall, all risk weights are a function of exposure, asset classes, risk categories or indices.

We propose a simplified methodology where each investment is risk-weighted by the volatility of the exposure and the sensitivity of the risk factors. Under the current methodology, a BBB bond at par receiving a 50 % risk weight amounts to a risk-weighted exposure of 50, making this approach very rigid. The new method proposed would simply estimate the volatility and sensitivity of the bond under a set of scenarios. Within a given level of historical volatility, one would be able to compute an annual or monthly price standard deviation to derive the first price sensitivity or delta, then gamma and theta.

Obviously the main advantage of the methodology, in addition to its simplicity, is the continuous alignment with the market conditions. Tiers 1 and 2 capital cannot technically be adjusted to market volatility, but collateral requirements can. A variable capital adequacy ratio based on market volatility and asset sensitivity would not only increase the responsiveness of the industry to changing market conditions but also provide the highly sought after countercyclical measures that have been debated in the aftermaths of the crisis.

10.1.1 Mark to time-weighted volatility

Measures of volatility and sensitivity always bear a notion of time. Volatility is measured as the square root of variance, which directly depends on the history used as sample data. Sensitivity, on the other hand, depends on the step chosen for the underlying and on the timeframe projected. The approach inevitably brings some level of complexity and choices in the effort to pinpoint the precise look back history and to consider projected investment timeframes. Yet those aspects were more or less neglected until now as far as the approach to risk-weighted assets was concerned. In contrast with the extreme levels of sophistication found in pure modelling of value-at-risk or curve and surface fitting, most systems are set on a 252 day history to retrieve the past volatilities and derive the steps for the simulation regardless of how long the investment has been held and was intended to be held. Our proposed methodology forces the search for the purpose of the investments, which is critical to their valuations.

A quick approach would be to measure the historical volatility of investments based on the intended holding period. Different inputs have a dramatic impact. For example, taking a very liquid blue chip listed around the world, the equity held for an intended 52 week investment can be measured with a historical volatility of 55 %. If the investor intends to sell the equity during the same month, a new measure of historical volatility would be 24 %. As the portfolio manager approaches a probable closing date, the volatility of an investment tends towards its daily standard deviation or sensitivity. The probability of default of an investment the manager intends to sell within a few weeks does not matter much in this case.

The implications of the above leads to a major departure from a well-established principle in finance and asset management, which states that long-term investments are less risky than short-term ones. The 'ancient dogma' relies on a false assumption of normality, where mean returns always end up rebalancing volatility. Edgar Peters,[1] building on the works of Benoit Mandelbrot, proves in *Fractal Markets* that the long memory processes of market return distribution might have confused the analysts of the 1960s and 1970s and been misinterpreted for mean returns. This critical point will be further elaborated in a later chapter. At this stage, we focus on the fact that time only gives more options for

---
[1] Edgar Peters, *Fractal Markets*, John Wiley & Sons, Ltd, Chichester, 1994.

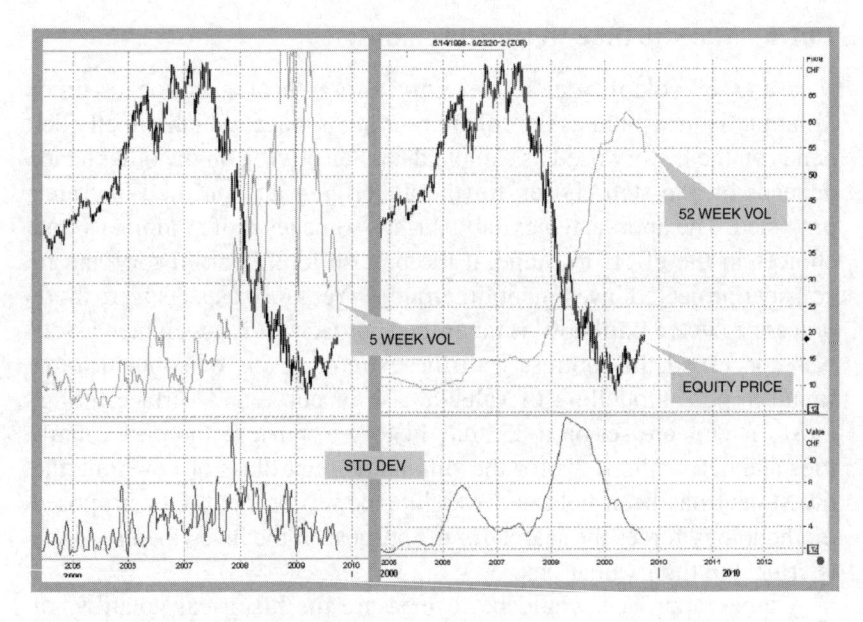

Figure 10.1 Timeframe impact
Source: Thomson Reuters 3000Xtra

prices and risks to evolve, and thereby volatility necessarily increases with time, thus making investments riskier, instead of the opposite. If it was not the case, then short-term options would not be cheaper than long-term ones.

Investments are as risky as they are volatile. Volatility is a function of the square root of time. Therefore the intended holding timeframe of each investment should directly drive the riskiness factored in its pricing or in risk weighting. The ancient dogmas of market efficiency theory assumed that all information available is encapsulated in a closing price. Modern markets do not necessarily prove the theory wrong but highlight the need for it to evolve. It appears that through a notion of a volatility and investment timeframe that the theory should evolve. The charts in Figure 10.1 display how the market for a similar financial instrument, with good market depth and liquidity, may appear volatile or not volatile depending on the chosen timeframe.

In reality, forward volatility does encapsulate all information expected to drive the prices forward: emotions, assumptions of market depth, liquidity, price slippage, credit risk, interest rates and time.

Based on volatility, risk weightings can be dynamically adjusted depending on market conditions, with the approaching liquidation date also accounted for. The methodology therefore integrates delta/gamma as well as vega and theta as measures used for risk weightings. In addition to market liquidity, market depth and elements of creditworthiness, forward volatility also encapsulates assumptions of correlations with other factors that might impact volatility.

10.1.2 Business resilience and countercyclical approaches

How does our proposed dynamic approach increase business resilience? Replacing a theoretical measure of default probability with actual measures of sensitivity and volatility fine-tuned with respect to the purpose and duration of an investment clearly positions the firm to be more responsive to internal changes such as portfolio structures and external factors such as market volatility. The risk weights obtained may not be necessarily higher compared to the previous methodology. With lower volatility, markets are less risky and therefore risk weights could immediately be adjusted. The principle can thus be used as a foundation for the countercyclical measures to be implemented in the aftermath of the crisis. It is much more realistic and dynamic than provisioning excess capital in so-called 'good times' in anticipation of the cyclical crises of the future. Recommended by some regulators, such an approach would no doubt be quite difficult to implement. Over a long period of growth and high liquidity, it is highly likely to be forgotten or circumvented.

Our recommended approach also facilitates compliance to internal rules and policies. By focusing on the volatility and sensitivity of investments, a firm is able precisely to describe the risk appetite of the company. Since risk targets are distributed in terms of sensitivity, the reconciliations with the risk profile received from the shareholders are straightforward. Risk-weighted assets should simply match the desired exposure. Whenever a mismatch occurs, it indicates that the exposure or the measured volatility is too high – a situation that calls for immediate adjustments.

When the number of days required for settling a transaction increases, the overall duration or holding period is prolonged, thereby increasing the risk of an investment. Likewise, clearing and settlement within 7 days as opposed to 3 days increase the volatility of an investment. The methodology is therefore an excellent tool for improving processing times by attaching performance measurement and linking capital efficiency measures to it. Overall, it encourages operational efficiency.

Part 3
Creating an Information Workflow for Continuous Feedback and Preventive Decision Making[1]

Executive Summary

A risk-based information workflow forms the backbone of the new culture.

This chapter describes the top-down and bottom-up exchanges of information that are necessary to lay out the foundations of a new generation risk management framework as described in the previous chapters. The whole concept of our proposed methodology relies on the capacity of the firm to exchange information internally and with external partners with a speed, precision and accuracy that allows risks to be minimized before they become losses.

Top-down, the workflow consists of translating the risk policies into practical, quantified risk targets that represent the sensitivity of each activity of the firm. Whether it is a vega target to a trading desk or a maximum number of failed settlements for a back-office department, each identified risk centre receives a sensitivity limit to manage. Those aggregated together must represent the risk policies of the firm, which in turn are the translation of the shareholders' appetite for risk. These are dynamic limits. It means that they are set in the context of defined scenarios. Should external market conditions or internal business conditions change significantly, the sensitivity limits in particular are set to adjust automatically.

---

[1] This part generally refers to an unpublished White Paper by Philippe Carrel, 'A risk based information workflow, backbone of the new culture'.

Such a framework improves dramatically the agility and adjustment accuracy of a firm if there is an efficient bottom-up feedback in return. The targets, limits, utilization and actual sensitivity figures need continuously to feed the management dashboards for them to be able to react and pre-empt on risks as soon as possible.

The essential bottom-up feedback consists of reaggregations that paint an overall picture of the risks pixel after pixel. Exposure and sensitivities are aggregated back from the business units to the management through the work of the risk managers and under the control of auditors. In addition, the scenarios are aggregated too. In our model of distributed accountabilities and responsibilities, business and risk units own their stress scenarios. Although the exercise is again coached and controlled by the risk management and the audit departments who define boundaries and methodologies, the business units are entirely free to build high-severity and catastrophic scenarios. These views are extremely important because they define the actual appetite for risk demonstrated by each unit through their everyday business activities. The aggregation of stress scenarios therefore provide a pixelized view of the actual appetite of the firm, which can be reconciled with the one initially expressed by the shareholders.

The control of valuation risks are absolutely critical to make sure the bottom-up and upside-down scenarios are efficient. Since the firm is now agile and relies on its capability to unwind positions or mitigate risks promptly, it actually runs market and credit risk as one huge operational risk. To ensure the integrity, consistency and accuracy of the risk-based information flow, firms will need to centralize all necessary data in a single repository, where prices, terms and conditions, corporate actions, risk events and generally any information that can possibly impact on the pricing of instruments, positions and collateral is stored, maintained and audited. In addition, a similar type of centralized platform should be created for all pricing models and auxiliaries such as curves, surfaces and matrices can be decoupled from their original application and used independently.

Finally, special consideration will be given to the legal and regulatory risks that can impact the firm's capability to unwind positions or hedge its exposure.

Managing risk, as opposed to measuring it, is to trigger a course of action that would mitigate or decrease risk exposure whenever some signal is given. Those signals would be triggered by risk-based information. Traders, for example, monitor (risk) sensitivity limits and targets. Information flows are set up so that risk-based information such as a vega or gamma limit can trigger timely action and the effect of unwinding can immediately be felt. The enterprise-wide information flow that we propose to establish must enable the same type of prompt reactions, pre-emptive action, informed decisions and overall make the firm as agile as possible in its approach to risk.

Implementing a corporate culture, to some extent, requires the involvement and engagement of every personnel in the firm. All generators of risks, among other objectives, can be assigned as risk targets from front-line units to back-office operations, extending all the way up to senior management and eventually to the board. Along the way, risk-based information will trigger executive decisions, transforming it into a management tool as well as a medium of both internal and external communication.

To lay down the foundation of a structure to enable communications based on risk facts, one needs to build a workflow of information where policies, instructions, events, feedback, score cards and alerts would be effectively transmitted throughout the enterprise alongside trades and customer information. In all due respects, this is far more complicated than just plugging IT systems together within or across division networks. To implement such a corporate culture successfully places the importance of information before building the systems. To begin with, it consists of identifying the inputs and outputs required by all potential generators of risks, and in each case to identify, assess, monitor, mitigate and report the exposure to those factors. Upholding this workflow will help achieve the firm's goal of successfully gathering insights with respect to risk exposure and potential developments as well as agility to shield against the effect of unexpected events.

The main aspects of an information workflow based on risk management would involve top-down target allocations translating the firm's appetite for risk into risk policies and turning these policies into risk-weighted performance objectives. As explored in Part 1, the risk targets will be respectively distributed across business units.

Top-down communications must be followed by a series of bottom-up activity feedback. These series comprise a risk exposure feedback, which is an aggregation of risk factors and risk units: dynamic sensitivity feedbacks based on multiple scenarios and scenario types involving dynamic alerts, limit breach, exceptions, volatility or correlation shifts.

Further to the basic exchange of information described in Part 1, some methodology feedback as described in Part 2 would also take place as part of the bottom-up communication flow. Specifically, feedback on methodology would require aggregated scenarios (baseline, high-severity and catastrophic), details of valuation and modelling methodology, descriptions of sensitivity under scenarios and statistics on the data utilization, maintenance, transformation and redistributions.

11
From Risk Appetite to Risk Policies

Thoroughly understanding the overall risk exposure borne by the firm has now become a corporate strategy priority. Following the 2008–2009 crisis, the adequacy of actual risk exposure versus expected risk exposure became a key aspect of CEOs' agendas. Some firms, hedge funds for example, were subsequently set up for business purposes that involved a concentration on a selection of risk factors. Others firms, on the other hand, were mandated with a high level of risk diversification in order to weather and survive any crisis. Implementation of policies by the executive management strongly reflected the shareholders' appetite for risk. All factors of risks related to market diversification, innovation, geopolitical risks and necessary deviations from the core business will now be under constant scrutiny.

To embed the shareholder's appetite for risk effectively into the corporate strategy, the expression of risk policies should at least cover the following: the amounts and nature of desired exposure (exposure to risk factors), mitigation strategies, the risk scenarios and the scenario expected impact.

11.1 RISK: THE NEW BOND

The purpose of the analysis of risk factors, as explained in Part 1, is to answer the following question: What are the risk factors the shareholders are willing to be exposed to? For example, do the shareholders of a European diversified insurance group know that they might be exposed to subprime real estate in California? If yes, to which extent, in which amount and with what level of sensitivity and volatility? Against this backdrop begs another question: Would such information be part of a top-down or bottom-up flow? At this high strategic level, the answer is actually both. Not only the shareholders must be informed of the risk the firm is truly exposed to, but the management team, or board, needs to acknowledge the risk factors the shareholders would like to expose the firm to. As part of this acknowledgement, the team or board must express their understanding of the risks and demonstrate confidence in their ability to mitigate, control and report them. In fact, this is neither top-down nor bottom-up, but rather a mission statement followed by an acknowledgement. In other words, the risk profile of the firm is therefore a bond between the shareholders and the executive team of the firm.

As part of the initial expression of risk profile, there must be an exhaustive list of structural factors that are directly and naturally related to the business purposes, such as securities prices, interest rates and counterparty risks.

There are also cyclical factors that may be related to new or temporary business conditions or to the conduct of specific business operations. In project finance, for example, the temporary exposure to the risk factors of the projects needs to be known, understood and accepted. Finally, both the shareholders and the executive team must be prepared for exceptional or unexpected factors to impact the firm. Low probability yet high severity events that can possibly impact the firm range from climate catastrophes to geopolitical events or unexpected correlation shifts, and so on. A simple review of those factors often provides a good heads-up and facilitates communications over risks.

11.2 DYNAMIC TWO-WAY INFORMATION WORKFLOW

The manner in which the shareholders' appetite for risk as a risk policy is expressed with detailed breakdown into factors, sensitivity, mitigation and reporting methodology is not set in stone. This is because the risk appetite of the shareholders may change over time with the overall business environment, the firm's competition, legal and regulatory constraints, etc. The executive management team should therefore hold the responsibility of providing advice and tools for the shareholders to make informed decisions concerning the risk strategies of the firm.

This dynamic two-way workflow of risk-based information and feedback is therefore critical to maintaining the desired alignment between the risk strategy of a firm and its actual risk policies as expressed and implemented. The workflow must provide the information necessary to trigger a course of action. What this implies is that both the sender and the recipient of information must speak the same 'language', so that the recipients are perfectly able to understand the issue as it is described and the parties involved know which decision to take to rebalance the

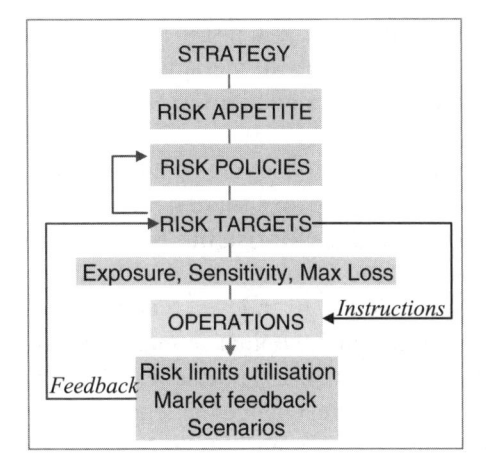

Figure 11.1 Dynamic risk information workflow

levels of exposure to the desired sensitivity. Figure 11.1 illustrates the fundamental workflow of risk-based information.

11.3 PREVENTIVE RULES FOR A PRE-EMPTIVE COURSE OF ACTION

The ultimate goal of the workflow is to minimize the time between the arrival of information loaded with risk implications and the adjustment of exposure or positions. A pre-emptive course of action, efficiently taken, will be a far better protection of the firm against risks and especially tail events than capital allocations set up in anticipation of losses.

The rule of pre-emptive action is not to predict market movements or loss events, but react promptly and cut loss or cover exposure as soon as it becomes obvious that some development will lead to losses. This requires reliable monitors, reliable information, tactics and rebalancing rules set in advance, as well as effective controls.

At a senior level, it is not advisable for the management team to sink into the details of risk exposure. For example, one does not expect the CEO to check on credit spreads and counterparty limits all day. Similarly, a counterparty default rarely occurs like a bolt of lightning and is usually announced by preliminary indicators such as the firm's limit utilization, overall exposure, changes in sensitivity levels, market volatility, correlation reversals, funding costs, just to name a few. It is worth noting that signals are not limited only to markets and externalities. Numbers of settlement failures, staff resignations, customer complaints or closed accounts can be also relevant.

The most important aspect of setting up an information flow that will trigger timely action is to prepare a set of dynamic rules. The rules must define not only the conditions for risk limits to be overridden but also a subsequent course of action. For example, if the value of collateral for mortgage loans falls below a given level, then the credit committee, the risk executive committee and the finance managers would immediately assess the implications and decide whether to refund the collateral, unwind some of the exposure, change the lending policies, etc. In order for them to find themselves in a position to make an informed decision, a top-down and bottom-up information flow involving the following points should have been well established:

- Collateralized loans priced and marked to value at an established frequency.
- Both the valuation frequency and repricing methodology dynamically adapted to the volatility of the underlying.
- Limits in collateral value established and monitored frequently.
- Underlying market conditions impact on collateral limits without new deals necessarily being added.
- Overridden threshold or limits would effectively trigger alerts.
- Overridden limits can be explained through drill-down.
- Valuation methodologies can be explored and back-engineered.
- Solutions to identified problems are recognized and scripted.
- The hierarchy is aware and has been involved in the scripting.
- The impact of decisions is immediately visible and measurable.
- The whole process, the valuation methodologies and the results are audited, analysed and archived.
- The incident is used as an increment to a body of knowledge.
- All valuations can be back-engineered.

11.4 THE DYNAMIC ASSESSMENTS OF RISK FACTOR SENSITIVITIES

One of the above points that deserves particular attention is the dynamic assessment of the sensitivity of the risk factors. It was established in Part 1 that the main point of focus to aggregate the overall exposure of the firm was the set of risk factors best suited to represent the business risks. Turning a selection of risk factors into a dynamic representation of risk sensitivities is the real challenge. The danger lies in simply looking in the wrong direction whenever tail events arise. There are two key aspects to maintaining an efficient assessment in place. First, the appropriateness of factors and root-risk factors must be continuously questioned and verified. Second, the pricing and sensitivity measurement rules must be continuously reviewed and their efficiency proved time and again. This is due to the changing nature of the financial markets and how the focus of investors and lenders tends to shift the rules driving market efficiency.

11.4.1 Risk factor appropriateness tests

At each level of the hierarchy, the macro- or micro-risk factors will be continuously monitored for efficiency and appropriateness. Back-testing is certainly a good starting point, but due to its self-assessing nature the test risks become a self-fulfilling prophecy. As long as there is no tail event, back-testing can pretty much justify any choice or any methodology. This is how value-at-risk, for example, which was supposed to be a dynamic forward assessment of correlated risks, ended up being a lullaby of risk management, justified by extensive histories in back-testing. Excellent models relying on wrong assumptions were perfectly efficient until derailed by tail events. Moreover, there were no pre-established alternatives to the methodology.

How can we know whether a particular risk factor and measure of sensitivity will be efficient and appropriate? We can recall the rules of the efficient market hypothesis (EMH), which states that all information available and market emotions that influence investors' behaviour drive prices. Earlier in Part 1, we have explored the evolution of EMH in modern finance and observed that volatility and sensitivity these days would provide a better ground to encapsulate information than solely a closing price. In other words, if a risk factor that was known to be a key driver of sensitivity for a particular asset no longer seems to be as effective as it should, then it is because the attention or emotion of investors have shifted to another factor of sensitivity. By observing the changes in sensitivity to the various risk factors, one can anticipate shifts to other sources of market volatility, if not directional changes.

The hypothesis of a mortgage loan department presents a good example. The exposure is known to be a function of the level of interest rates versus funding costs. The prepayment rates, the volatility of collateral value and the probability of default of borrowers are sources of sensitivity. Let us assume that the sensitivity limits have been defined and distributed evenly to each of these factors. In times of normal market conditions, the collateral value would rise at a rate of, say, 3 % per year with fairly stable default rates. During these times, the P/L would be truly created through management of interest rates and funding costs, sensitivity limits would be based on such a spread, the term structures and gap analysis, basis risks and the cap of profits implied by prepayments.

Assuming a tail event of a sudden 10 % drop on collateral value takes place. If the firm is aware of it and structured to adapt, it can immediately write off losses, avoid loading additional exposure through undercollateralized assets, refocus sensitivity limits on default rates and collateral value, and try to weather the crisis at its best. While traders know that it is impossible to predict the future, being the first to know and first to act is key to damage control or profit taking. Good traders do not read newspapers. They make news.

In the above example, successful management of the event comes from awareness of the facts, their sources and effect. Efficiency in the information flow is the key, as the best information is of little use if people receive it but are not prepared to interpret it. The second factor of success is the accuracy of valuations. In our example, the firm is able to mark collateral to value even in the context of a tail event, which would have presumably changed the market characteristics in terms of liquidity, depth, spread, etc. This means that the scenario has been considered before, leading to the third factor of success, the preparedness of the firm. The best information and valuations are totally useless if one does not know what to do with it. This presumes that some sort of 'war game' should have been carried out in anticipation of a situation of pre-established severity.

11.5 SENSITIVITY RULES AND STRESS TESTS

How realistic is it to try figuring out high-severity scenarios and pre-establish emergency procedures? Clearly this is not about predicting the future but defining 'state-of-the-world' types of scenarios. Hedging tools, sensitivity calculations and controls must depend on the market situation. Option or convertibility models, for example, require different volatility surfaces and interpolation rules when the markets get chaotic than when returns are between one and two standard deviations. In our example above based on mortgage loans, there was no direct hedging possibility, but all limits were frozen. At which point should they have only been reduced instead of being totally locked? Should it be when the collateral value had fallen by 10 % or by 15 % or more? In reality, only stress tests can possibly measure the severity of a scenario and assess the cascading impacts of events as they might unfold. These should be more appropriately seen as 'war games' instead of stress tests. For several reasons the firm must roll them out. First, as previously suggested, it is an important exercise to try and draw the chain of events and consequences that might arise from a sudden expected market shock. Second, and more importantly, it pushes further the internal levels of risk awareness, since the 'games' should in practice involve everyone. It is also the only way that the staff can truly rehearse and practice emergency procedures.

The procedures should contain at least three types of information: (1) the conditions defining the state of emergency – the factor, event, sensitivity figure, threshold that would trigger the alerts; (2) the mitigation tactics – the hedging tool, haircut rule and valuation methodologies that would prevail; (3) the procedures – comprising the responsibilities, information flow, controls and reports.

11.5.1 Triggers

The aim is to define the monitors and triggers that would allow the firm to gain the necessary awareness when it finds itself within a different set of business conditions. The sensitivity threshold seems to be a most direct approach since it relates to the risk factors deemed relevant to the firm. An example of the sensitivity threshold for a given risk and set of risk factors defining applicable scenarios is given by Figure 11.2.

In the preceding example, a number of triggers would be defined in order to set the rule for a changed business and risk environment. Beyond the threshold level on one or more of the critical factors, even if the other factors remain within the 'normal' boundaries, the overall business environment is said to be changed from baseline to high severity for instance. This is a methodology learned and adapted from other industries and sectors, such as fighting wildfires or epidemics. The importance of this rule in post-crisis risk management cannot be further emphasized as it fully focuses on prevention, raising the levels of awareness, rounding up skills and expertise to place the firm in a focused and highly alerted mode when the markets become volatile or

RISK UNIT NAME		Baseline	Severity 1	Catastrophic
Risk factors	Sub-factors	Sensitivity Threshold	Sensitivity Threshold	Alert
Retail clients	Eco Growth			
	CPI			
	Rho			
	Basis			
	Default			
	Credit Scores			
Collateral	Mortgage Value			
	Liquidity			
	Vega			
	Rho			
Hedges	Pre-Payment rates			
	FMAC spread			
	FNMAE spread			
	Portfolio Delta			

Figure 11.2 Sensitivity threshold example

shift from one liquidity status to another. This is a major departure from the pre-crisis typical frameworks where trading and hedging were confined to the profit centres while enterprise-wide reports would merely sum up VaR and potential future exposure (PFE) figures. By the time the respective parties would be impacted by the new business environment and the reports reviewed by decision makers, the devastating effects of tail events would have unravelled a very different picture from the reported version.

While timely information to notify that the firm has entered into rough seas is precious, a significant difference can only be made if the firm swiftly and wisely changes its course. Risk mitigation tactics, notably, would need to be adapted.

11.5.2 Dynamic, swappable mitigation tactics

What truly makes a difference is if a firm is able to receive and understand early warnings on higher volatilities, to tail events or disasters and to modify its tactics promptly enough to control damages. For example, when a credit event strikes – be it default, simple payment or downgrading – the information is available on agency networks at a given time, which could be within or outside the scope of market opening hours. At this point, some traders are aware of the event and some others are not, for various reasons that could be as simple as being in a remote time zone. Those who are aware typically try to unwind their positions as soon as possible. If the bond or paper markets are not deep enough, they will go around all available equity execution venues and try to unwind or hedge existing exposure or even go short. Electronic books get instantly filled, regardless of limit and stop orders. Those who were not aware find themselves suddenly bearing a much greater exposure to the counterparty. To avoid this, the firm could have set up some risk intelligence workflow whereby a credit event on a given counterparty immediately locks all limits on the upside at all desks, triggers alarms and may even send emergency messages. A single event may create a very different environment, impact perceptions, reverse correlations and create massive price slippage. The sooner the firm adapts its risk management tactics the less likely it is to suffer extensive damage.

To understand the importance of this strategic adaptability, one must remember that tail events do not happen by coincidence. The nature of their course means that the events are bound to happen and when they do, the likelihood is that they will repeat. Tail risk is not idiosyncratic in nature. When changes are so sudden and so deep, the firm must be ready to adapt not only the trading and hedging tactics but also the valuation methodologies. Option traders, for example, do not use the same volatility curves or surfaces depending on the level of volatility and the nature of return distributions. Volatility, unlike market price, always moves from a state of compression to a state of expansion.

It is in the nature of markets to create price and volume accumulation zones, where large orders are progressively filled against numerous smaller ones. Institutional investors build their blocks in the context of their valuations and of the available market liquidity. As they work out their weighted average prices (WAP), rates typically remain within range during those periods, allowing volatility levels to fall. Suddenly large orders are filled and price can move away from the range, even in low volumes. Volatility then rises.

Another case scenario is a steady price trend upward or downward. Since volatility is measured as a standard deviation, it will fall as long as the trend continues steadily, in spite of a common belief that volatility only rises when prices move up or down. When the prices eventually reverse, volatility rises again. For example, the volatility levels have been consistently declining between 2003 and 2007 on most equity and foreign exchange markets in spite of large price movements. Volatility traders were desperate and many hedge funds had given up some of the long volatility strategies when the trend finally reversed in 2007, only to reach unheard of levels 2 years later. Volatility is not a market return or a trading item. It is a measure of market emotions and trading liquidity conditions. Therefore it is meant to expand and compress as the market will eventually reverse. Firms implementing a dynamic culture of risk management are well advised to investigate their specific exposure to volatility and prepare for the inevitable changes.

12
Bottom-Up Activity Feedback

When risk management has reached the status of a corporate culture, with business units empowered with the capability of identifying their own exposure and tasked with defining their own scenarios to mitigate their risks based on the targets and limits derived from the corporate strategy, the efficiency of this framework will be intricately linked to the feedback from the business units to the management. Also, the feedback will be channelled to the Executive Risk Committee (ERC), which should continuously monitor the exposure, appraise the assessments of sensitivity and approve the relevance and coherence of scenarios.

12.1 KEEPING A FINGER ON THE PULSE

To achieve this, a number of 'sensors' need to be installed on the nerve centres, where risks directly or indirectly originate. Some of the nodes may be obvious. For example, if a trading unit manages bond portfolios with sensitivity limits and compliance targets, the feedback would involve the overall convexity or basis point value (BPV) of the desk, the exposure concentration per bond category, ratings, currency, and so on. Initially, monitoring the key risk generators of a back-office department might seem to be unnatural or unusual. Items such as the number of failed executions, client exceptions or settlement errors can be easily quantified but the reputational risks due to the repetitive mishandling of operations would be more difficult to estimate. Regardless of those difficulties, the appropriate sensors must be designed and set up for the management and all people involved to keep a finger on the pulse.

Ideally, the risk units themselves would have been involved in the definition of what they deem to be the most critical aspects of their market: credit and operational risk exposure. They are best placed to figure out the baseline and high-severity scenarios that might seriously disrupt their operations and to estimate the potential cost of those disruptions. Assigning them the task of identifying and reporting those risks is certainly a way to raise their awareness and commit them to the risk issues. It is yet another important step towards making risk management a culture.

12.1.1 Continuous efficiency monitoring

Risk and business units should be tasked with risk mitigation. The efficiency of hedges must be continuously monitored. With trading units exposed to quantitative risks and portfolio effects, this raises new issues such as valuations, slippage, market liquidity and overall volatility. For back-office and purely functional units, the mitigation of risks can consist of a process, supplement resources or a disaster recovery procedure for example. The feedback must therefore include elements of appropriateness and efficiency. In the case of a disaster recovery centre, tests would involve factors such as the number of critical functions covered, the timescale required to restore critical functions and completion of simulations.

One way to facilitate the understanding and reliability of mitigation tactics is to store and document all facts. For example, recording loss events, failed hedges and inappropriate scenarios will eventually improve the understanding of this type of issue and sharpen the analysis.

No matter how dynamic and accurate it might be, the feedback only becomes an unparalleled powerful management tool when it enables prompt action by the management. In other words, we need a 'feedback on feedback'. If an alert is triggered, if the exposure to a given risk factor reaches a critical level, the executive risk manager in charge of that particular factor needs to be perfectly aware of the nature of the exposure and of the mitigation tools that can be used to react timely and adjust the exposure. This implies that the efficiency of the hedging methodology should periodically undergo testing and reviews. This very important step towards turning risk management into a corporate culture involves a continuous review of issues and permanent commitment to the mitigation processes. The firm, at this stage, is now gaining agility in the face of risk exposure. The complementary periodic reviews of the consistency and integrity of the mitigation techniques should also be in use. This is yet another step that makes the firm 'risk intelligent'.

12.1.2 Test and result certification

In large organizations, processes to reach such a level of agility and reactivity require controls and certification of hedges, hedge tests, scenarios and methods. Some of the typical tests would involve answering the following questions: Are risk factors properly identified and assessed? Are the mitigation tools and techniques efficient enough and adapted to the scenarios considered? Are the scenarios aligned with market realities? Did anyone check and certify that they were? Has a name been attached to each reply to each of those tests?

Those tests need to be instilled within the business operations and then certified as part of the risk diligence process, which ensures that they remain relevant. Alerts triggering reviews will be raised otherwise.

The certification process consists of validating the measurements, the valuation and assessments as well as the efficiency of the risk mitigation. Attaching a name to each certification of each test ensures that responsibilities are properly allocated – yet another step towards the cultural shift.

Risk factors are identified and sorted according to their sensitivity. Data attached to each factor involve sensitivity, mitigation techniques, hedge efficiency and back-testing records. As part of the bottom-up feedback, risk managers or executives assigned by the ERC need to sign off and certify the relevance and the integrity of the tests in use.

Ideally, an instant messaging and communication network would provide immediate requests, such as drill-in concentrations or customer credit decisions for example. Traceable instant messaging tools can increase the level of transparency and agility in the face of fast changing risk factors.

12.2 AGGREGATING SCENARIOS: THE ACTUAL RISK APPETITE OF THE FIRM

A crucial aspect of implementing a corporate culture consists of identifying the root-risk factors a firm is exposed to and assessing their sensitivity, as discussed throughout Part 1. For this reason, sets of baseline, high-severity and catastrophic scenarios have been designed and regularly updated based on market conditions. The cultural shift consists of allocating this task to the business owners themselves as opposed to having the scenarios defined in isolation by some specialists. Auditors and controllers can coach and guide the definition of relevant and realistic scenarios, but the view remains that the risk centres themselves are best placed to express how catastrophic a situation can be, estimate its potential impact and assess its potentially contagious effects. This is a major departure from the predictive models, which relied on calibrations

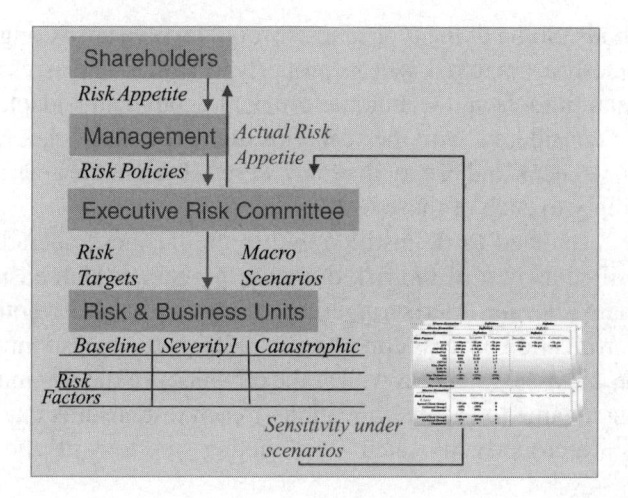

Figure 12.1 Risk allocation and scenario feedback

themselves based on underlying assumptions, variable distributions and probabilities in particular.

One of the main benefits of the new approach is that an aggregated view of the scenarios arising from the business operational and functional units will appropriately reflect the views and understanding of risks as they are perceived by the operating agents themselves. In other words, the ERC or the auditors will be able to draw a picture of the risk appetite of the firm observed through the day-to-day operations coupled with perceptions of what constitutes high-impact or catastrophic events. The management will now be in a position to reconcile such a risk appetite with the one initially portrayed by the shareholders through the risk policies (see Figure 12.1).

12.3 TOWARDS A RISK INFORMATION BUS FOR IT PURPOSES

The workflow of risk information described here is the nervous system of the firm. It commands operations, conveys data and triggers a course of actions or spontaneous reactions. As such, the workflow is the firm's risk intelligence provider. It conveys shareholders' expectations as well as distributes multiple layers of feedback and instructions. Additionally, it warehouses risk-based information that can be used for calculation, back-testing or auditing purposes at a later stage. Market and credit events of either high or low severity, whether expected or unexpected, can be stored and reused to refine scenarios, discuss limit utilization or sharpen the risk policies.

The overall efficiency in the information workflow is critical to maintaining the balance among risk and business managing units, risk committees and audit controls. The information workflow cannot solely rest on the shoulders of the IT department. It should provide a culture of open, sincere and transparent communication across the firm, supported by IT. The audit and control departments are responsible for the workflow as they need to foster the culture, maintain the alignment with the risk policies and ensure the consistency of methodologies without hindering the free flow of data and information.

To achieve this, the IT framework should no longer stack up disparate applications initially created for silo purposes. Instead, it should chain together the calculation engines and analytical tools revolving around a purpose-built flow of external and internal data – a Risk Information Bus. Risk information can consist of details such as prices, valuations, counterparty data, scenarios, sensitivities, P/L and performance. Further information can include events such as ticket inputs, corporate actions, sudden changes in volatility, collateral adjustments and any information that may affect the exposure, mitigation or compliance to risk policies. A trade execution, for example, can trigger a message related to another trade of collateral. This message immediately feeds a margining and collateral pricing system, which will henceforth listen to any changes in value, news related to the counterparty, margin accounts servicing and so on, successfully demonstrating the evolution of the IT network into a dynamic workflow linking the publishers and listeners of risk information (see Figure 12.2).

A listener, in turn, can select the information needed, compute a new output and republish through the network. Continuing from the preceding example, the net collateralized exposure computed by the margining system would be republished and used by credit officers, controllers or compliance departments. The respective entities would compute related risk-weighted liquidity impact or concentration statistics to publish them again for the likely use of regulatory compliance officers and so on.

Far from only being a simple middleware message bus, the information bus is 'risk intelligent'. Essentially, it is capable of identifying news, data, events or computed items that can potentially impact the firm's exposure to market, credit, liquidity, legal or reputational risks. By definition, an exhaustive list of items required for risk management

```
Trades    Loans    Collateral    Funding     Regulatory
                                 Deals       driven data
```

Risk Information Bus

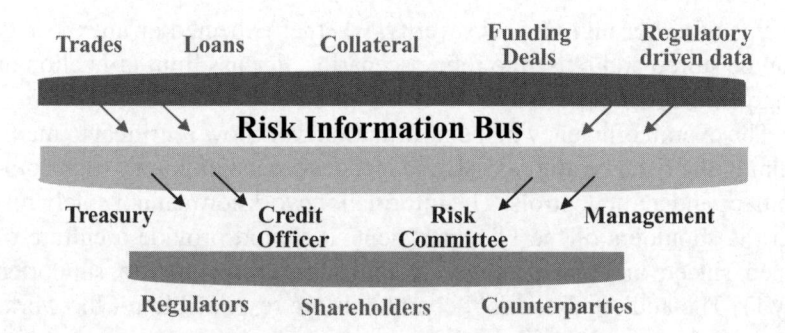

```
Treasury      Credit        Risk         Management
              Officer       Committee

        Regulators   Shareholders   Counterparties
```

Figure 12.2 A trade execution

cannot be firmly established. Such a list would only be sustained for a brief period as each day brings its own load of unpredictable developments and raises new risk factors to dismiss some of the old ones. The key is to allow each risk centre or business unit to be in control of the risk data that they need and generate the requirements themselves. The support in this task by the IT departments, audits and risk executive who will drive and coach the implementation is indispensible. With this final step, a giant leap is made towards turning risk into a corporate culture.

13
Enterprise-Wide Aggregation

Clearly the main challenge of feeding back risk events and sensitivity to the management lies in the diversity of exposure. The greater the diversity of the firm, the more complications in cross-asset and cross-division reconciliations, particularly in defining the proper alerts and triggers that will occur.

13.1 CROSS-ASSET SENSITIVITY AGGREGATION

Value-at-risk (VaR) has been a convenient tool to compare apples with oranges, but the concept has shown its limitations. VaR is a combination of backward-looking methodology and predictive statistic modelling. As such, it presents two major deficiencies: history may distort the statistical analysis while predictive modelling relies on assumptions and calibrations themselves derived from history. In other words, the concept is poorly adapted to tail events, falsely validated by back-testing. It is fine to apply it for benchmarking purposes but no longer as a measurement of risks on which to base sensitivity reports, risk assessments, capital allocations or traders' compensations.

To replace VaR with a reliable view of risk sensitivities, the input of every business division and every person in charge of risk targets will be necessary. The importance of deploying a culture of risk management is obvious, but this raises other challenges. The risks and sensitivities from every unit must be understood by them if they have to be accountable for it. This means sensitivities will be collected with different means, interpreted with different cultures and reported with different supports.

Risk managers tasked with gathering the input that will later be aggregated must therefore define the rules and granularity of the dollar sensitivity being collected and reported. Figure 13.1 illustrates how different scenarios and different subfactors impacting the same macro-factor at different frequencies can produce an auditable $ sensitivity set of figures that the risk managers can quickly aggregate and discuss directly with the persons responsible and accountable for the mitigation of the risks they assess and report themselves.

116   The Handbook of Risk Management

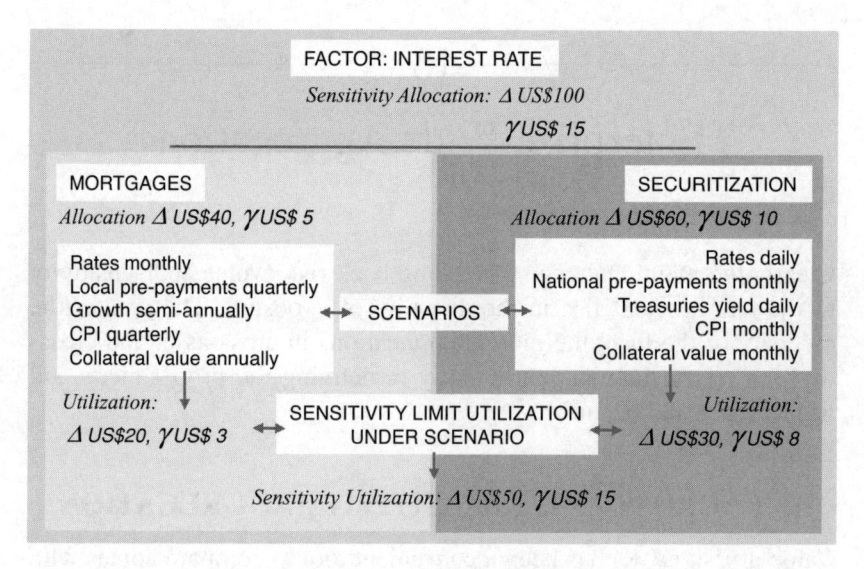

```
┌─────────────────────────────────────────────────────────────────────┐
│                      FACTOR: INTEREST RATE                          │
│                    Sensitivity Allocation: Δ US$100                 │
│                                            γ US$ 15                 │
│  ┌──────────────────────────┐        ┌──────────────────────────┐   │
│  │       MORTGAGES          │        │      SECURITIZATION      │   │
│  │ Allocation Δ US$40, γUS$5│        │Allocation Δ US$60, γUS$10│   │
│  └──────────────────────────┘        └──────────────────────────┘   │
│   Rates monthly                               Rates daily           │
│   Local pre-payments quarterly       National pre-payments monthly  │
│   Growth semi-annually    ↔ SCENARIOS ↔   Treasuries yield daily    │
│   CPI quarterly                               CPI monthly           │
│   Collateral value annually           Collateral value monthly      │
│                                                                     │
│   Utilization:                                       Utilization:   │
│   Δ US$20, γUS$3  ↔  SENSITIVITY LIMIT UTILIZATION ↔ Δ US$30, γUS$8 │
│                         UNDER SCENARIO                              │
│                                  ↓                                  │
│            Sensitivity Utilization: Δ US$50, γ US$ 15               │
└─────────────────────────────────────────────────────────────────────┘
```

Figure 13.1   Aggregating the $ sensitivity enterprise-wide

In the above example, a diversified banking group has identified that the 'interest rates' were a key risk factor. The management and the executive risk committee have derived sensitivity limits from the size and risk appetite of the company. The permitted sensitivity under the macro-factor 'interest rates' is then distributed to the various divisions and centre of exposure, in this case a retail mortgage loan department and a securitization division at the investment bank. Both departments are in the business of collecting loans against the value of mortgages but obviously in a very different way for varying purposes. Stemming from very different corporate cultures, both departments will most likely derive the delta and gamma sensitivity of their exposure with dissimilar methods and inputs and at different times and granularity. Somehow, however, each will manage to use their own capabilities to produce $ sensitivity figures, at least a delta and gamma. Vega and theta could probably be easily added. Whichever way they proceed, all calculations can be audited, archived and restored if need be. Not only does the output reflect the sensitivity of the exposure of each group but it also reflects their corporate culture. If figures produced are inconsistent, implausible or irrelevant, the risk managers and the audit will get a chance to investigate the sources of the issue and to fix the corporate culture rather than the models. If the overall $ sensitivity is too high across the board, then the risk management can quickly narrow down the risk centre from which the excesses have arisen.

Whether this particular way to compare apples and oranges is more accurate than VaR is not the issue. The efficiency of this suggested way is not absolute but it is certainly more transparent, participatory and can be discussed bottom-up or top-down by any one within the firm. VaR can still play a great role in the process: VaR was typically computed through models fed with rate sets and scenarios. In other words, the distribution of price returns and cross-items covariance was the input and the measure of risk was the output. If this workflow is reversed, we can use the measure of risks derived from the above methodology and back-engineer the distribution assumed by the collective estimations of the entire company across divisions. The result would be a valuable description of the risk acceptance of the company. It is not its risk appetite but the actual amount of risk that they manage through their operation based on an implied set of price distribution – an implied 'state of the world' – that will be attained.

13.2 CROSS-DIVISION AGGREGATION POTENTIAL PITFALLS

In large diversified groups in particular, the task of aggregating all scenario-based sensitivities may become daunting. Any failure, any negligence in collecting data with an established level of transparency and granularity, will quickly become unmanageable. Worse, our principle of aggregated sensitivity values will not tolerate delays of missing input.

The only way to ensure that each risk centre fully abides by the rules is to help them individually define their risk sensitivity assessment methodologies. As explained above, each risk centre will need to turn the macro-factors into micro-factors of sensitivity that are relevant to the nature of their activity. This particular exercise is to be closely watched by the risk management committee and formally agreed with respect to the sensitivity calculation methodology, granularity, frequency and reporting media. The audit and control department can be called in to arbitrate in the case of uncertainty or disagreement.

In addition to issues that may arise at the department level, the enterprise-wide aggregation concept is likely to raise eyebrows among the VaR specialists, who may object on correlation issues.

13.2.1 Cross-market effects and correlations

The VaR methodology was supposed to reflect cross-market correlations through the complex covariance matrices necessary in input. Whether used in historical simulations or Monte Carlo processes, the covariance matrices would have driven the impact of correlations in the final VaR output.

The proposed simplified methodology to aggregate sensitivity across the enterprise obviously does not attempt to model correlations, since it only wants to tell the reality, not model it. Exposure of opposite directions based on correlated or uncorrelated factors will naturally offset each other when different departments estimate the sensitivity of opposite signs. The most important aspect is that correlations will become forward looking as they are now based on people's assessment of volatility looking forward. With statistical analysis, covariance is obviously a backward looking measure that highly depends on the sample. In most cases, VaR calculations have been based on an arbitrary 252 day history, corresponding to a fiscal year. The dangers are obvious when one thinks, for example, of the sudden jumps in volatility to unheard-of levels between October and December 2008. During those times all correlations and covariance measures were entirely corrupted by the liquidity crunch, market panic, fire sales and uneven depths of the markets. Risk managers were left divided on the issue of whether to include these figures with full weight or minimize their impact. On the contrary, suggestions have been made to extend the historical analysis instead of suddenly removing exceptional levels of volatility from the charts. Either way, the sudden jumps will appear on one day and disappear on another, which will not be a diffusion learning process but just a technical bias. During those periods, analysts cannot even decide to ignore correlations as this has massive implications on the levels of VaR. Finally, VaR measurements, being based on models, are themselves calibrated on price and return distributions. It is clear that any measurements done between September 2008 and March 2009 would be of little relevance.

13.2.2 Of correlation and liquidity

The key issue, as demonstrated by Carlo Acerbi[1] in his 2009 analysis of liquidity risk, is that the entire portfolio theory is based on an assumption

---

[1] C. Acerbi and G. Scandolo, Liquidity risk theory and coherent measures of risk, *Quantitative Finance*, **8** (7), 2008.

of market efficiency that presupposes the depth and liquidity of assets. Market correlations are in reality often based on the movements of liquidity, the market depth or shallowness and how they translate into volatility. We will discuss liquidity risk and the importance of its management in adequacy with the risk profile of the firm throughout Part 4. At this stage, we can already emphasize the fact that enormous distortions in correlations and volatility arise from liquidity issues and translate into further liquidity issues. The relation is complex, nonlinear and barely predictable. If we try to explain the links, we can say that correlations derive from perception and that perceptions are influenced by liquidity. The charts in Figure 13.2, for example, exhibit the weekly price paths of two major Swiss banks that are normally correlated with each other. The charts illustrate how each sudden reversal in correlation corresponds to a spike in the traded volumes of both equities.

13.2.3 Model and valuation risks[2]

Valuation risks, identified in Part 1 as a combination of model risk, data management risk and pricing process operational risks, are an important aspect of the enterprise-wide aggregation of sensitivity and exposure.

In addition to being exposed to mispricing and data issues, the risk management committees need to ensure the integrity of the decentralized pricing methodologies. For example, the various divisions and departments can have a very different sensitivity assessment of the same financial instrument or asset if they have a different exposure to it or a different investment timeframe, but not if it is only due to different model methodologies or discrepancies in data input. Different accounting methodologies can be justified by different investment purposes, provided there is integrity in the process and that it is all documented, audited and archived.

The solution requires a risk and pricing intelligence workflow drawing all information from a single source, whether data are amended or not, and feeding back all the changes and valuations for different purposes. For the trading books, it will consist of a securities and instrument repository where each item traded or held can be described with terms

---

[2] This section has been inspired by a White Paper by Philippe Carrel, 'Valuation risk', May 2008.

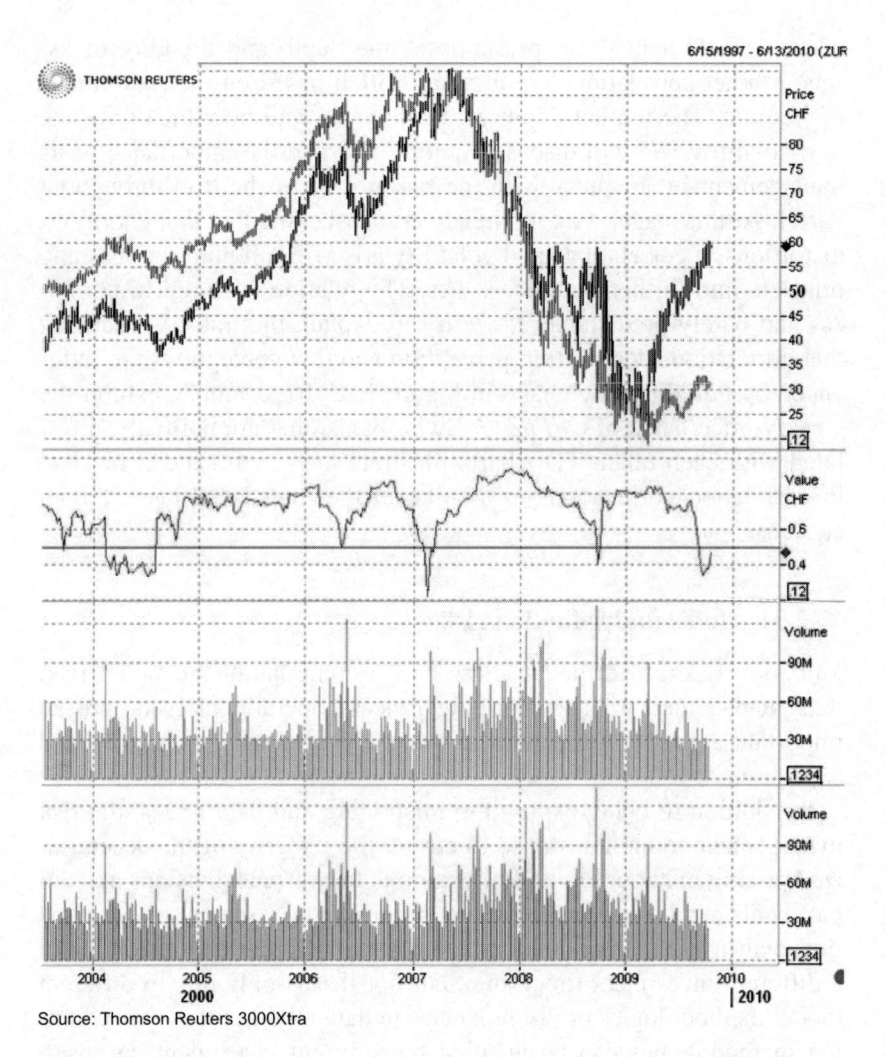

Figure 13.2 Weekly price paths of two major Swiss banks, correlation and respective volumes traded

and conditions as well as cash flow projections, pay-off profiles, absolute sensitivity, index-based sensitivity, source of price and information. The responsibility and accountability for maintaining the data alive and the workflow operational should be clearly allocated.

Once all the securities and traded instruments are set in the operational datastore, then a similar task needs to be carried out for over-the-counter (OTC) instruments and all calculated items for which there is little or no price available from market sources. The models must be documented, together with the curves, surfaces and matrices, with their interpolation methodologies. Their inputs and fittings must be understood and archived. Models should be decoupled from their original applications. Option pricing models, for example, may produce results for pre-trade analytics, which would be time consuming to reconcile with what the back-office computes. In reality there is nothing wrong with allowing front-office traders to compute their own options with their market making curves while the back-office uses a different frequency and end-of-day input, for example. It is not an issue as long as the processes are known, recorded, audited and accepted by all. When the trading desk is requested to indicate their own sensitivities to risk factors such as volatility or interest rates, they can perform the calculations based on the models and on the curves they use to give prices to their clients. When the back-office is requested to indicate their assessment of sensitivity to risk factors such as personnel qualification, delivery issues or accounting failure, there is no reason why they would not use different curves and methodology. The aggregated sensitivity will truly represent the total risks with those options – credit, market and operational – from all imaginable points of view. The key to keeping the whole framework manageable and dynamically adaptable is to ensure that the original data are controlled – the nomenclature description of the options and the market data sources – and that the price base of all desk and departments are given enough historical detail to ensure back-engineering of the valuations. Figure 13.3 exhibits the main flow of an enterprise-wide platform of this format.

The platform must be open to model changes, alternative curves and matrices, external sources of pricing and input. It should be the central piece of the architecture for risk and auditing purposes.

A critical aspect is that centralizing all risk intelligence sources on to a single platform does not create uniformity and standardization, which would create more operational risk than it would eliminate and also impede making people responsible and accountable for the risk they generate and mitigate.

For banking books, retail banking and corporate loans the items and tools are similar. The fund transfer pricing (FTP) systems and asset and liability management (ALM) tools must refer to a single platform where all values of loans and collateral, all counterparty data, limit, resources and analysis should possibly be documented, archived and audited.

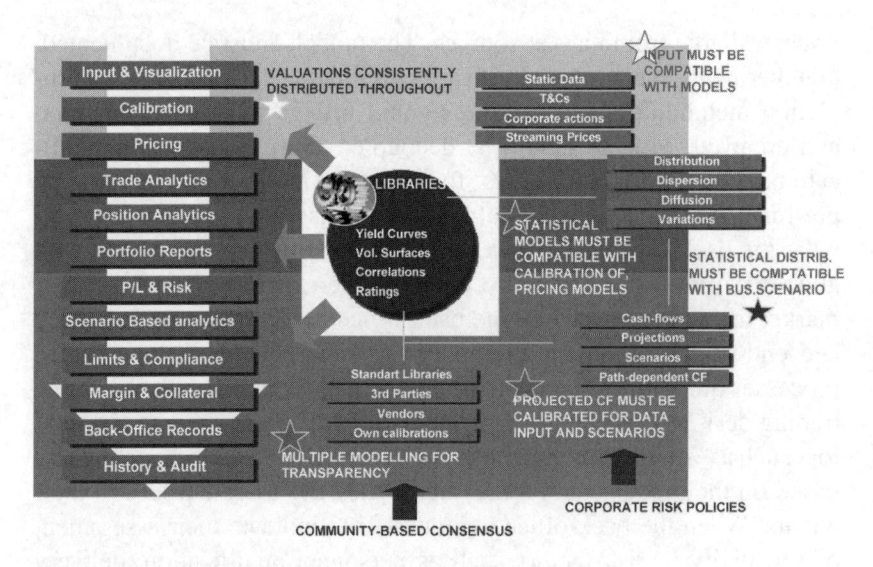

Figure 13.3 Securities pricing and modelling an open platform

13.2.4 Technology risks

These result from the above discussion, where the role of IT is crucial to implementing a workflow that can turn the bottom-up feedback into a source of risk-based information allowing the firm clearly to see the risks deriving from its day-to-day activities. The technology used therefore becomes an operational risk in itself. Not only must the technology keep functioning at all times and under any circumstances, and provide adequate scalability and reliability, but also the IT process must itself be audited and stick to the spirit of the risk management framework.

In particular, the concept should allow for a supervised autonomy of all the stakeholders. It is very important that the IT department enables such autonomy without trying to impose technocratic rules with respect to data availability, IT processes, availability of information or of resources – to name just a few.

From a technical point of view, the technology in use should focus on openness and scalability. The system we want to create is thought to be self-adaptive. The business complexity that will result from it requires a distributed approach to pricers and handlers, valuation tools, open database structures and data visualization.

14
Top-Down Decisions and Feedback

Once risk-based information reaches the management layers, it needs to be made available, understandable and usable in order to trigger decisions and produce effect. The aim is to create an 'if...then' relationship so that intelligence of misalignment of risk taken with risk policies can timely trigger a change of course and rebalance the desired with the actual exposure. The first element of the top-down workflow is therefore a risk management dashboard.

14.1 RISK DASHBOARDS

Providing a risk management dashboard to the senior management featuring market, credit and operational risks, trade statistics and P/L breakdown has been the most sought-after type of project since VaR was created, the ultimate dream of any risk management consultant. Some actually managed to pull off some integrated dashboards, to the least risk reports featuring VaR, credit VaR and limit utilization. Yet in most cases those reports have not been properly used.

The first reason is that the entire culture of risk management has consistently rewarded only one value, namely capital efficiency. In other words, CEOs could hardly be bothered with VaR figures, not only because they were not understandable but because they would rather be concerned with their return on risk adjusted capital (RAROC), though these too failed to produce the announced breakthrough.

The second issue is that VaR – and to some extent modelled sensitivity figures – are not directly functional as management tools. Although the linear function between VaR and exposure could be explained by the risk managers or investigated by drilling down through the reports, there is no natural link between the risk measure and actionable tactics the management can quickly decide upon. Being a statistic analytical tool, VaR would always remain in the toolbox of analysts rather than decision makers.

Third, it was always understood that there were overlaps and dependencies between market risk, credit risks and operational risks. No matter how thorough and sophisticated the research went, it failed to produce any reliable modelling. We would all intuitively be certain of a credit risk dimension within market risks and vice versa, that the operational risks of mismanaging this relation could lead to serious losses and that it all ultimately boiled down to liquidity issues, but no one, no model, has ever been able to describe this complex and nonlinear relationship. From that point of view, VaR has remained a dead end, in spite of recent improvements with particular respect to tail risk.

The tilting point, at which the VaR-based risk management dashboard became a mere reporting and compliance tool, was the first series of tail events that hit the world economy in the early 2000s. Following the failure of Long-Term Capital Management (LTCM), the burst of the Internet bubble and fallen angels such as Enron, Worldcom and Parmalat, it was clear that predictive modelling based on backward-looking analyses could not produce the monitors and decision tools the managers would need. Again, if there is only one error, it is not within the models. It is the attempt to superimpose regulatory-driven methodologies on a corporate culture. Those at the wheel need pre-emptive decision tools formatted for the nature of their activity and expressed in a language they can understand. They also need to see the effect of their decisions and whether turning the wheel actually changes their course.

14.2 PRE-EMPTIVE DECISION FRAMEWORKS

The essence of managing risk is not to be able to predict the future or to comply with some regulatory language. Managing risk is to create the ability to receive information relating to exposure, sensitivity, limits and losses followed by a trigger of action so that those risks remain within the defined boundaries in line with the risk policies. Each and every corporation would therefore have its own definition and policies and would set up levels of reactivity adapted to their risk tolerance.

The top-down decision framework must fulfil two essential roles. First, it must build on a risk sensitivity dashboard, which points out the sensitivity to the risk factors, with drill down capabilities, under the various scenario types – baseline, high severity, catastrophic. Valuations under stress and their impact on limits must appear so that the management will be alerted as risk builds up. Such a dashboard must be active. For example, volatility levels could change, thus overriding vega limits without any deal being entered. This market fact should trigger some instructions leading to unwinding of some of the vega exposure. Credit events such as downgrade or negative watch could impact the value of securities or derivatives, triggering some hedging instructions.

These mechanisms must be in place and fully supported by the risk information dashboard so that the framework can be as preemptive as possible. This presupposes that a valuation platform can sensibly price all instruments and aggregate their sensitivity, as previously described.

Second, the decision framework must also be as adaptable to external market conditions as it is to internal exposure and sensitivity bottom-up feedback. Limit values, mark-to-value frequencies, collateral management and risk targets can be dynamically adapted to external market conditions. The process is described in Figure 14.1. The role of the risk management committee is central when translating the risks assessed by the division into aggregated factor exposure, sensitivity and liquidity requirements that the management committee or senior executive management team can immediately use for decision making. The role

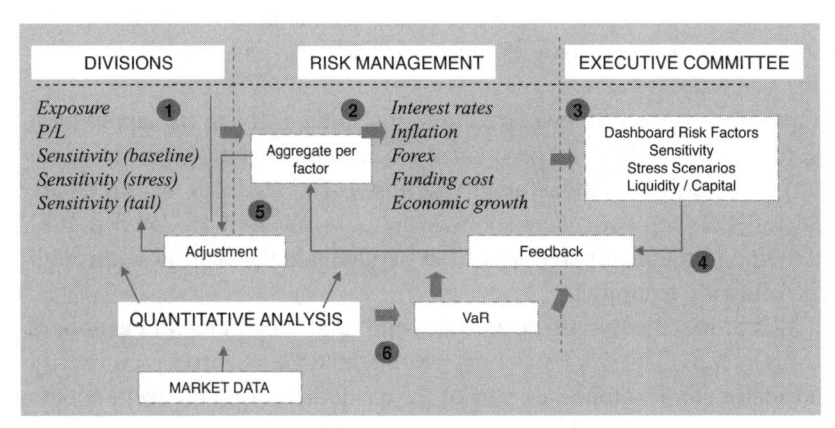

DIVISIONS	RISK MANAGEMENT	EXECUTIVE COMMITTEE
Exposure ① P/L Sensitivity (baseline) Sensitivity (stress) Sensitivity (tail)	② Interest rates Aggregate per factor — Inflation Forex Funding cost Economic growth	③ Dashboard Risk Factors Sensitivity Stress Scenarios Liquidity / Capital
Adjustment ⑤	Feedback ④
QUANTITATIVE ANALYSIS → VaR
⑥ MARKET DATA

① Each business division computes fundamental risk figures such as exposure, P/L and sensitivity under baseline, stress and extreme scenarios. Divisions are supported by the quantitative analysis team in this task

② The Risk Committee aggregates sensitivity per factor, scenario and business division. The quantitative analysis team maintains consistency with the valuations performed by the divisions.

③ The executive management receives a dashboard with sensitivities and expected liquidity impact under scenarios. The figures can be directly reconciled with the risk objectives.

④ The executive management feeds back with quantitative and qualitative adjustments

⑤ The Risk Committee translates the adjustments into quantitative limits per risk factor and advises on pricing and valuation methodologies accordingly

⑥ The quantitative analysis team supports the provision of market data, maintains integrity of methodologies, computes VaR and feeds back as a benchmark

Figure 14.1 Top-down risk information workflow

of the quantitative analysis team, supervised by the risk management committee, is to ensure the consistency and integrity of pricing and valuations throughout the process, maintain the quality of data and adjust the models and pricing methodologies to the market conditions. VaR is still computed in the end, no longer used as a risk management tool but rather as a benchmark.

14.3 AN INTERACTIVE AND ADAPTIVE WORKFLOW

The most important aspect of the workflow is to keep it dynamic and adaptive in times of poor liquidity, of spread increase and of volatility rises. Above a given threshold, the nature of the markets and the profile of the return distribution will be drastically modified. At such a point a dynamic risk management framework must be able to adapt its customer margins, trader limits and sensitivity limits. This, however, cannot be done in isolation, as the quantitative analysis team must at that stage adapt the curves, surfaces and model parameters to the new market status. It is therefore critical that the workflow remains transparent along all of the feedback processes in order for the quantitative team and risk managers to proceed with the necessary adjustments after an alert has been released.

In doing so, the framework continuously adapts to the risk appetite of the firm (which might not be set in stone and could change depending on market conditions and customer reactions). The feedback is immediate and reflects the changes as soon as the adjustments have been implemented and the results reported. Let us navigate the workflow through the following example.

A fixed income trading desk trades and funds positions for customers through repos. The risk factors such as interest rate sensitivity, convexity and sector credit spreads are part of the dashboard. A credit event occurs on one of the issuers, which raises the credit spread of an entire industrial sector. All of a sudden, the credit dv01 sensitivity and cost of funding rise. At the level of the trading desk, the sensitivity under the baseline scenario is not much higher but the perspective of potential defaults within a sector raises the cost of catastrophic scenarios substantially higher.

The risk management aggregates the expected sensitivity to those same factors across the various desks impacted and reports it at end-of-day to the senior management with some recommendations. All aggregations, valuations and modelling are supported by the quantitative analysis team in the process.

The management receives the alert and decides the risk is not acceptable, so makes an order to remain within the accepted boundaries even though the new situation has dramatically increased the risks. The risk committee takes the order and translates it into an instruction of lower exposure to the trading desk. After a discussion initiated by the risk management and supported by the quantitative analysts, the decision is made to raise the haircut levels for all clients exposed to this sector. Complementary analysis is also ordered to estimate the potential repercussions of the same incident on other types of positions or on the customers directly. The trading desk adjusts haircut levels, while the quantitative analysts check if there is no implication on pricing and valuation methodologies. The adjustment lowers the overall sensitivity of exposure, which is immediately reflected in the risk factor aggregation and the management dashboard.

In a diversified banking group exposed to a very large number of customers potentially exposed to the deficient issuers, the whole process described above might have taken a few days to a week at the maximum. In traditional risk management frameworks, the hedging haircuts would be decoupled from risk calculations. By the time the VaR figures would have raised concerns in management spheres, the origin of the issue would have been located and the traders would or would not have already covered the additional exposure. Sensitivity limits and even VaR limits do exist in most modern frameworks, but they are not dynamically adjusted to external market conditions and to the ever-changing nature of liquidity and funding conditions or to the evolutions of the risk appetite of the firm. The system may be efficient as far as calculations and modelling go but is not responsive to changes.

14.4 HIERARCHY, DECISIONS, OVERRULING

A key aspect of creating an adaptive and dynamic framework where risk events trigger risk management action is to make sure that the hierarchical decision model allows for overruling risk management tactics such as hedges or exposure in case alert levels are reached or deficiencies arise. For example, when a trader's vega limit is reached in his absence because market volatility moves against a position, the alert usually reaches a deputy or manager who can take immediate action to unwind some of the vega exposure. When the overall collateral value of a portfolio held for margin trading reaches the threshold for margin calls, systems automatically inform the credit officers and the clients of the imminent readjustment. When the value of large collateralized loans held by a bank fall below a given threshold, there must be a similar approach. If hedges that were supposed to cover exposure start to drift apart, the decision must be transferred to a higher hierarchical level automatically so that a decision to maintain or amend positions can be reached.

In our proposed framework, the decision to hedge an exposure and how it is carried out belongs to the person accountable for the sensitivity – trader, credit officer, head of division. A sensitivity limit threshold is reached for several reasons: (a) the hedging tactic is not efficient or the hedges drift apart because of external factors (such as market movements, volatility, liquidity); (b) there is excessive exposure due to the activity of that particular unit; (c) the activity of other units adds up to the aggregated sensitivity to the same risk factor so that the threshold levels themselves have to be amended.

In the first case, two further case scenarios can take place. The trader is aware of the issue or not. If the trader is aware and present, the alert simply triggers the routine information, discussion, amendment procedure. If the trader is not aware, then the hierarchy of responsibilities has to be set up so that someone else can immediately be allocated the responsibility to take action and be accountable for such action without a further authorization process. Typically, the second level of responsibility for risk should be outside the business division and in the risk management division, for example. The second level must be empowered to make an executive decision such as cutting traders' lines,

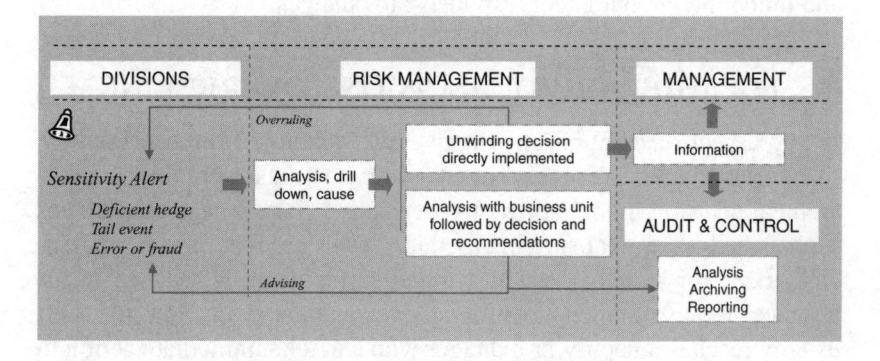

Figure 14.2 Risk management hierarchy and overruling

unwinding deals, freezing transactions or setting limits or escalating issues. In the interest of keeping the whole process dynamic, responsive and alert, no further permission is requested once the responsibilities have been allocated, but there is a duty of information. The original desk or trader as well as the audit department and the senior management team should be informed that it has become necessary to overrule existing risk mitigation tactics or decisions and that pre-emptive action is being taken. Figure 14.2 exhibits this decision workflow.

15
Deriving a Firm's Actual Observed Risk Appetite

There is no such thing as good risk or bad risk. There are risks a firm is supposed and tasked to take, in line of its corporate policies, and the risk exposure that is clearly undesired by the shareholders, if they could express themselves directly on the issues.

Shareholders are typically delivered risk reports attached to end-of-year statements and documentation that describe the exposure in generic terms and strongly focus on VaR figures, such as the example in Figure 15.1, which is drawn out of a Tier 1 investment bank report.

Of course, quantitative reports are always accompanied by extensive comments but those are typically focused on the methodology used to compute the results or are merely comment statistics. There has been little relationship established between the firm strategy and the risk strategy. The main reason that risk was not seen as a strategy in itself was that risk was perceived as a side effect of the growth and expansion policies that needed to be managed in accordance with the regulations.

In post-crisis risk management, risk is a key factor of the core strategy, balancing the drive towards capital efficiency. The task of the management is therefore to draw a qualitative and quantitative picture of the actual risk appetite of the firm – as expressed through its everyday's actions, strategies and tactics – and reconcile it as often as possible with the appetite expressed by the shareholders, the funding partners of the firm as well as its customers.

To compare the risk one is supposed to take with the risk actually taken, there is no better way than considering the risk factors to which the management has exposed the firm. Obviously the sensitivity to the factors must then be explained in detail together with the scenario underneath the sensitivity measures. Finally, the scenarios themselves are the real expression of risk as understood by the very actors exposing the firm to risk day in and day out. What they call baseline versus high-severity versus catastrophic needs to be reconciled with the views of the shareholders, client and partners. If there is a discrepancy, then it must

Investment Bank: Value at Risk (10-day, 99% confidence, five years of historical data) [1] Source: UBS

CHF million	Quarter ended 30.9.08				Quarter ended 30.6.08			
	Min.	Max.	Average	30.9.08	Min.	Max.	Average	30.6.08
Risk type								
Equities	104	137	119	121	117	150	128	126
Interest rates (including credit spreads)	362	659	511	575	257	478	312	422
Foreign exchange	17	58	30	29	16	51	34	32
Energy, metals and commodities	18	33	25	24	20	60	37	21
Diversification effect	[2]	[2]	(223)	(231)	[2]	[2]	(201)	(206)
Total regulatory VaR	342	601	461	519	254	426	310	396
Diversification effect (%)			(33)	(31)			(39)	(34)
Management VaR [1,3]	253	390	303	339	249	443	313	388

1 From 1 January 2008, excludes US residential sub-prime and Alt-A mortgage-related exposures, super senior RMBS CDOs and the US reference-linked note program. 2 As the minimum and maximum occur on different days for different risk types, it is not meaningful to calculate a portfolio diversification effect. 3 Includes all positions (including CVAs) subject to internal management VaR limits.

Figure 15.1   Investment bank risk report

be addressed at this level. Risk is essentially an in-depth understanding of 'what could be happening'. Managing risk is therefore anticipating the adverse developments that can be foreseen. Strictly modelling them will only instill a false sense of safety and control.

15.1   MODELLING WORST CASE SCENARIOS

We have seen in Part 1 that scenarios designed and controlled by the business risk units were eventually aggregated into one 'view of the world' for the management to present to the shareholders. We present hereafter a methodology that is part of a risk-based information workflow. Is this part of a bottom-up or top-down feedback? It is actually both. It is an exchange of views that is necessary for creating the culture of risk management. The more constructive discussions triggered by the information workflow, the deeper the culture of risk management will embed in the culture of every firm.

Aggregating back catastrophic scenarios is the key to building or modelling 'worst case' scenarios, nowadays usually called stress testing. The goal of extreme scenarios in traditional risk frameworks is to be able to compute VaR under such a scenario. In most cases, risk managers have stress-tested their models rather than their firms' ability to weather a serious crisis where tail events might arise and multiply. They would usually use the extreme conditions they knew from the past, sometimes with a little add-on, and recompute all the models with those rate sets.

There are three major problems with this method. First, the models may not have been calibrated for sets of rates that would not include the extreme levels used in stress tests. Second, even if they were, they may no longer be compatible with each other under those conditions. Finally, the entire exercise is only based on market measures of risk. Extreme business conditions may translate in extreme prices, but it is not the essence of a crisis. The central mechanism of an unfolding crisis is in how tail events trigger one another, how the crisis is compounded by their combined effect and how it impacts perceptions – and hence correlations – with a dramatic effect on liquidity, volatility and hence prices. Working backwards from the prices does not recreate the conditions that allowed the crisis to develop in the first place; therefore it is only the models that would be stress-tested rather than the capability of a company to address a serious crisis.

In our proposed methodology we aggregate the worst case scenarios used for computing each unit's extreme sensitivity into a unique corporate drawing of what the firm understands as 'extreme business conditions'. Inevitably, the aggregation will need to focus on the risk factors, where sensitivities are understood and aggregated in the first place. A consolidated view from all parts of the firm follows, with a common language established. In a 'state of the world' scenario, not only do extreme figures need to be communicated but qualitative developments as well.

15.1.1 Aggregating figures

The first step is to take all common risk factors and aggregate the extreme figures considered as worst case developments. For example, a trading desk may consider that, under extreme conditions, the level of short-term interest rates could reach 12 %, typically in a hyperinflation type of environment.

The table in Figure 15.2 gives an idea of such a model. Almost like a questionnaire, a known macro-scenario is first presented, typically one of the macro-scenarios each unit has been working on to define their micro-factors and work out their sensitivities. At this stage, each unit can be requested to enter the very figures they have already used to compute the sensitivity. Then, since the review is ongoing and most likely triggered internal reviews within the units, other factors than just market facts can be examined: what would then be the turnover of our resources, what would be the evolution of their base salaries, how many clients within our weakest categories could go bankrupt, what would be the changes in typical recovery rates, what would be the impact on our cost of funding, and so on. The correlations are here, within the thought process. The point to note is that they are intellectually thought through instead of being mathematically modelled or empirically estimated.

MACRO-SCENARIO: INFLATION 1	Trade Unit 1	Trade Unit 2	Retail Division	Wholesale	...
Inflation Rate 10%					
Economic growth 5%					
STIR					
US$1m					
US$3m					
...					
Energy					
Crude					
Elec					
Gas					
Cost of Resources					
Salary growth					
Pensions					
Overhead					
Counterparty failures					
Default rates in T1 clients					
Default rates in T2 clients					
LGDs					
....					

Figure 15.2 Table showing a macro-scenario of inflation

In the process, however, some elements can be mathematically aggregated. Interest rate input, for example, can be used to interpolate yield curves. Curves can be mapped on to each other to derive a view. Each unit may have only its own end of the curve as a true focus, but the overall shape derived gives a pretty good understanding of where the firm's liquidity or volatility will move.

15.1.2 Aggregating qualitative assessments

The shapes of yield curves and volatility surfaces are links between quantitative and qualitative assessments. A yield curve is a collective expression of liquidity in movement. It points out the main areas of focus, hints at stresses and indicates fears of the markets. Volatility surfaces point out the areas of emotion, the main expectation. It hints at the type of distribution the markets factor into their quantitative approach.

The risk factors used by the various units are not only market based. Inevitably, front-line units would deal with more market-based quantitative elements than operations or accounting. Yet each department of each division would have received macro-factors, such as staff turnover or customer loyalty, which would not be directly based on market rates. The questions raised would be such as: How many customers would leave us in that case? What would it take to retain our best resources? The responses may be quantitatively expressed, and the very point would have raised extensive discussions with regard to the side effects of the scenarios and the internal operational risks under stress conditions. We have reached the point where risk management processes focused on external sources of distortions start to raise concerns over internal risk management. We are now in the presence of a self-adapting framework since the culture eventually becomes the source of its own evolution.

The risk managers will then need to work on an aggregated view of the qualitative aspects and internal risk factors that would be driven by a stress scenario. The input can be averaged or centred through a median and extremes can be shaved off; whatever the methodology, it needs to be as fair a representation as possible of the spirit of the worst case imagined by the largest possible number of people within the firm. The format to represent the scenarios should be as close as possible to the one initially received by the management from the shareholders. The risk factors, the policies, the nature of exposure, acceptable sensitivity and maximum loss must be the main points.

15.2 RISK POLICIES RECONCILIATION

The very purpose of our proposed post-crisis risk management approach is to align the risks a financial institution bears with the risk appetite expressed by the shareholders and the customers of the institution. This appetite is not set in stone but evolves with the markets and the economic perspectives. It may also be restrained or developed depending on market conditions. This is a major departure from most of today's precepts. Isn't a fixed Cooke ratio (be it 8 % or something else), for example, a rigid expression of risk appetite?

Achieving quantitative and qualitative reconciliations of risk taken and risk appetite amounts to a map of the various business activities of a firm with the types of risk it may face. The missing link between the business division's correlated types of exposure and the shareholders' aggregated views of banking risks, such as market, credit, liquidity, etc., has been the notion of risk factors. Replacing it with VaR has created a very opaque and theoretical approach falsely supported by back-testing. The influence of regulators to normalize and even enforce the practice has created systemic risk and definitively disconnected the shareholders' goals from the reality of the global banking business. With risk factors, everyone speaks the same language. The table in Figure 15.3 describes how the approach by risk factors reconciles the micro-measurements of sensitivity recorded by the operational units with the high-level expression of risk appetite from the shareholders.

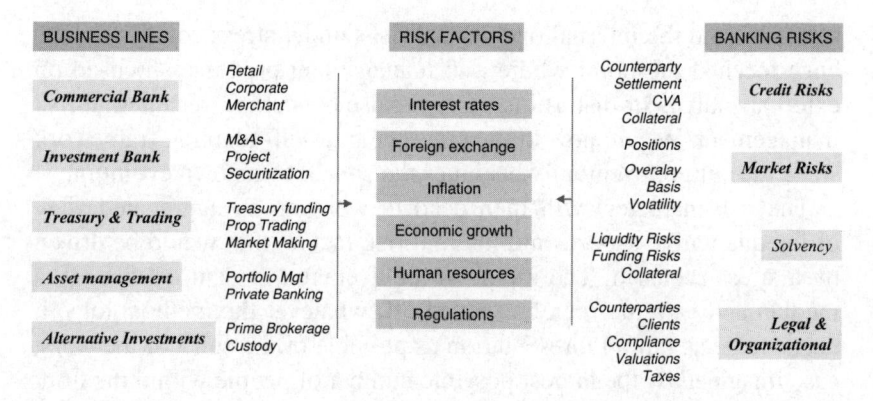

BUSINESS LINES		RISK FACTORS		BANKING RISKS
Commercial Bank	Retail Corporate Merchant	Interest rates	Counterparty Settlement CVA Collateral	*Credit Risks*
Investment Bank	M&As Project Securitization	Foreign exchange	Positions Overalay Basis	*Market Risks*
Treasury & Trading	Treasury funding Prop Trading Market Making	Inflation Economic growth	Volatility Liquidity Risks Funding Risks	*Solvency*
Asset management	Portfolio Mgt Private Banking	Human resources	Collateral Counterparties	
Alternative Investments	Prime Brokerage Custody	Regulations	Clients Compliance Valuations Taxes	*Legal & Organizational*

Figure 15.3 The approach showing how risk factors reconcile sensitivity with risk appetite

The risk appetite of the shareholders will be reconciled with the risk profile of the company using the following methodology: first, the quantitative aspects, exposure, P/L, sensitivity under scenarios (at least three types: baseline, severity, catastrophic) and the qualitative definition of risks with respect to the implied understanding of counterparty risks, market distribution and business conditions implied by the figures within the stress scenarios; second, the implications of the previous points on the overall solvency of the firm, the funding strategy, liquidity tactics and collateral management policies; third, the impact of the external scenarios on the systematic risks, the potential reactions of competitors and their likely impact on the firm or its customers; fourth, the regulatory risks, which are not only the risks and constraints imposed through regulatory compliance requirements but also the potential implications of regulatory entanglements, systemic risks or regulatory-driven bubble effects.

Let us explore the reconciliation process in more detail, as this is a key aspect of our proposed methodology.

15.2.1 Quantitative: risk factors, sensitivity, scenarios

These are certainly the most straightforward elements to be reconciled. The CEO and the Executive Committee have accepted a risk management objective in addition to performance targets and have expressed it in terms of the maximum net exposure, sensitivity and maximum loss. Those objectives have been spread on risk factors themselves distributed to the risk units. Sensitivity limits have been defined and managed accordingly; the bottom-up feedback workflow has efficiently conveyed the exposure and sensitivity back to the management who can now proceed with a quarterly reconciliation with the initial objectives defined in agreement with the shareholders. Although it is already a giant leap forward to be able to formally balance performance measurement with hard figures of risks and sensitivity, it would be an inaccurate representation of the risks borne by the company to stick to quantitative reconciliations.

Just like a RAROC figure does not say much about the nature of risks underlying performance, a pure reconciliation of net sensitivity could hide significant discrepancies in terms of the nature of the actual versus desired risks taken. For example, the firm could decide to reduce rate sensitivity levels with fixed income securities that would be illiquid, where low sensitivity would actually hide huge convexity. The desired figures could be reached but the nature of the exposure would not match the desired risk profile of the firm.

The sample table in Figure 15.4 exhibits the results per risk factor in terms of expected sensitivity versus achieved results. More importantly, it aims to quantify the impact of any difference or slippage in terms of corporate performance. For example, if a failure to maintain the desired level of interest rate sensitivity within boundaries results in a substantial loss for the company, then what is the estimated impact on the equity price, funding costs or capital value? If the economic growth was overestimated and ends up impacting results significantly, how does this impact wind out on the customer base, the firm's reputation and so on. Not all cells in this table will be filled and many side remarks or

RISK FACTORS		LIMIT S1 S2 S3	ACTUAL	SLIPPAGE	LINK TO PERFORMANCE				
					Equity	Cap	Return	CAGR	Cust base	Reputation
Interest rates	P/L Sensitivity Curve effects Basis									
Foreign exchange	P/L Sensitivity Liquidity									
Inflation	Cost Clients Financial trading									
Economic growth	Clients Ctpy failures Business dev									
Human resources	Costs Qualification issues									
Regulations	Compliance costs Regulatory costs Systemic issues									

Figure 15.4 Quarterly risk reconciliation process

drill-downs will be necessary, but we have made a first attempt truly to present a balanced view of risk estimation, actual risk exposure and performance in a single report.

15.2.2 Qualitative: implied assumptions, distributions, correlations, market evolutions, back-testing

Inevitably, the above attempt to link risk management quality to performance will raise many questions and discussions with respect to qualitative aspects such as the type of business environment the firm found itself within or the unexpected tail events it had to weather. The issue is no longer to explain model deficiencies or the unpredictable nature of the tail risks that could not be foreseen in modelled stress tests. There are worst case scenarios and results. Since they are no longer a matter concerning mathematics only, the worst case scenarios necessarily refer to a view of the world that is important to describe as part of a qualitative assessment of the risk management results.

For example, a worst case scenario based on an assumption that the world economy is going to continue deteriorating and that the recession will deepen may estimate that short rates will remain around zero, while long bonds will keep tense due to a confidence crisis keeping yield curves tight and almost vertical. These assumptions need to match with the other expected developments related to resourcing, customer base, funding cost, and so on. The integrity of each risk factor and how it is expected to evolve should correspond to an agreed upon state of the world.

Implied qualitative expectations will also be reconciled with those of the shareholders. The skills of the firm's expert risk managers, quants and researchers may outshine by far those of the shareholders or whoever represent their interests when it comes to predicting potential macroeconomic and microeconomic outcomes or the likely changes in financial regulations. Therefore the experts need to be invited to propose and present their views of the world and express views on what should logically be the next sensitivity or commercial growth targets. Whichever way it is built, it is this bond between the execution and the ownership of the firm that is the backbone of the risk culture. It needs to be created and strongly remain the leading driver of the risk policies. Then there will no longer be any disconnection between the management and the shareholders, as reflected in the compensation policies or in the business development strategies, for example.

Traditional Full Monte Carlo Approach

Model Stochastic Processes — Return Distributions → Fitting: Derive model from history, Generate random distribution → VaR under confidence level

Reverse VaR

Estimated Sensitivity Δ, γ, ϖ, τ, ζ → Stochastic Distributions → Estimate distribution, Validate scenario

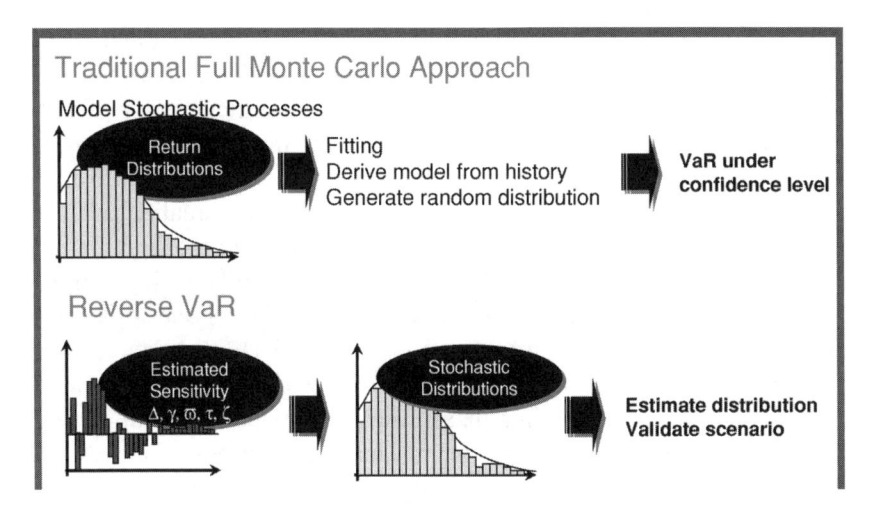

Figure 15.5 Reverse VaR distribution validation

Paradoxally, an interesting use of quantitative analysis could arise for qualitative reconciliation purposes. We have extensively discussed the limitations of the VaR model approaches, the main one being model based. The most sophisticated cut, full Monte Carlo simulations, even models stochastic distributions, instead of using historical steps for forward-looking random distribution generation. While we prefer professionals' expert estimations to stochastic modelling, the concept of translating a return distribution into an amount at risk can be reversed to derive an implied distribution that the sensitivity analysis could have been based on. The method sometimes used in back-testing derives the actual distribution from VaR. Here the delta, gamma, vega, theta and zeta sensitivities we derive from scenario-based estimations will be used as a substitute to VaR to derive a distribution. Such an implied 'state of the world' can then be reconciled to the aggregated scenario, presented to the scenario owners and obviously gaps can be analysed. Figure 15.5 describes this process.

15.2.3 Solvency and liquidity management

The next critical element to reconcile, which would be discussed in detail throughout Part 4, is the management of liquidity or funding strategy.

The funding strategy is an important aspect of the shareholders' appetite for risk: first, because the shareholders are themselves funders and, second, because liquidity management is a critical factor of risk and the risk mitigation tools depend on it. The most usual example is the case of funding long-term illiquid assets with a short-term floating rate or any treasury tool with a short call notice. The reality is more complex and valuation risks again play a most critical role in all asset and liability management (ALM) purposes. The rapid development of global finance, moreover, has recently complicated the issues by bringing foreign exchange and cross-currency basis risks to the picture.

Here again most ALM systems have been designed and implemented with a single purpose in mind, measuring performance and minimizing funding costs. Our new culture of risk management now imposes the rule that the asset and liability funding strategy corresponds to the risk appetite of the company. How can a funding strategy and liquidity tactics be reconciled with a risk appetite?

The method again focuses on risk factors. Single currency and cross-currency asset funding necessarily generates gaps that have a measurable sensitivity. Since our initial distribution of exposure by risk factors must have integrated commercial margins and margins on internal prices, the risk remains that of financing the balance sheet or immunization. Measuring achieved gaps and actual sensitivity is not a measurement of risk but only performance. VaR models would be even further from reality as assets and liabilities outside trading books would be even more unpredictable to model.

At this stage, the task is to translate the shareholders' understanding of funding risks and funding costs into a desired risk concentration and maximum loss. Quantitatively, a limit on liquidity gaps and their costs is a straightforward reconciliation. Limits on basis risks should be added as well, together with vega limits highlighting the potential volatility issues and their pricing with the gaps. To the quantitative measures of ALM gaps it is necessary to add some scenario-based sensitivities relating to funding strategies and liquidity management tactics. A risk profile can then be created and reconciled with the one that the funders of the firm have assumed. By monitoring concentrations and leverage ratios, it will be possible to derive a good qualitative approach to the funding risk and to estimate whether the solvency of the firm is truly at risk. The technique of monitoring concentrations in order to anticipate bubble effects or unexpected liquidity issues is presented in full detail in Part 4.

Finally, since gaps are usually hedged or managed using derivatives, the correlations between interest rates plays here a greater role than with other financial instruments.

15.2.4 Systematic risks

The business scenarios used for assessments of sensitivities would, if they occurred, necessarily have an impact on the firm's competitors, its clients and partners and on the entire sector it operates within. In other words, the high-severity and catastrophic scenarios envisioned would trigger systematic risks that cannot be ignored since they would also impact the firm itself or its capacity to mitigate or unwind risks.

As part of the reconciliation with the risk strategy expressed by the shareholders, the systematic risks implied by the scenarios deemed of high severity – yet plausible – should be reconciled with the initial understanding of the shareholders.

For example, a macro-scenario involving further depreciation of real estate mortgage prices would necessarily translate into higher sensitivity, funding costs and potential write-down losses. However, the risks do not stop there. A significant sector-wide deterioration would also lead the firm's competitors to seek further liquidity, adjust haircuts due to the depreciation of collateral and liquidate some of their assets through fire sales. These types of secondary developments, also defined as systematic risks, must be presented as part of the scenarios and accepted by the shareholders when they validate the macro-scenario.

The notion of risk diversification was inherited from asset management theories of the 1960s; systematic risk remains generally described as the undiversifiable part of market exposure, typically the risks related to an entire sector or market. Undiversifiable does not equate to unhedgeable. In the deregulated global banking business of the 21st century, there are virtually no market or credit risks one would not find any hedge for, by means of structured derivatives or a hybrid instrument. Even the risk of an overall business downturn could be in theory mitigated by means of securitization or portable alpha strategies, sometimes called systematic alpha. The risk remains, however, that the hedges themselves are inefficient or malfunction to the point that they end up creating or exacerbating the risks they were supposed to mitigate. There are two sources of systematic risks in the 21st century: the one inherited from the externalities of idiosyncratic risks and the tail risks that hit the markets unexpectedly.

Figure 15.6 represents graphically the main flows that create liquidity holes and externalize idiosyncratic risks into systematic risk. Clearly the key triggers and accelerators of the process are linked to valuations and materialize as liquidity issues. It is therefore in valuation gaps due to market or sector practices that risk managers may find a source of uncontrolled risks.

The risk policies must be specific and descriptive of valuation methodologies. Whenever they may diverge significantly from the usual market practice, even if recommended by the regulators, then the divergence should be explained, documented and officially endorsed by the management. Although it would be unrealistic to imagine involving the shareholders in details of accounting techniques, a reconciliation of the concept with the corporate risk policies is important as the chosen valuation methodology may result in a loss of opportunities and weight in performance reports. For example, many mortgage loan collaterals were only evaluated at inception in securitization processes, and cease after. A firm choosing to revalue periodically its securitized portfolios – provided it finds the data – would write off substantial losses during a real-estate meltdown compared to its competitors, who might stick to the previous methodology. The choice of accuracy versus absolute performance is not only an option but also depends on the investment timeframe. Therefore it must be individually aligned with the specific risk policies of each firm.

The second aspect is the leveraged interdependence of all sectors of the system. The current structures of both the market and the regulatory frameworks had not been designed for those interdependent cross-system leverages. In particular, they had assumed continuously linear relationships across asset classes, which proved to be untrue. The mitigation here is to control the exposure (and overall leverage levels) to potential tail events. Although tail events are unpredictable in nature, the exposure sectors and industries where tail events can occur can be monitored and reconciled with risk policies. For example, it may or may not be acceptable for a Tier 2 European bank with a tradition of prudent and diligent strategy funding the local farmers to invest in real estate in US. The very principle of getting exposed to this particular nature of risks can be questioned. Furthermore, some exposure deemed acceptable may expose unacceptable risk factors. In the case of US mortgages, for example, a foreign entity would not be legally entitled to participate in the market and would be driven to securitized investments, raising numerous additional issues related to operational and legal risks, valuations,

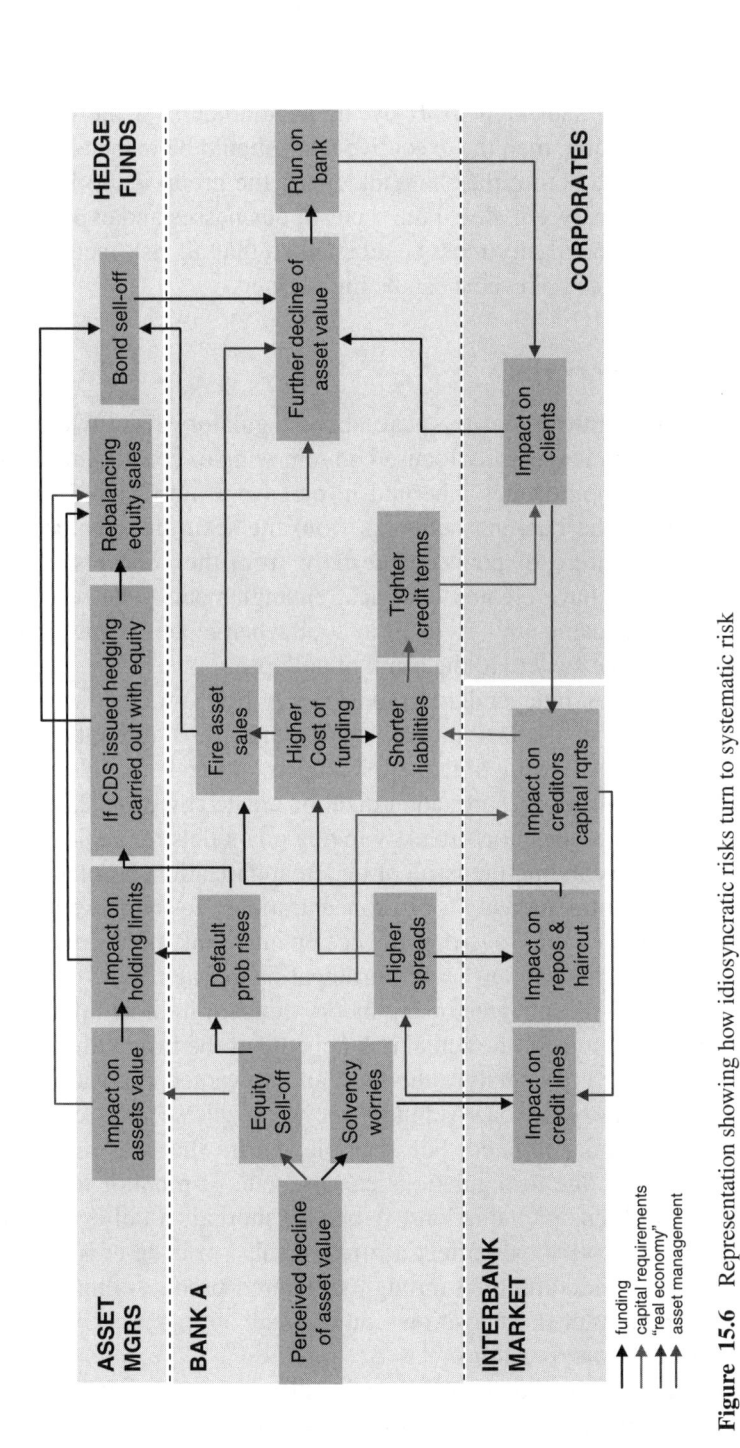

Figure 15.6 Representation showing how idiosyncratic risks turn to systematic risk

market liquidity, etc. What the firm invests in and how is part of the corporate risk policies signed off by the shareholders. If the policies are not clear enough, then the executive team should be responsible for bringing the issue before the shareholders. If the group is too large or too complex to analyse in detail the types of businesses and exposure it faces, then the granularity must be adapted so that all risk factors that can present risks of tail events can be highlighted.

15.2.5 Regulatory risks

It may sound controversial to speak about regulatory risks while the regulators' action is precisely focused on removing or controlling risks. Yet the various approaches inherited in part from the Glass–Steagall Act, separating the banking networks from the securities companies, and from the culture of convergence born from the concepts of the European Union have created historical entanglements. The resulting systemic risks became obvious to all in 2008 when repetitive tail events brought the whole system to the brink of collapse.

The issue is that, independent from its risk policies and its own strategy, a firm might be dragged into tail events and risks it did not choose to be exposed to, as a result of regulatory constraints and entanglements. The culture of uniformity and standardization created by Basel 2, for example, has allowed the entire industry to rely on models for capital allocations. Notwithstanding the issue of undercapitalization, similar strategies across an entire industry led to concentrations. To some extent, the excessive leverage ratios, overdependence on interbank money markets, exposure to securitized loans or the participation to fragmented pools of liquidity were all incentivized by regulatory direct or indirect influence.

The reconciliations of the actual risk appetite of the firm with its risk policies must therefore analyse the risks and unwanted exposures that might be regulatory driven. Although inevitable, those risks can still be anticipated and mitigated. For example, a firm that was driven to securitized debts due to regulations can mitigate or monitor the risks with a special focus on valuations. A ban on shorts is a tail event that can, for instance, seriously affect a firm's results, or even create legal risks if the firm is committed through structured products engineered with combinations of short positions and long call options, or if it carries out convertible bond positions.

Firms required to abide by credit ratings because of regulations can run parallel approaches to factor more accurately the value of credit into their market prices. The costs are substantial and the concern keeps growing among banks in particular that having separate risk frameworks for regulatory and business purposes drains resources. Regulatory-driven risks should therefore be attached to systematic risks and accounted for in the review of financial activities that can lead to tail events and analysis of potential mitigations.

Part 4
Aligning Funding Strategies and Liquidity Management Tactics with Corporate Risk Policies[1]

Executive Summary

This part emphasizes the need for a funding strategy and liquidity risk management tactics that truly reflect both the risk policies of the firm and the actual characteristics of the exposure, especially in terms of term structure, sensitivity and currency.

The management of funding and liquidity risks consists of maintaining a balance between the risk characteristics of assets, liabilities and collateral. These are functions of the term structures, volatility and valuations of the underlying instruments and also the valuation methodologies and market depth. The proposed methodology suggests data management and market monitoring methodologies in order to maintain the accuracy and integrity of the measures as efficiently as possible.

The hinge between business risks and financial risks is at the fund transfer pricing stage, which drives the asset and liability management. It is at this level that we re-emphasize the issues related to valuations, model risks, market depth and volatility.

Managing liquidity risk involves special attention to risk and exposure concentrations. Our proposed methodology suggests a dynamic approach to concentrations for buy-side and sell-side organizations. These are estimated and reported at a very high frequency to enable the firm to monitor potential risk bubbles as they form and assess its own exposure to the bubble.

---

[1] Chapters 16 to 19, Section 19.2, have been strongly inspired by a White Paper by Philippe Carrel, 'Implementing a new culture of risk management: liquidity, the ultimate operational risk', made public by Thomson Reuters in June 2009.

Once the concentration is identified, it needs to be reconciled with the risk policies expressed by the shareholders and validated by them if appropriate. A risk concentration is in itself no danger if it fits the desired exposure of the firm.

Managing liquidity risk is not an exercise to be carried out in isolation. It requires communications with the rest of the sector, preferably with the participation of the regulators. A body of knowledge is necessary throughout the sector to establish market conditions such as high severity and catastrophic and to define the corresponding 'regimes' that, in themselves, can trigger new series of updated processes.

Liquidity risk is a complex operational risk. It arises from the unexpected – tail risks, internal imbalances, counterparty failures, market crises, systemic risks or from the combined effects of those shocks. Therefore it cannot be hedged with a process but through a culture of risk management aiming to establish a routine around the unexpected. When firms have developed rules of corporate governance and risk management tactics deeply rooted within their corporate culture, as an immune system, then managing risks will become part of the solution to the growth equation, simply by involving more people within the firm.

Reconnecting with the fundamental principle of risk management where diversity mitigates risks while uniformity concentrates them further, the regulators need to implement the same type of risk-based communication network that would keep the system as agile as an individual firm. Liquidity risk is not a standalone risk. It can't be hedged with a set of remedies uniformly imposed on patients not yet ill. It is a system-wide exchange of information and transparent communications that can keep the whole industry and the regulators aware of risks as they develop and better prepared to face the unexpected.

In this part, we highlight the key issues used to identify the sources of liquidity risks and measure their potential impact. Then we propose a methodology to design and implement a liquidity risk management framework that sticks to the corporate culture of risk management that we propose. The funding strategy and the liquidity tactics of the firm must reflect its risk structures or they would become a risk of their own. Therefore they must evolve with the firm's strategy and its ever-changing exposure and risk factors. The liquidity strategy must also adapt to the constraints from the external world. Managing liquidity is maintaining this balance by permanently making adjustments.

16
Liquidity, the Ultimate Operational Risk

Liquidity risk is not a standalone risk. It derives from the management of all types of exposure, which may result from a firm's allocation of assets, from its funding strategy, from collateral policies or from any mismanagement of risks. Liquidity risk mitigation is achieved through continuous adjustments of the balance sheet structures; liquidity management tactics are the hedge. Unsurprisingly, each firm, professional group or government entity would have an individual definition of liquidity risk, since it is as specific as operational risks can be.

Imbalances arise when market conditions change the value of assets and collateral or when external factors disrupt the funding sources. Managing liquidity risks consists of maintaining a fine balance between the three internal variables (asset allocations, funding and collateral) within a sphere of external changes and potential shocks, which consistently challenge this equilibrium (see Figure 16.1). Liquidity issues also arise when manifestations of the internal balances misalign with the external factors – an ultimate operational risk.

16.1 MAINTAINING THE INTERNAL BALANCE

Any factor that is disruptive to the asset and liability equilibrium over time can be seen as a potential source of liquidity risks since asset liability risks are leveraged in nature – the Cook ratio of financial institutions is rarely above 12 %.

Conceived in the early 1980s after a sudden yield curve reversal had brought huge losses to banks relying on accrual accounting, asset liability management (ALM) evolved over time, to cope with the fast growth of interest rates and credit derivatives, embedded options and off-balance-sheet exposure. Most ALM techniques involve value accounting, gap analyses, duration analyses, foreign exchange exposure and basis risk analyses, at least.

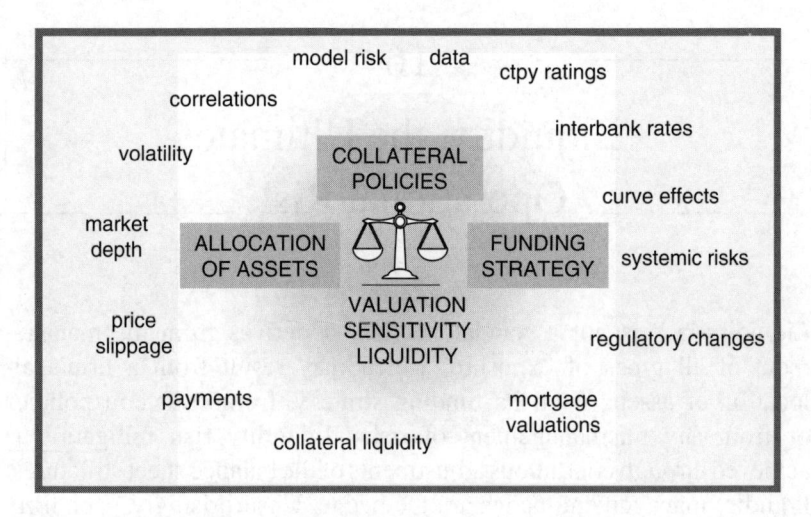

Figure 16.1 Internal balance and external shocks

The 2007–2008 crisis, however, challenged these methodologies by exposing firms to liquidity risk factors coming from external sources. The global reach of modern institutions, the deregulation, wide-spread securitizations, structured products, the active management of collateral and many other aspects of 'universal banking' have blurred the traditional funding channels. The liquidity crunch exposed obsolete models and inefficient liquidity tactics. Regulators acknowledge the need for change and led the effort.

16.2 INTERNAL SOURCES OF LIQUIDITY RISKS

Company-specific factors leading to liquidity risks are defined by the impact they can have on the balance sheet structure of financial institutions. The valuations of assets, be it securities or loans, has a direct impact on the effective duration and sensitivity of the portfolio, thus affecting its overall liquidity. The type, term structure and typical sensitivity of liabilities used for funding the portfolios are often legacy inherited from the bank's history and culture. The challenge of timely adjustments of liabilities in line with asset characteristics is complicated by the liquidity and volatility of pledged collateral.

Overall, we get a very complex equation of asset–liability–collateral coherence, which normally relies on linear functions of value

LIABILITIES	ASSETS	COLLATERAL
Liquidity	*Allocations*	*Cash Payments*
Concentrations	*Concentrations*	*Securities Liquidity*
Term structure	*Duration*	*Asset valuations*
Credit ratings	*Conditional Exposure*	*Implicit duration*
Credit events	*Sensitivity*	*Reg. & Legal Framework*
Payments	*Volatility*	
Regulatory impact	*Mkt Depth*	
	Valuations	

Figure 16.2 Internal factors of liquidity risks

(see Figure 16.2). This condition of linearity may not be verified in the presence of liquidity risk.[1]

Although a combination of the above factors applies uniquely and specifically to each individual firm, liquidity risk is generally recognized by the industry and by the regulators[2] as arising from the following categories:

1. **Valuation risks** are the risks that assets held in portfolio (securities or loans) or pledged as collateral may be mispriced or simply impossible to sell due to adverse market conditions. Such risks arise from:
   - **Market depth** is generally defined as the volume that it is possible to trade without bias on either the prices or the spreads. This very theoretical notion impacts massively on liquidity risks and valuations. Market depth is one of the key hypotheses of market theories such as the arbitrage pricing model. Its suitability to nonsecurities markets remains questionable.
   - **Nonlinearity of valuation functions** was recently termed as 'lack of transparency' during the liquidity crunch. In the presence of liquidity risks, the valuations of assets, and hence portfolios, tend to become nonlinear as it may not always be possible to obtain or estimate prices that reflect a consensus or fair values without further discussion on timeframe and trading purposes. The estimation of

---

[1] See C. Acerbi and G. Scandolo, Liquidity risk theory and coherent measures of risk, *Quantitative Finance*, 8 (7), 2008.

[2] CEBS Technical Advice to the European Commission on Liquidity Risk Management, June 2008.

methodologies is discussed in later chapters based on the most recent research.
2. **Funding risks** arise from the difficulties and costs of providing liquidity that meet the term structures and sensitivities of the balance sheet. The liquidity crisis of October 2008 highlighted the fact that transparency and counterparty risks were critical to maintain the liquidity of the funding channels, regardless of even the G7 governments' backing.

In addition to these endogenous variables, we see new external sources of liquidity risks playing a major role in the post-2007–2009 crisis era.

16.3 EXTERNAL SOURCES OF LIQUIDITY RISK

The most important lesson of the 2007–2008 credit crunch and subsequent global crisis is that risk can no longer be managed in isolation. So far the potential impact of external variables on internal risk factors (i.e. portfolio risk and asset valuations) has been well observed. It appears that liquidity issues can also be imported from outside. We will next consider risks arising from the counterparties (systematic sources) and from the system itself (systemic sources):

1. **Counterparty-linked** liquidity risks are related to the counterparty's unfulfilled obligations, missed or overdue settlements. Causes may stem from either financial problems faced by the counterparty itself, from connectivity failures or data mismanagement. The latter occurs across straight-through processing systems linking risk takers with their execution venues, brokers, custodians and administrators – these systems require complex and frequent database alignment. On OTC markets, failures to process transactions in a timely manner have had an impact on assessments of credit risks, in particular when the backlog of unsettled credit default swap (CDS) transactions had clouded liabilities and off-balance-sheet exposures.
2. **Regulatory-driven** liquidity risks related to the combined evolution of the regulatory frameworks of the banking, asset management, insurance and brokerage systems allow the entire financial system to be greatly exposed to errors or misconceptions from the regulators and policy makers. This is a new type of systemic-operational risk that cannot be ignored.

The current crisis has exposed the risks created by uniform regulatory rules indiscriminately applied to countries or sectors. Regulatory entanglements against a backdrop of deregulation and subsequent arbitrages have created layers of opacity that potentially disrupt or bias the normal flows of funds. They present real threats to the systems they were initially designed to protect.

17
Analysing and Measuring Liquidity Risks

17.1 VALUATION-DRIVEN LIQUIDITY RISKS

In the presence of liquidity risk, the value of portfolios is no longer a linear function of the sum of the weighted prices of each asset. The basis of coherent risk diversification functions, usually represented as

$$P = \sum_{ni} Ai$$

is no longer true.

However, most portfolio management and asset valuation techniques are still based on assumptions from the *arbitrage pricing theory*, which supposes no restrictions on trade. Recognizing this inadequacy, Jarrow and Protter[1] had introduced the notion of a *stochastic supply curve* featuring trade price, size and direction (buy or sell) in an attempt to model *price inelasticities* as a function of timing and size of the trades. In their 2009 paper, Acerbi and Scandolo[2] further describe *marginal supply–demand curves* and define the value of portfolios as a function of the proceeds that it is possible to obtain within a given timeframe defined by the trader of the risk policies.

The 'liquidation value' of assets is given by $L(P)$, the sum of proceeds from the liquidation, or

$$L(P) = \sum_{i=0}^{N} Pi = p_0 + \sum_{i=1}^{N} p \int_{0}^{pi} mi(x)dx$$

The difference between this estimation and a usual mark-to-market portfolio $U(p)$ is the cost of the liquidity risk

$$C(P) = L(P) - U(P)$$

---

[1] R. A. Jarrow and P Protter, Liquidity risk and risk measure computation, *Review of Futures Markets*, 27 February 2005.

[2] Carlo Acerbi and Giacomo Scandolo, Liquidity risk theory and coherent measures of risk, (white paper, available on the internet) 22 April 2009.

This innovative approach therefore includes two extremely important notions, timeframe and risk policy, to the measures of valuation slippage leading to liquidity risk. Measurements of liquidity costs or exposure to liquidity risks should therefore factor in a projected timeframe. Scenarios should involve such a timeframe and should be designed in the context of the risk and accounting policies (liquidation, mark-to-market, mark-to-value, fair value or accrual).

17.2 MARKET DEPTH

The marginal supply–demand curves depend on market depth, which we can define as aggregates of *price/time/volume* trading opportunities. At a pace regulated by the implied volatility, the markets move prices from one liquidity pool to another. The depth of those pools depends on the overall sentiment and on the investors' focus, which leads to price/volume concentrations. It also relies on the transparency and credibility of prices and on the perceived settlement risks. It can thus be estimated by observation of past areas of price and volume accumulations, where volatility typically narrows. The rationale is that those accumulation periods are loaded with market emotions. They create dramatic price levels such as breakeven, average weighted prices, stop losses, option barriers and so on. When hit, those price levels trigger volatility expansion phases and might create liquidity holes depending on the focus, the emotion and the market depth.

In mathematical terms, price return distributions prove to be autoregressive (most recent data influence the next ones) and feature memory processes (repeating patterns). The issue is that most asset management models are still based on the assumption of a Brownian motion (random walk), where dispersion keeps increasing with the square root of time until mean reversals eventually return to a zero mean and a variance of 1. It is usually accounted for using a monthly factor such as

$$\sigma(R) x \sqrt{12}$$

Building on Benoit Mandelbrot's fractal distribution approach (chaos theory), Edgar Peters[3] found that the hypothesis of a fractional Brownian motion with antipersistent long memory processes better described the financial markets. Random shocks keep the market from ever reaching equilibrium and add to the memory, while the autoregressive process

---

[3] Edgar Peters, *Fractal Markets*, John Wiley & Sons, Ltd, Chichester, 1994.

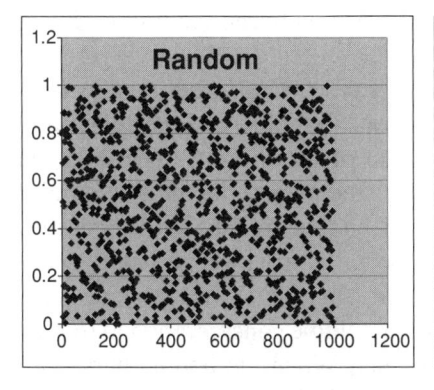

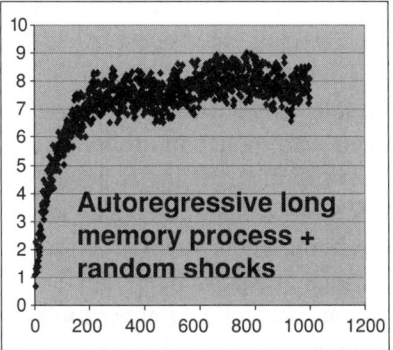

Figure 17.1 Assumptions and dispersion models

maintains the bias. The consequence of the new approach is that there were no mean reversals but a memory process that had been confusing the analysts.

The graphics in Figure 17.1 illustrate how assumptions and dispersion models redefine the build-up processes of price–volume accumulation areas. These concentrations of liquidity have a massive impact on future volatility and market depth. In other words, mining data to highlight the diffusion patterns provide invaluable insights into the nature of the market concentrations that lead to high volatility and correlation shifts. Future volatility surges, price gaps and liquidity holes will arise from random shocks, which initially often appear to be benign.

17.3 OVER-THE-COUNTER MARKETS

Over-the-counter (OTC) deals are often described as customized versions of exchange traded transactions. Managing liquidity risks therefore consists of replicating the parameters of credibility of the exchanges, such as existence of natural matching exposures, diversity of investors' timeframes, fair and transparent pricing and absence of settlement risks.

The phenomenal liquidity of the credit default swap (CDS) market from 2003 to 2007 was due to a virtuous combination of those ingredients. The depth of the market was provided by the natural exposure arising from product structuring activities, which matched with yield enhancement and arbitrage strategies of the buy-side. The perceived price transparency came from the market depth. As the latter depended on the price transparency itself, a weak link was exposed. The OTC market lacked the exchange-like disconnect between the trading floors and the clearing processes.

There is no other way to estimate this type of risk other than by continuously assessing market concentrations (bubbles) and benchmarking one's own concentrations against those of the market. Whenever the diversity of matching exposures creates the market depth, the liquidity risk is low. It builds up as investment bubbles inflate until it reaches the point where the market depth is actually provided by risk concentrations. At such a point the liquidity risk is huge but keeps growing since the market increasingly requires further volume concentration to remain in balance. It is unfortunately temporary. When the bubble bursts, all traders forget their investment timeframe and try to exit in panic; the previous price–volume accumulation zone instantly becomes a liquidity hole.

18
Funding Risk

Up until 2007, issues relating to asset and liability structure or balance sheet immunization would essentially boil down to a cost of funding or loss of opportunity. The liquidity crunch made it a survival issue, epitomized by the Northern Rock's bankruptcy whose funding structure turned unsustainable amid fast-changing market conditions. In the aftermath of the liquidity crunch, it was generally advised that banks should build some special reserve buffers to counterbalance potential liquidity shortages. Yet the unpredictable nature of those risks meant that this type of risk mitigation could easily turn into a false sense of security.

18.1 ASSET LIABILITY RISKS

The duration and sensitivity of banks' assets, the type of collateral requested and the funding sources are deeply rooted in the history of each bank. Indeed, the historic customer base of a bank drives its funding habits. It can be perceived as its DNA, which, among other things, defines how its funds are sourced, to whom and for which purpose they are redistributed and how they are collateralized, amortized and evaluated. Liquidity risks typically arise from mismatching term structures of assets versus liabilities or from diverging sensitivities, usually derived from diversification, mergers and mispricing, which lead to unbalanced concentrations of exposures. Regrettably the bank may sometimes not be aware of those imbalances. For example, a known Tier 1 bank was doubly exposed to the duration and liquidity of the US real estate markets, initially through its traditional involvement in retail mortgage markets and subsequently through the securitization arm of its investment banking divisions. The liquidity crunch and subsequent plunge in real estate price then unveiled a highly illiquid situation.

Regardless of their varying root causes, when liquidity risks materialize they appear through valuation and funding issues. Banks have established fund transfer pricing procedures with collateralization processes appropriate to their types of activities. Liquidity issues typically arise when these procedures fail to properly estimate the depth and liquidity of the markets, or by misreading their sensitivity. The impact of liquidity and depth of the markets is significant on the effective duration of assets, while price slippage can considerably impair sensitivity measurements.

18.2 SYSTEMATIC SOURCES OF LIQUIDITY RISKS

Banks have different marginal costs of funding. Those are generally estimated as the opportunity cost of collateral pledged for obtaining funding from the central banks. An interbank market occurs when disparities among banks justify intermediation.[1] Cash, short-term securities, repos and forex swaps are the underlying tools. Derivatives are mainly interest rate swaps and futures. Spreads between reference rates such as Eonia, Euribor and Libor and the central bank reference rates are the key indicators of the difficulties the banking system faces to obtain liquidity against collateral. As the spread is a manifestation of market tension, it can be used as a measure of liquidity cost.

Neyers and Wiemer measure this cost as a quadratic function resulting from the needs of the sector, the credit risk among interbank market participants, the cost of transactions, the opportunity cost of pledged collateral and the concentrations of collateral across the sector.

The total cost of liquidity C for a bank i is given by

$$C(i) = K_i l + B_i e + Q_i + Z_i \quad \text{if } B_i > 0$$
$$C(i) = K_i l + B_i e p + Q_i + Z_i \quad \text{if } B_i < 0$$

where K_i is the amount a bank i needs to borrow from the central bank, B_i is the net position of bank i on the interbank market, Z_i is the cost of transactions, l is the central bank interest rate, Q_i is the opportunity cost of holding collateral, e is the interbank market rate and p is the credit risk.

In times of high tension, expressed by high liquidity costs, banks become particularly vulnerable to imbalances from the term structure of assets versus liabilities, as their dependence on the interbank market for refinancing purposes is greater.

Decreasing the central bank rates normally reduces interbank market rates by a greater proportion. If such a relation is broken, as was the case late in 2008, the spreads will become a mere measure of credit risk

---

[1] Ulrike Neyer and Jurgen Wiemers, Why do we have an Internet market?, Discussion paper number 182 on Internet market dynamics, Institut für Witshaftsforshung Halle (IWH), 2003.

Funding Risk   161

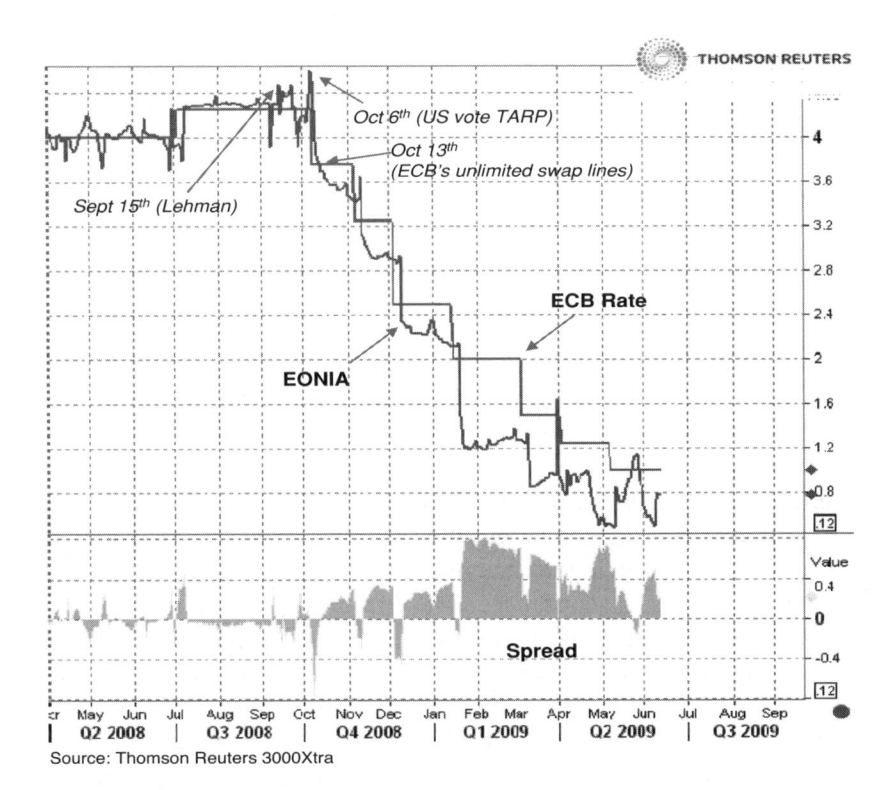

Figure 18.1 Euro currency rates

and opportunity cost of holding collateral. Liquidity risk, at this point, is at its highest.

Figure 18.1 displays the euro currency rates of the European Central Bank (ECB) and Eonia. The subchart is the spread. It clearly shows how the central bank struggled to maintain liquidity through multiple rate cuts late in 2008 and the very large excesses throughout Q1 of 2009.

18.3 CONCENTRATION RISKS

The true measure of exposure to liquidity risks is the level of concentration to the root factors of those risks. As diversification remains a fundamental mean of risk mitigation, concentration of any kind, such as asset types, funding channels, currencies, sectors, time bands, option strikes, counterparties, etc., are potential sources of liquidity issues. A bank holds portfolios of loans, of counterparties (creditors or debtors), securities, commercial and residential real estate, fleets and so on.

Asset Mgt	→ Fund shares	→ Securities	→ Risk Factors ?
Investment Bk	→ Securities/Derivatives	↗ Funding ← Valuations ↘ Funding	Correlations? → Risk Factors ? Correlations?
Commercial Bk	→ Loans	→ Securitized Collateral	→ Risk Factors ?

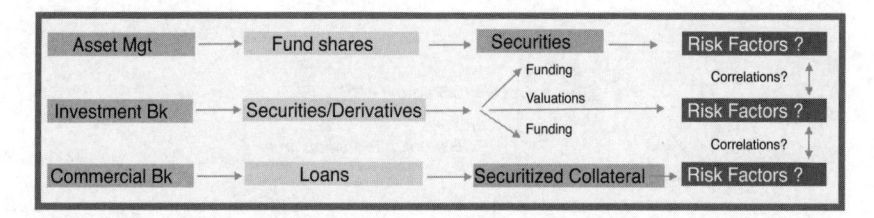

Figure 18.2 Liquidity risk is concentration risk

Each portfolio is subject to a number of risk factors, the sensitivity of which is directly linked to the concentration factor of the items within the portfolio. Sensitivities leading to liquidity risks are tail-dependent. Their dependence is an asymptotic function of factor concentrations.[2] In other words, liquidity risks are directly linked to portfolio concentrations and proportionally sensitive to systematic shocks as levels of concentration increase. One can therefore use measures of factor concentrations to estimate liquidity risks under scenarios involving tail events.

To highlight their concentrations, each bank should pursue an introspective search of their actual sources of exposure. Identifying the true variables of the risk equations is not always straightforward. Multiple layers of derivatives, complex legal frameworks and the innovative hybrid products have sometimes hidden or blurred the true generators of risks, impeding or corrupting sensitivity measurements. Figure 18.2 highlights how the actual factors of sensitivity, the root-risk factors, may be hidden, making risk concentrations even more difficult to spot.

Commercial banking activities, for example, traditionally expose a firm to private, individual or corporate counterparties. Structural risk factors involve the competitiveness of offered rates, the costs of operations and collateral management, and the transparency of collateral values, inflation rates and reputational risks. Asset management activities, on the other hand, depend on factors such as the volatility of underlying prices, unpredicted correlations or issuer defaults. All buy-side and sell-side institutions and funds depend on business continuity, the provision of IT services and legal and regulatory issues.

Every funding source (retail, wholesale, interbank market, securities issuance) and all types of assets (loans, securities, holdings or collateral)

---

[2] Gabriel Bonti, Michael Kalkbrener, Christopher Lotz and Gerhard Stahl, Credit risk concentrations under stress, Discussion, Deutsche Bundesbank, Basel Committee on Banking Supervision and the Journal of Credit Risk, Eltville, 18 November 2005.

expose firms directly or indirectly to specific risk factors. Concentrations within asset or liability groups will thus increase their dependence on systematic risk. Liquidity scenarios should therefore shock several systematic risk factors weighted by the concentration to each specific factor.

Systematic weights are unfortunately not static and have to be reviewed and readjusted to their relative importance at different times, according to their correlations with the specific factors.

18.3.1 Dynamic concentrations

As a result of internal changes within portfolios, risk concentrations can develop spontaneously. Defaults, deterioration of asset value and collateral value changes can dramatically impact on the risk profile of a loan or security portfolio without any action being taken, as a secondary effect of the impact of tail risks.

There is relatively little literature available with regards to this problem, outside the BIS 1999 Forum[3] on risk concentrations and the stress testing of concentration risks under the Basel 2 framework, which are limited to credit portfolios.

A new approach based on benchmarking is proposed as follows. We have seen that tail-risk impacts were a function of risk concentrations. They also increase the procyclicality of risks. The impact of the concentrations on liquidity therefore depends on the concentration of the other banks to similar factors. In other words, a bank should be able to benchmark its own concentrations against those of the rest of the sector, country or system, to assess the potential impact a tail event may have on its liquidity and which type of liquidity factor it may be affecting (funding, market depth or collateral). The benchmarks can be based on measures of the Gini index to highlight concentrations to each factor of each category without unveiling proprietary information.

The Gini index and Lorenz curves are commonly used to measure concentrations (see Figure 18.3). The method provides a graphical representation of the cumulative distribution functions. It allows, for example, a measure of dispersion with absolute mean difference, which represents tensions within a portfolio better than standard deviations.

---

[3] BIS 1999, Risk concentration principles, paper presented at The Joint Forum: Basel Committee on Banking Supervision, International Organizations of Securities Commissions and International Association of Insurance Supervisors, Basel, December 1999.

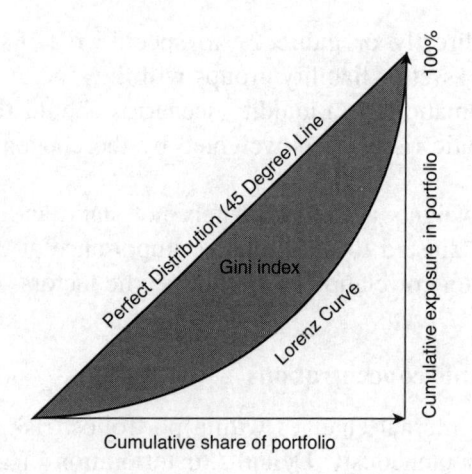

Figure 18.3 Gini index and Lorenz curves used to measure concentrations

Measuring concentrations and dispersions for the major risk classes periodically and benchmarking them to an aggregated figure from the rest of the industry would provide an accurate estimation of the potential effect on volatility and liquidity of tail events impacting concentrated portfolios.

The proposed framework consists of gathering each financial institution's exposure concentration periodically, expressed as a Gini index and mean difference, for the factors given below. A professional association, a third party aggregator or a regulator can aggregate the data periodically and produce a monograph of the industry's concentrations, thereby allowing each firm to be in a position to benchmark their own concentration to those of the market. At this stage, the purpose of this document is not to expose the technical arrangements involved but to review the risk concentration factors and granularity categories as follows:

For sell-side institutions:
- Asset allocations by counterparty type or ratings, country, underlying groups, mark-to-market (or value) frequency, time band, convertibility, optionality and vega bucket
- Liabilities by time bucket, currency, country, funding channel, creditors' group, issuer, settlement type, collateral group, convertibility, optionality, vega bucket
- Leverage ratios by client type, collateral, liquidity groups, derivative types
- Cyclical factors such as inflation, energy and interest rates.

For buy-side institutions:

- Portfolio concentrations by sector, market, trading counterparties, issuers, underlying asset type, mark-to-market frequency
- Leveraged exposure by derivative types, market, settlement type, volatility and sensitivity groups
- Pledged collateral by instrument, sector, haircut ratio
- Cyclical factors.

18.3.2 Concentration risk measurements

Statistical analyses of cumulative distribution functions are widely used to represent unevenly distributed concentrations, such as population wealth. The y axis represents the total value of the exposure to a given risk factor and the x axis is the cumulative categories for each factor, say the number of currencies, issuers, issuer ratings, etc. (see Figure 18.4).

Initially created to evaluate disparities within societies and across countries, the Lorenz curves are a perfect tool to use for benchmarking and comparing concentrations internally among traders, books or divisions, for example. They could also be used by professional associations or regulators to compare banks and to benchmark their risk concentrations across sectors, countries or systems. The methodology can be used to regulate the industry and monitor the speculative bubbles as they inflate and anticipate their burst.

Internal concentrations of liquidity exposure, whether arising from asset concentrations or reliance on a small number of funding channels,

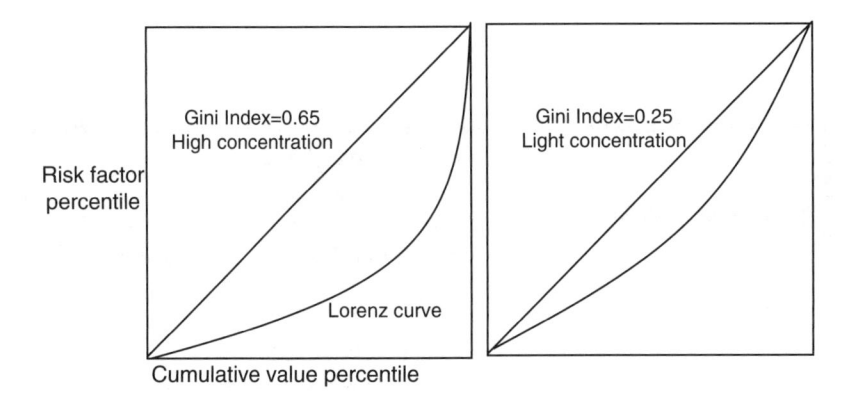

Figure 18.4 Cumulative distribution functions

Risk Policies → Root risk factors identification → Exposure & Concentrations → Sensitivity Scenarios → Potential Impact on Liquidity → Identification of risk mitigation → Alignment with risk policies → Liquidity Strategy

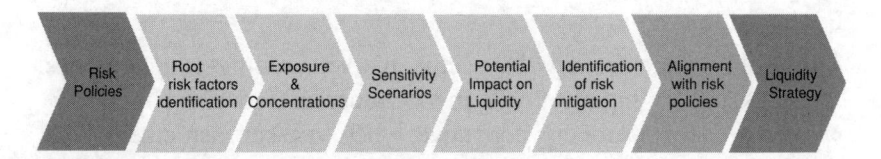

Figure 18.5 Progression of the workflow

are not necessarily dangerous or misaligned with corporate policies. By continuously measuring concentrations to each type of risk factor, the firm is in a position to reconcile the risks taken – and their potential impact on liquidity – with the defined risk policies. The workflow has progressed as shown in Figure 18.5.

18.3.3 Counterparty interdependence

The main lesson from the 2007–2009 crisis is that risks can no longer be managed in isolation. Exposure may come from indirect sources and issues may arise from others' failure to evaluate properly their own exposure or mitigate their own risks. In the deregulated global environment where absolute return (hence speculative) strategies have flourished, a banker's credit risk is a client's market risk. A fund manager's liquidity risk is the prime broker's credit risk. Corporate operational risk is a counterparty risk to the bank. These are just a few illustrations of the infinite interrelations with correlations arising and disappearing unpredictably (see Figure 18.6).

Since 2007, financial markets have grown so sensitive to facts and rumours that the mere inkling of being perceived as funding illiquid

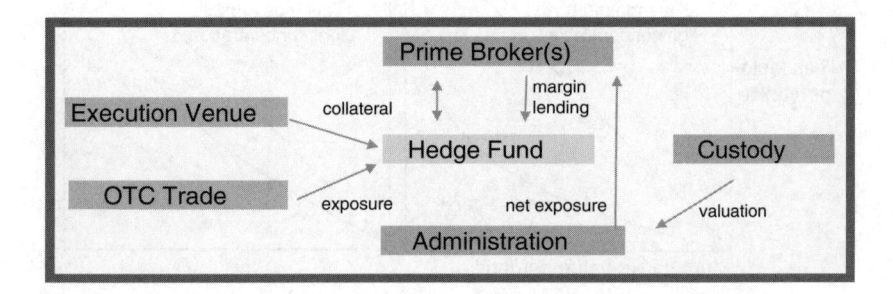

Figure 18.6 Liquidity risk may arise from trading and settlement counterparties

portfolios or running opaque positions can bring immediate repercussions on a prime broker's own funding costs. Wasting little time, Goldman Sachs and Morgan Stanley set up automatic credit line adjustments that depended on their own credit spreads, probably as an attempt to self-regulate their cost of funding through the exposure inherited from clients.

This type of liquidity risk can only be anticipated and mitigated through transparency. Critical paths, dependencies, mitigation rules, alternative strategies and project management tactics are the usual means. To obtain and maintain the necessary insights into a counterparty's own exposure requires a high level of back-office efficiency, where awareness and risk-educated people at all levels of the hierarchy should be attained.

18.3.4 Regulatory-driven liquidity risk

As explained in Part 3, regulatory entanglements may have complicated cross-asset management and resulted in unexpected liquidity movements or arbitrage generating uncontrollable flows across regions through the various segments of the financial industry.

We explain in Part 6 on regulatory issues how Basel 2 had indirectly encouraged securitization. Although highly risky and opaque in pricing, the instruments created ended up in risk-averse institutional portfolios thanks to the new UCITSIII regulation. Meanwhile, the Markets in Financial Instruments Directive (MIFID) had fragmented liquidity pools which led to even less transparency and shallower markets.

All these changes decided and implemented within jurisdictional silos created opportunities of regulatory arbitrage and incentives for entire business activities such as bespoke product structuring for example. But it drove financial institutions to engineer similar strategies and tactics under similar conditions, leading to even more concentrations of assets and liabilities. New regulatory initiatives have vowed to address those issues but it will realistically take a long time to design, pass and implement.

In the meantime, the potential consequences of regulatory-driven tactics on the funding channels should be accounted for by financial institutions in their market scenarios. These institutions need to anticipate how periods of euphoria and panic bias the markets during bubble 'inflate-and-burst' processes.

19
Managing and Mitigating Liquidity Risks

The above analysis leads to the following results. Liquidity risks arise from multiple sources, due to the consequence of multiple operational risks and of their combined effects. Liquidity risks have been identified as the main cause of failure of Tier 1 institutions that were previously thought to be 'too big to fail' in 2008 and 2009.

Our proposition is to implement a framework, not a system, which supports the progressive development of a culture based on risk management. It focuses on agility, responsiveness, and adaptability. The IT architecture and the whole framework is meant to enable corporate governance, not to replace it. A solid foundation is needed, to provide the content, the workflow and the monitoring tools that are necessary to ensure transparency and to allow the firm to develop its agility to tackle liquidity issues over time.

A framework for liquidity management designed to fit the specific corporate risk policies of any firm should involve three key elements: tracking and monitoring risk concentrations, keeping a particular focus on valuations and measures of sensitivity, and obviously asset liability management (ALM). Adapting funding strategies and liquidity tactics to a risk profile consists of permanently maintaining a balance between those three poles, as illustrated by Figure 19.1.

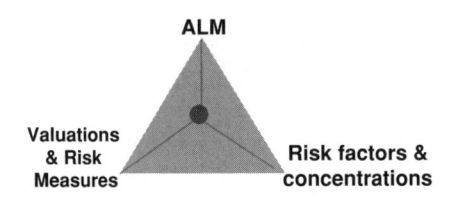

Figure 19.1 The essential components of a liquidity management strategy

19.1 LAYING DOWN THE FOUNDATIONS OF A CORPORATE STRATEGY

Developing a strategy and governance structures for liquidity risk management first requires answering the following questions. What is the firm risk strategy or appetite for risk? Which accounting rules would apply for different investment time horizons? What are the known root causes of liquidity risks or risk factors? What are the regulatory requirements? What governance rules are there? How are responsibilities distributed?

19.1.1 Chosen risk factors and appetite for risk

The corporate risk strategy is defined as a balance of risk factors with governance and compliance rules (see Figure 19.2).

The risk appetite of a firm makes it vulnerable (see Figure 19.3). The key to understand those vulnerabilities – to liquidity and to other risks - is to uncover the actual factors of sensitivity to which the firm is exposed. For example, a firm holding a portfolio of loans whose clients are directly or indirectly exposed to commodity prices would get only a partial view of its risk exposure through simulation credit ratings and interest rates shifts. Not only might the fluctuations of the underlying commodities have a greater effect on the clients' equity and creditworthiness but tail events are more likely to come from that side. As far as liquidity risk is concerned, tail risk is where the focus should be.

Each firm should therefore embark on a course in identifying all root-risk factors, paying particular attention to those that could create tail risk. An identical process should then be rolled out for pledged collateral and contingent exposure (covenants, guarantees and options). The exposure to each root-risk factor then needs to be measured with a particular focus on risk concentrations.

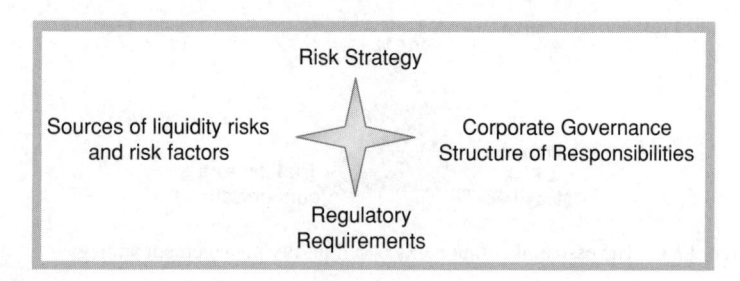

Figure 19.2 The balance of risk exposure and governance rules.

Managing and Mitigating Liquidity Risks

ALM

Valuations & Risk Measures

Risk factors & concentrations

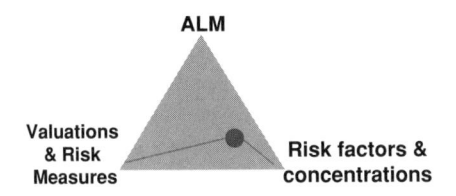

Figure 19.3 Development of the concentration factor

Following this categorization, data sources (human or electronic) can be aggregated to identify the sensitivity of all root-risk factors. By designing risk scenarios with various levels of shocks and tail events impacting the factors, one can highlight the main areas of vulnerability to liquidity risks. It is an analysis of cause and effects, as illustrated by Figure 19.4.

Through a bottom-up computation of market and credit risks, one can identify where sensitivities originate from and analyse them with the drill-down functions. Key risk factor categories where concentrations can be closely monitored are thus identified. The details of sensitivities measured at trading desks are aggregated into a total sensitivity by exposure categories (curves, rates, ratings, etc.). Most importantly, the system should recompute all exposure and risks with different marking methodologies. This is crucial for each unit and risk manager to be able to align the accounting methodology (accrued, value, market, model, etc.) to the risk profile of the unit.

These precautions are particularly important to address the issue of the valuation risks. To reach a satisfactory level of integration it is necessary to combine the power of IT with manual input and human judgement at many stages. The hybrid approach fosters a transparent workflow, which will be adapted to grow and evolve along with the firm. These are the key steps towards establishing a corporate culture based on risk.

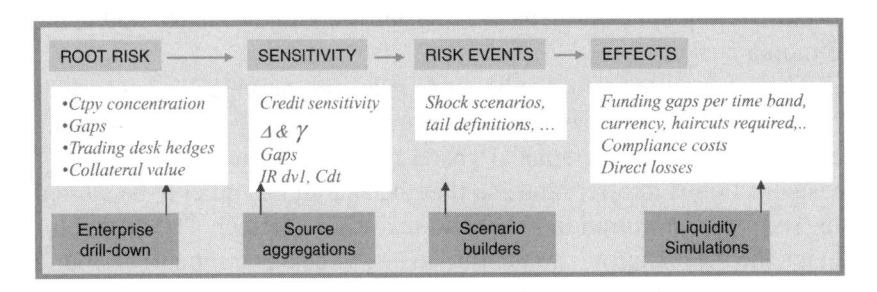

ROOT RISK	SENSITIVITY	RISK EVENTS	EFFECTS
•Ctpy concentration •Gaps •Trading desk hedges •Collateral value	Credit sensitivity Δ & γ Gaps IR dvl, Cdt	Shock scenarios, tail definitions, ...	Funding gaps per time band, currency, haircuts required,... Compliance costs Direct losses
Enterprise drill-down	Source aggregations	Scenario builders	Liquidity Simulations

Figure 19.4 Causes, events and impacts under scenarios

Risk Policies → Root risk factors identification → Exposure & Concentrations → Sensitivity Scenarios → Potential Impact on Liquidity

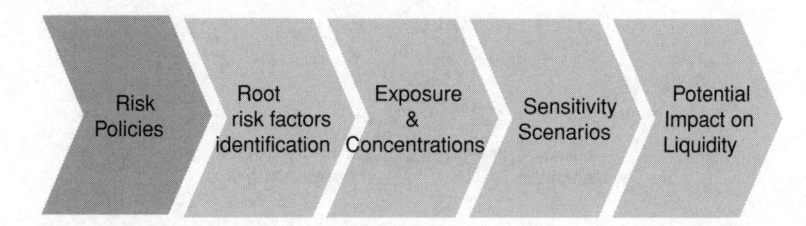

Figure 19.5 Flowchart of the process

19.2 MONITORING CONCENTRATIONS

Once the risk factors are identified, the risk manager will learn to understand the scope of the framework and how to review the factors. The next step is to identify all concentrations within or across factors and associate those with a potential loss under scenario(s). This aspect has been extensively discussed above. The flowchart in Figure 19.5 indicates the process.

19.3 WORKING WITH RISK CONCENTRATIONS

Concentrations are the main cause of liquidity issues as they increase the dependence on tail risks. Special flags should therefore be set up to highlight high levels of concentrations and their dependency on potential tail events. Internal monitoring can be supported by IT and audit departments to project cash flows from both the banking and trading books under a variety of scenarios.

Risk concentrations may come from a natural exposure or from a particular business focus, say exposure to the euro, for example. They may also arise from combinations of variables within books. For example, a bank may not have any particular concentration of euros with respect to other currencies and may not have high exposure to the 3 month tenor overall. It might, however, have an all euro exposure concentrated in the 3 month bucket.

There are systems to display concentrations graphically but visualization of imbalances is not a measure of risk in itself. Due to scale effects on monitors, graphical charts can be misleading. The goal of visualization is to offer hints, so that the analyst can quickly be alerted to 'risks of concentration risks' and investigate further. The quest also helps the most appropriate measurements of concentration to be found and to identify appropriate shocks for the scenarios to contain.

19.3.1 Reconciliations or risk concentrations and risk policies

A heat map of risk concentrations is critical to reconcile actual risks with expected risks. The risk policies have highlighted an appetite, a selection of risk factors, acceptable sensitivity numbers and maximum losses. The risk concentrations measured by the firm must meet those requirements.

In traditional risk management frameworks, the issue of concentration risk has been merely an approach from the point of view of concentrations within ratings matrices. Abundant literature exists where the main focus is to model credit concentrations within portfolios and compute the distribution of credit losses. Here the main driver of the approach was to comply with Basel 2 requirements of modelling expected and unexpected credit losses in order to be able to fine-tune capital allocations. As far as market risk is concerned, most analyses also focus on portfolio diversification, using the most traditional CAPM-based approach to reduce portfolio risk to systematic risk, as described by Figure 19.6.

This has led firms to hold portfolios of systematic risks, leaving them exposed to tail events and, in most cases, totally unsuited to tail events that hit several types of systematic exposure simultaneously.

Our proposed methodology is to analyse concentrations within portfolios by risk factors, and not only by portfolio components. In doing so, it is possible to reconcile concentrations to risks across the enterprise. Figure 19.7 exhibits polar charts pointing out concentrations within the different business units. While some of the risk factors may be specific, others would be common to all units, making it possible to assess the exposure to tail events enterprise-wide.

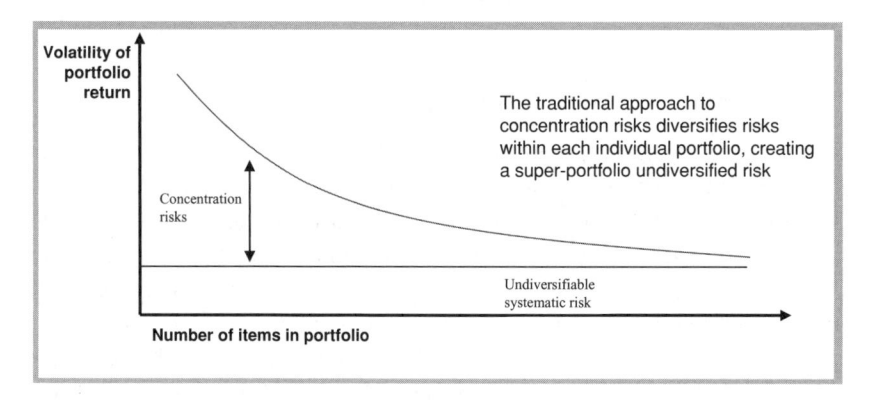

Figure 19.6 Approach used to reduce portfolio risk to systematic risk

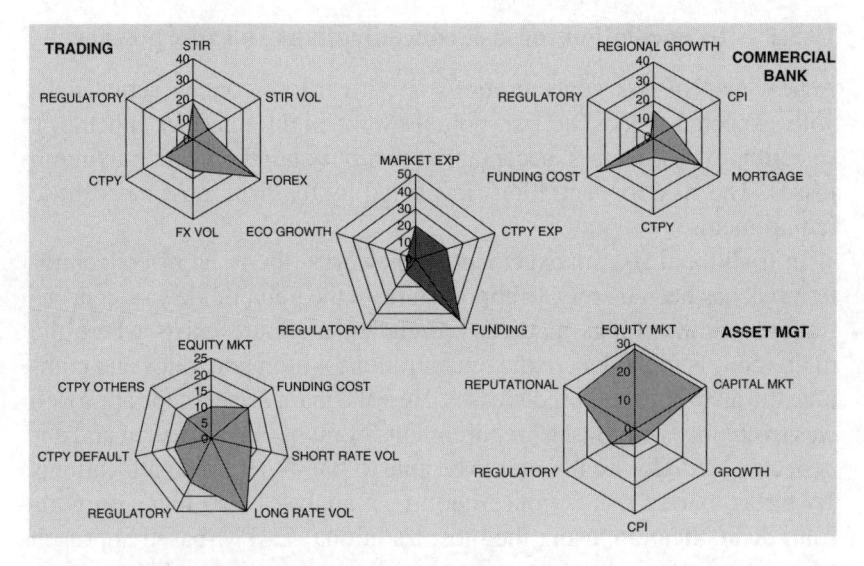

Figure 19.7 Enterprise-wide study of concentrations

Clearly the approach does not replace the typical allocation concentration studies, which are designed to measure specific risks. It is an additional enterprise view of risks designed to anticipate the effects of known and unknown concentrations. In the aftermath of the real-estate meltdown in 2008 in the US, for example, a large Tier 1 diversified banking group admitted, through the voice of its own CEO, to being doubly exposed to the same risk factor – real estate prices – through its mortgage lending division and its securitization business. At the enterprise level, such concentration was previously unknown.

19.3.2 Managing concentrations

Liquidity problems typically appear in times of great market emotion and turmoil – when a bubble bursts, for example. A firm may suffer from liquidity imbalances if it was exposed to the same risk concentrations as the rest of the market but was caught unprepared for the burst. Manifestations of liquidity risks reveal imbalances previously existing until a catalyst, a tail event or a crisis, comes and turns them into losses. Until then, the imbalances existed but were overlooked. This was the case of LTCM in 1998, of the Internet bubble of 2000–2001 and of the complex exposure to structured finance in 2007.

By benchmarking the internal risk concentrations to those of the rest of its segment, country or system, a firm can properly assess the amplitude of potential liquidity issues or bubble bursts. Unfortunately, such benchmarks do not exist and we can only encourage the industry representatives, professional associations and regulators to work together in a most constructive way to make this information publicly available. It would require each bank to contribute its own concentration factors – in the form of concentration indices to keep sensitive information undisclosed – and an aggregator to send back a monograph of the sector.

In the meantime, financial institutions are left with a purely idiosyncratic view and management of their liquidity risks. The impact of volatility and correlations on market liquidity is massive and complex. The unpredictable nature of correlations under stressed conditions makes predictive quantitative models less reliable. The interaction of volatility, liquidity and correlation is three-dimensional and nonlinear. Simulations based on history can be misleading too, since financial markets typically suffer from remedies or structures derived from a previous crisis and so the next crisis will necessarily be different from previous ones.

19.4 ALM ANALYSES AND LIQUIDITY MANAGEMENT

Triggers that spark off a sell-off, a market panic or balance sheet adjustments are, by definition, unpredictable (see Figure 19.8). Managing liquidity risks is to understand the potential impact that the firm's concentrations (whether wanted or unwanted) might have on the structures of its balance sheet. With such knowledge, an asset management firm can prepare portfolio rebalancing tactics, a bank can establish alternative funding channels, while a risk-averse corporate can adjust their own exposures.

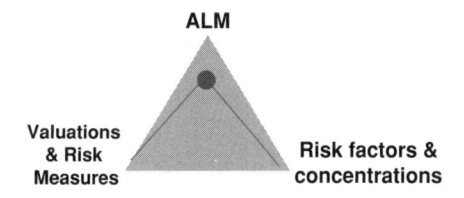

Figure 19.8 Development of the ALM factor

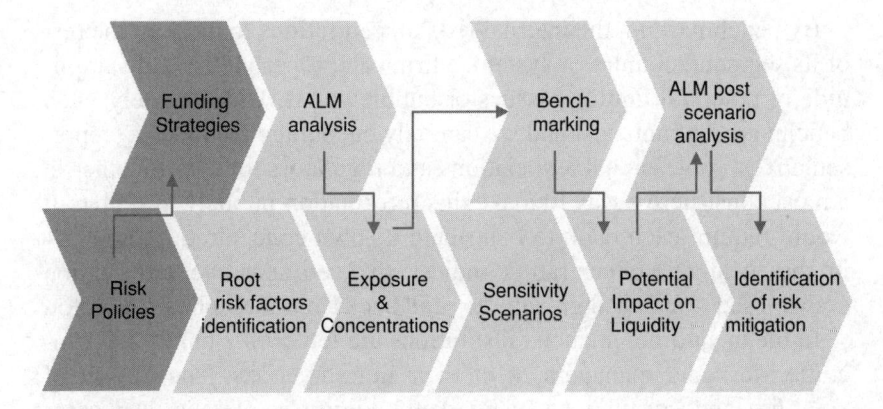

```
        Funding      ALM              Bench-      ALM post
        Strategies   analysis         marking     scenario
                                                  analysis

  Risk     Root        Exposure                  Potential    Identification
  Policies risk factors    &        Sensitivity  Impact on    of risk
           identification Concentrations Scenarios Liquidity   mitigation
```

Figure 19.9 A second stream in the framework

This implies a perfect knowledge of the traditional funding channels and cash flows of the bank. An enterprise-wide mapping of all cash flows is required at this stage so that the liquidity impact of the above scenarios can be estimated in terms of balance sheet risk. This is a second stream in our framework, as exhibited by Figure 19.9.

The ALM analysis is expected to unveil risk return implications of potential changes in risk variables, as well as the vulnerabilities and key dependencies in funding. It highlights a critical path to liquidity management and is a true analysis of the firm's business risk. Pre- and post-scenario analyses unveil the potential gaps resulting from the concentrations under the stress scenarios. As ALM simulations will combine the exposure from both the business and funding risks, they will add valuable input to the heat map of exposure and concentrations. Most ALM techniques have typically relied on scenario analyses and less on predictive modelling such as VaR, for example. The main factors of risks are the business margins, the duration gaps and the convexity gaps. To these one might add implied option effects and portfolio or correlation effects.

19.4.1 Margin and business risk analysis

The ALM analysis is essential to the assessment of risks to the extent that it measures the performance of the internal management and the performance margins of a firm. It defines the economic benchmarks for internal and external pricing and as such is a reflection of the risk policies. The pricing policies are supposedly risk-based and if any risk is not properly compensated for, it should trigger a review so that either

Managing and Mitigating Liquidity Risks

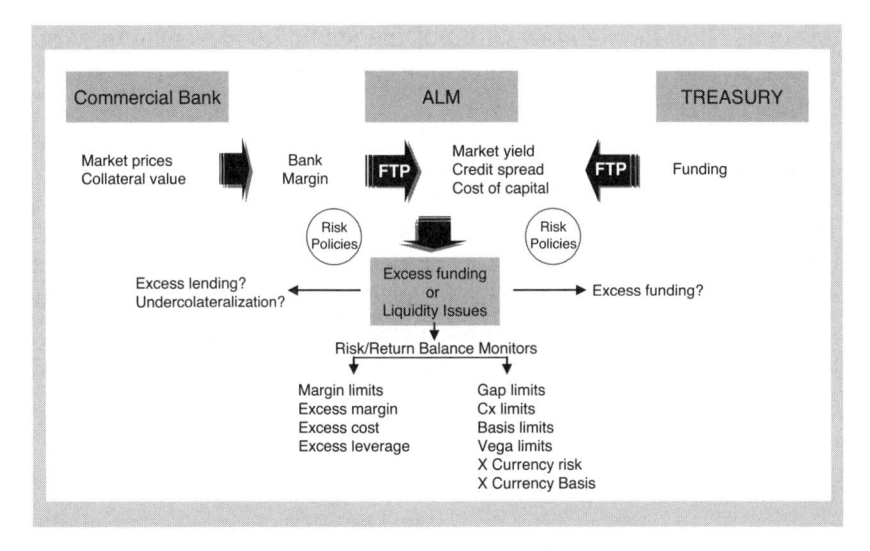

Figure 19.10 Capturing the implied risk policies at fund transfer pricing

the margins can be upgraded or the business abandoned – the subprime credit crisis of 2007 springs to mind.

The data necessary for the assessment can be collected at the fund transfer pricing (FTP) stage. An FTP system or process is the link between the commercial and the funding sides of a firm. It is therefore where business risk is conveyed into the enterprise and turns into financial risk. It makes a perfect spot to monitor whether risk policies are accurately reflected in business policies. Transparency, accuracy and integrity there is therefore essential.

Figure 19.10 illustrates the process. Based on its business policies, the commercial divisions of a bank grant collateralized loans. Their margins, lending targets and pledged collateral assets depend on how aggressive their policies are, in other words it depends on their risk policies. What is essential as part of our risk culture implementation is that the risk policies implied by their lending style matches those decided by the shareholders and that the risk policies of the funding divisions match that profile too. This can be achieved at the ALM level, where the bank margins will be reconciled with the cost of funding – a combination of rates, credit spread and cost of capital. Banks typically have excess short-term resources and long-term extra needs. Hedging tactics involving derivatives such as interest swaps, futures or interbank loans will be deployed. As a result the balance between desired returns and acceptable risk is maintained by sets of limits. Everything in excess should be hedged. Excessive lending or undercollateralization can be unwound. It is through the set-up of the lending limits (margin, cost, collateral) and funding limits (duration gaps, convexity gaps, basis, etc.) that the balance can be maintained.

19.4.2 Sensitivity of duration gaps

The sensitivity of duration, or modified duration, measures the changes in value for a shift of interest rates or yield curves. The general formula assumes a flat yield curve, but as such a thing does not exist most simulation works model various changes in curve shapes.[1]

Duration is generally described as

$$D = \frac{\sum_{t=1}^{N}[tCt/(1+y_t)^t]}{\sum_{t=1}^{N}[Ct/(1+y_t)^t]}$$

where Ct and y_t are respectively the cash flow and the market yield at time t. Modified duration is described as a sensitivity of duration and is given as

$$\Delta V/V = -[D/(1+y)]\Delta y$$

In other words, the rate sensitivity at a given tenor is a function of the discounted cash flow and of the forward rates differential under a given scenario. The routine risk management task of a bank is to immunize the bank's margins against potential gaps between the value of assets and liabilities due to interest rates or yield curve changes over the entire term structure of position exposures. The immunization condition is described as

$$VA \times DA = VL \times DL$$

To put this in words, it requires the value of assets multiplied by the duration of assets to equate those of the liabilities.

Any gap measured in this equation is interest rate risk and any gap differential between tenors is basis risk. The exposure is generally multiplied by the leverage ratio between assets and liabilities.

The issue with this most traditional approach is that it assumes that there is no volatility in the price of assets, that liquidity risk does not exist and the cost of funding (and hence the price of liabilities) is unchanged

---

[1] See Joel Bessis, *Risk Management in Banking*, John Wiley & Sons, Ltd, Chichester, 2002.

regardless of which scenario the firm finds itself in. If a firm funds long-term assets with short-term liabilities, for example, then the equation requires either an overestimation of the discounted value of assets or an underestimation of the future value of liabilities. Should the yield curve turn negative, the funding costs would rise dramatically and if the market's perceptions adds a rising credit spread on top of it, then the situation might quickly become unsustainable, as infamously happened in the case of Northern Rock.

Our proposed methodology described in Part 1 would have necessarily highlighted rates and curves as risk factors. High-severity and stress scenarios would estimate the level of duration gap sensitivity that would be considered sustainable to the firm.

The adequacy of the risk policies with the ALM gap analysis relies on matching durations and modified durations across the whole term structure of exposure. However, few items are as volatile and sensitive to investors' moods as a yield curve. Alerts with respect to valuation risks should therefore be set up specifically to focus on valuation gaps that could threaten the immunization of the books. As the duration gaps are usually controlled using derivatives, an early alert should allow for timely adjustments.

Interest rate volatility is certainly part of the equation too. Whether the firm runs books with options or not, the volatility of interest rates increases dramatically the basis risk and also instils an element of convexity in the sensitivity or durations. Again, modelling these complex nonlinear interactions can be a mathematically challenging achievement, but it would not bring much risk management to those who are responsible and accountable for the immunization. It is best to monitor the combined evolution of these factors and trigger alerts whenever they start impacting on the available liquidity of the firm. At such a point, alternative liquidity management tactics must be predefined. As exhibited in Figure 19.11, duration and convexity gap analyses based on scenarios should at least encompass the combined and reciprocal effects of shifts in credit spread, yield curve movements and a term structure view of interest rate volatility.

19.4.3 Convexity gaps

Convexity exists in each instrument valuation that depends on one or several factors through a supposedly linear function. Whether it is interest rates and bond values or an option premium with 'moneyness' (how

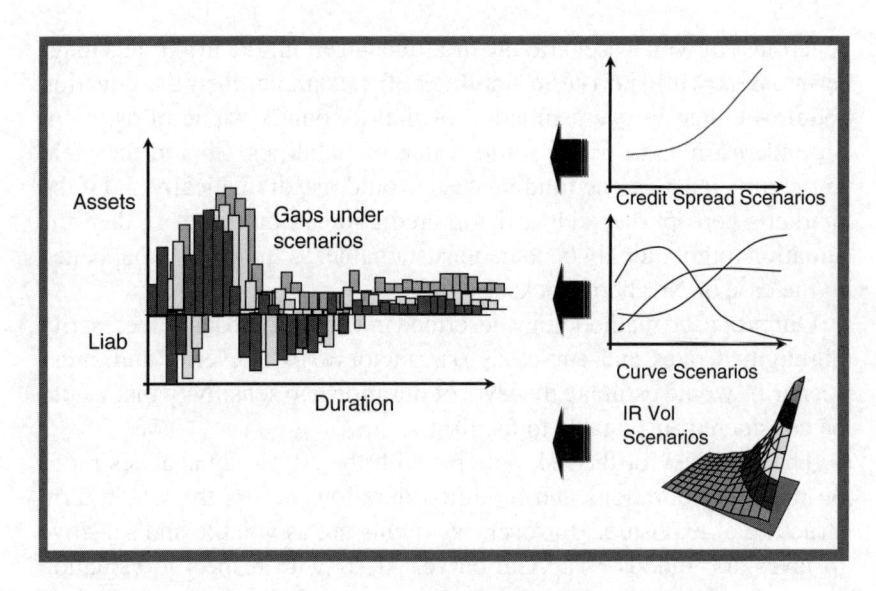

Figure 19.11 Minimum input into scenario-based duration gap analysis

much in or out-of-money an option can be), there are critical points at which the function changes straight lines into curves.

A typical issue of this well-known type of sensitivity is that it has been mostly approached as a mathematical function for hedging purposes. Convexity is always computed out of discount factors and implied volatility, and is rarely understood as a manifestation of investors' emotions. It significantly complicates VaR calculations as it makes some of the simulated projections forward of net present value (NPV) irrelevant, yet skewing the end statistical results. Methods to compensate for the sensitivity effect in VaR are often based on an arbitrary cap on interest rates set by the analyst, which raises many other modelling issues with respect to mean returns in particular. Again, an empirical approach based on scenarios and experience, while less comforting in terms of mathematical foundation, would bring much more sense to the risk mitigation processes.

Credit spreads and ratings directly influence convexity, to the point that it can be reversed into an implied assessment of credit quality. In the midst of the 2008–2009 meltdown, for example, some long G7 government bonds started to have some convexity, an extremely rare development highlighting a lack of confidence in even some of the G7 Treasuries. The other key 'predictive' function of convexity regards the volatility of interest rates, whether or not the portfolio contains

Managing and Mitigating Liquidity Risks

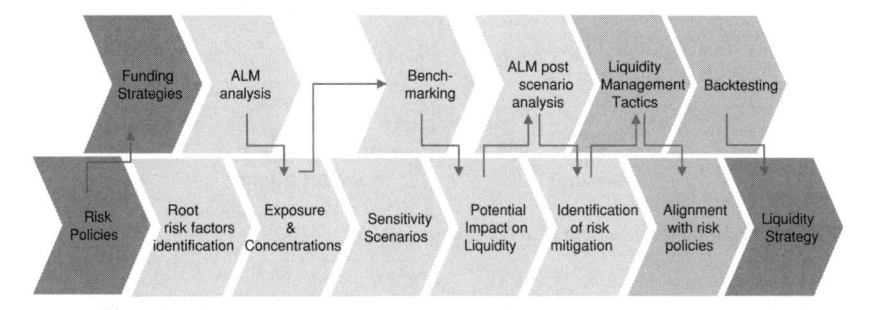

Figure 19.12 Further progress in the framework

explicit optionality such as caps, floors, bond options or convertible securities.

In conclusion, convexity levels should be added to our display and monitored as an advanced indicator of market sentiment, used as an alert trigger that can possibly come ahead of tail events. The impact on liquidity management is at such a level. The reconciliation with corporate policies should also integrate convexity targets as an element of the risk profile with respect to the volatility and credit quality of the instruments in use.

Following the post-scenario ALM analysis and the identification of mitigation tactics, the firm is in a position to add liquidity risk management tactics to its policies. This is a crucial aspect of implementing risk as a corporate culture since it allows the alignment of the funding strategy to be maintained with the corporate strategies.

In case of discrepancy, the gaps will be the base for adjustments. It is an important step to let the risk management framework evolve with the nature of the company's business, its volume growth and changing environment.

The progress of our liquidity risk management framework is displayed by Figure 19.12.

19.5 VALUATION RISKS

As previously established, the validity and integrity of valuations is the cornerstone of the entire framework (see Figure 19.13). It is not simply an issue of accuracy in pricing or valuations. Since the proposed risk management methodology consists of shocking prices, curves and surfaces by significant proportions to mimic tail risks, the valuations need continuous adjustments to fit the scenarios. Under a stress scenario,

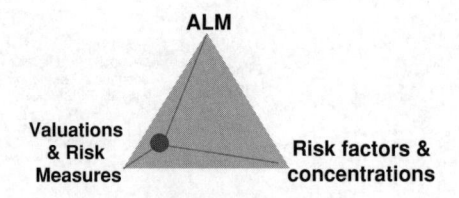

Figure 19.13 Development of the valuations factor

not only the price changes. Trading books are also impacted by path-dependent exposure, changes in curves shapes and rating matrices. Banking books may be subject to clauses triggered by a ratings shift. The behaviour of customers and investors may be different as well. Clearly, no mathematical model can represent such an intricate combination of cross-influences. At best it needs to be empirically built and maintained. To avoid creating more operational risks and to maintain consistency over time, the risk system needs to be built on the same framework where valuations are carried out.

19.5.1 Market depth

Anticipating the potential consequences of liquidity concentrations consists of estimating the factors of market tension and their impact on market depth. With respect to trading books, the price movements and volume aggregations provide precious indications of potential concentration build-ups. They point out the degree of emotion in which securities or financial instruments are traded. Well-balanced markets where buyers meet sellers in a steady volume tend to return normally distributed prices and P/L changes. Before a market loses balance and experiences a massive drawdown, typical distortions are often noticeable, such as directional volumes imbalance, unexpected changes in correlations, unusual standard deviations, and so on. Simultaneously, news releases accelerate with new frequent sources of information and the market sentiment tends to point in a single direction. The market liquidity may actually be at its highest at such a point, but it becomes increasingly vulnerable.

With collateralized banking books, the notion of market depth is obviously much more difficult to assess. Since the underlying won't trade on a secondary market, issues of market depth and liquidity purely relate to collateral. With the exception of cash and securities collateral, the accounting methodology is more relevant than the market depth

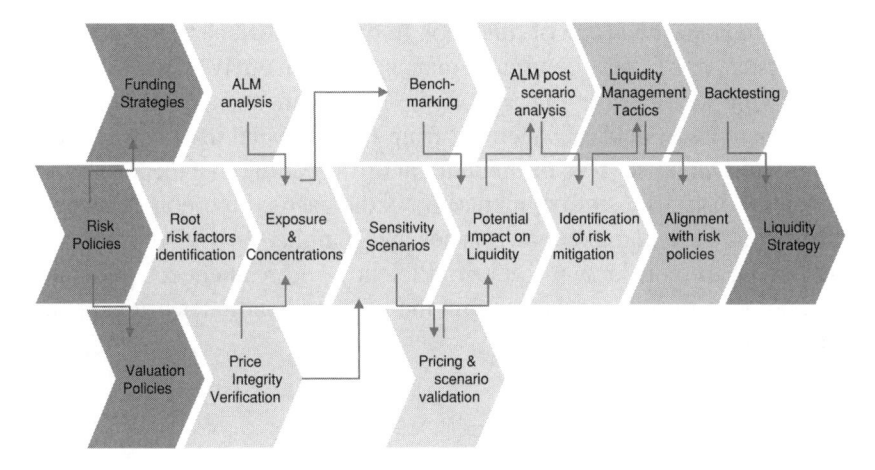

Figure 19.14 A third stream in the framework

(or lack of it). There has been extensive discussion on the role that value-based accounting played in the crisis – whether it compounded issues and added to the procyclicality effects.

With direct links between valuations and scenario-based risk assessments for identifying the potential effects of tail risks during stress tests, our liquidity risk framework benefits from the best possible levels of price integrity, consistency and transparency (see Figure 19.14).

The impact of external constraints should not be underestimated. Although counterparty risks are part of the risk factor identification and risk concentration measurement processes, liquidity risks arising from external counterparties should be objects of particular attention.

19.5.2 Counterparty-related liquidity risks

Managing this type of risk consists of building charts of dependencies and contingencies to highlight the points where any failure could create liquidity issues for the firm. The analysis is not redundant with the concentration analysis of counterparty risks since the former are related to the creditworthiness of counterparties. The present analysis instead focuses on payments, litigations and all operational risks related to external counterparties, such as service providers, custodians, transfer agents, data providers and so on. From a 'critical path of liquidity provision' the firm will be able to design alternative strategies and risk mitigation.

It is beyond the scope of this book to display flowcharts and discuss the aspects of business continuity management that may create liquidity risks. One key aspect, however, is the management of data. Frequent discrepancies in data management from one financial institution to another are typical sources of operational error leading to exceptions and potential disruptions of payments. As is the case with credit exposure, firms can rate external counterparties and liquidity provision processes according to their known level of efficiency and resilience. This practice helps to raise awareness within the firm and facilitates critical path monitoring.

19.5.3 Corporate governance

Addressing liquidity issues, when they occur, require the firm to be particularly agile in times of market turmoil. Needless to say, it cannot be the sole responsibility of the risk managers. All executive managers who might influence the volumes and concentrations of assets or liabilities, the management of collateral, need to be prepared and trained to react to liquidity issues as if they were emergency procedures.

Countless surveys have highlighted the fact that the most effective way to drive these efforts is through incentive and compensation schemes. Few banks, however, have yet considered incentive schemes that were not merely linked to P/L performance.

A widely-held misconception is that risk management is subsequent to business priorities. Once the management of liquidity and other operational risks is rooted deeply in the processes and business operations, the firm is in a position to prioritize products or business plans according to their risk profiles and to their fit with the corporate risk policies. Risk-adjusted profitability is a notion that will get more traction in the aftermath of the crisis.

19.6 REGULATORY RISK

The regulatory entanglements discussed earlier have been identified as one of the root causes of the crisis and of the so-called liquidity crunch. In response to the pressing requirements of the industry and of the policy makers, several regulatory entities decided to propose new arrangements to prevent the devastating effects of a future liquidity crisis.

Exceptionally adverse market conditions have underlined the fact that financial markets do not follow any kind of normality. Therefore the very concept of turning a probability into a frequency of occurrence and risk weighting capital accordingly may not protect a firm facing repeated tail events. Furthermore, it may expose the entire sector or industry to systemic risks if uniform tactics are deployed when rare exceptional events occur and especially when they generalize.

We suggest a three-pronged approach involving:

1. Assessing net exposure quantitatively and dynamically through observable market-based measurements of price, sensitivity and liquidity
2. Benchmarking risk and liquidity concentrations against the rest of the industry to identify areas of tensions and exuberance
3. Provisioning for worst case developments as opposed to most probable scenarios.

The recommendations of the Financial Services Authority standard FSA CP 09/13[2] call for an in-depth revision of liquidity risk management well beyond adjustments of capital requirements or creation of counterbalancing capabilities.

The screen in Figure 19.15 is an example of a regulatory report on liquidity provided by Thomson Reuters Top Office. It is designed to provide a comprehensive regulatory reporting tool compliant with FSA CP 09/13 as an integral part of the liquidity management framework.

We note that the FSA encourages the implementation of dynamic frameworks, associating internal liquidity risks with market-generated ones. The notion of idiosyncratic stress testing and market stress testing is an acknowledgement of the tail risks and systematic risks, which were largely overlooked by previous regulations.

We understand that there is currently a dialogue between industry participants and regulators with regards to the costs and difficulties of implementing a compliance framework. The cost of compliance is a never ending debate, which can only be settled when capacities of anticipation, communication and transparency enhancements resulting from the effort eventually turn into a profit. Risk-based strategy plans, risk-based cost analysis and especially risk-based external communications are to become value generators in the near future. This aspect is extensively discussed in Part 5 of this book.

---

[2] FSA CP 09/13, *Strengthening Liquidity Standards 2: Liquidity Reporting*, Financial Services Authority, April 2009.

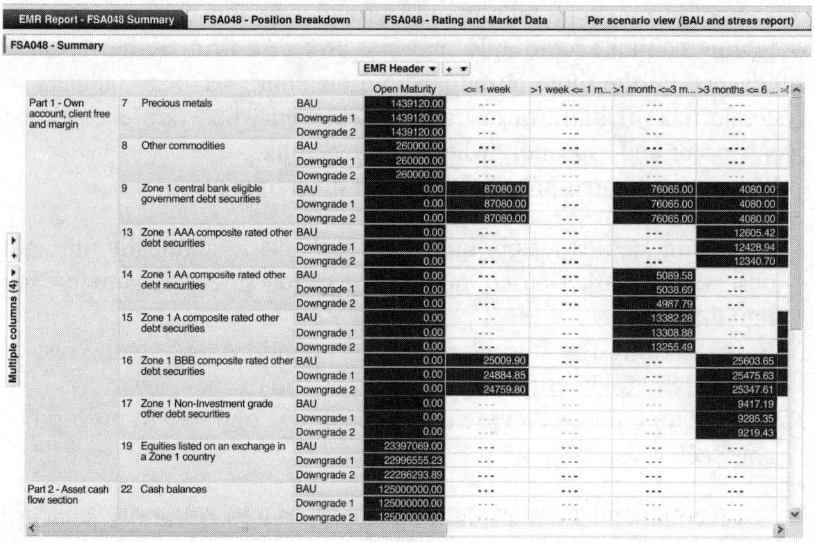
EMR Report - FSA048 Summary | FSA048 - Position Breakdown | FSA048 - Rating and Market Data | Per scenario view (BAU and stress report)

FSA048 - Summary

EMR Header

				Open Maturity	<= 1 week	>1 week <= 1 m...	>1 month <=3 m...	>3 months <= 6 ...
Part 1 - Own account, client free and margin	7	Precious metals	BAU	1439120.00	---	---	---	---
			Downgrade 1	1439120.00	---	---	---	---
			Downgrade 2	1439120.00	---	---	---	---
	8	Other commodities	BAU	260000.00	---	---	---	---
			Downgrade 1	260000.00	---	---	---	---
			Downgrade 2	260000.00	---	---	---	---
	9	Zone 1 central bank eligible government debt securities	BAU	0.00	87080.00	---	76065.00	4080.00
			Downgrade 1	0.00	87080.00	---	76065.00	4080.00
			Downgrade 2	0.00	87080.00	---	76065.00	4080.00
	13	Zone 1 AAA composite rated other debt securities	BAU	0.00	---	---	---	12605.42
			Downgrade 1	0.00	---	---	---	12428.94
			Downgrade 2	0.00	---	---	---	12340.70
	14	Zone 1 AA composite rated other debt securities	BAU	0.00	---	---	5089.58	---
			Downgrade 1	0.00	---	---	5038.69	---
			Downgrade 2	0.00	---	---	4987.79	---
	15	Zone 1 A composite rated other debt securities	BAU	0.00	---	---	13382.28	---
			Downgrade 1	0.00	---	---	13308.88	---
			Downgrade 2	0.00	---	---	13255.49	---
	16	Zone 1 BBB composite rated other debt securities	BAU	0.00	25009.90	---	---	25603.65
			Downgrade 1	0.00	24884.85	---	---	25475.63
			Downgrade 2	0.00	24759.80	---	---	25347.61
	17	Zone 1 Non-Investment grade other debt securities	BAU	0.00	---	---	---	9417.19
			Downgrade 1	0.00	---	---	---	9285.35
			Downgrade 2	0.00	---	---	---	9219.43
	19	Equities listed on an exchange in a Zone 1 country	BAU	23397069.00	---	---	---	---
			Downgrade 1	22996555.23	---	---	---	---
			Downgrade 2	22286293.89	---	---	---	---
Part 2 - Asset cash flow section	22	Cash balances	BAU	125000000.00	---	---	---	---
			Downgrade 1	125000000.00	---	---	---	---
			Downgrade 2	125000000.00	---	---	---	---

Multiple columns (4)

Source: Thomson Reuters Top Office

Figure 19.15 Example of a regulatory report on liquidity

Featuring this final aspect, regulatory compliance finalizes the implementation of a comprehensive and adaptive liquidity risk management framework, as illustrated with the flowchart in Figure 19.16.

19.7 OF LIQUIDITY RISK AND CORRELATION

In the proposed framework the risk policies lead to monitoring risk factors and their sensitivity. Regardless of their complexity, a deeply rooted culture of risk management operates as a front-line protection against the risk factors' sensitivity and volatility. Each factor is turned into a micro-factor and monitored as a limit, distributed with performance objectives to responsible and accountable business specialists. One type of exposure, however, cannot be turned into a target; it is the correlation effects within a portfolio, among activities, across regions or currencies. Correlations are unpredictable by nature, either through modelling or expert estimation. Correlations reflect associations of sentiment and technical difficulties. Any attempt to define any sort of limits involving simulated correlation effects in modelling generally leads to disaster. Correlations are tightly related with market liquidity and volatility. They spontaneously arise through tail events as investors are forced to look for

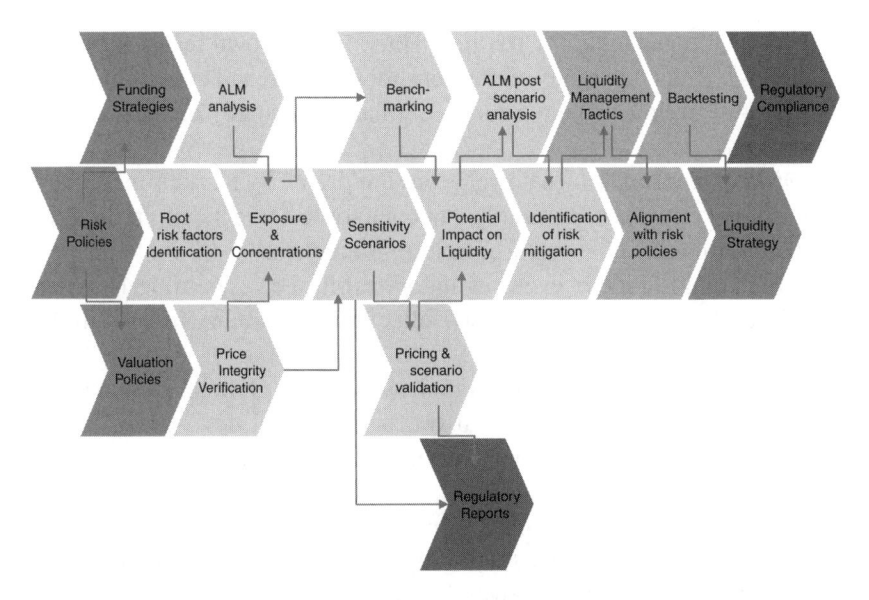

Figure 19.16 The liquidity risk management framework

alternative assets to cut their losses in fire sales or for alternative funding channels when market shocks suddenly change well-established trading and hedging rules.

Since our established risk policies are expected to be reflected in pricing policies and commercial strategies, they necessarily imply a distribution of correlations. Those should not be approached through statistical analysis as the sensitivity resulting from the correlations can remain unchanged while underlying correlations change dramatically. Only then can a description of assumed correlations among macro-risk factors be monitored. In finance, correlations are even more volatile and unpredictable due to the effect of leverage.

One should not confuse a multivariate analysis with correlations. Variables can be linked without being dependent. Acharya and Schaefer[3] discuss the fact that liquidity shocks are usually preceded by asset shocks. The triple effect comes from forced liquidations, funding needs arising from lower collateral value and raising haircut requirements due to higher credit risks in adverse market conditions. The issue may be compounded if the shocks have lasting effects by the fact that less capital

---

[3] Viral V. Acharya and Stephan Schaefer, Liquidity risk and correlation risk: implications for risk management, Draft article, London Business School, 8 September 2006.

will be made available for trading. Thus, in their own terms there are 'regimes', which are times of market shocks, where tail events multiply, as opposed to times where returns seem to be normally or lognormally distributed.

Clearly in normal times correlations are driven by market fundamentals, industry purposes or simply a beta factor to some index. In times of high volatility and tail events, correlations are driven by flight to quality, loss financing, fears or even regulatory arbitrage. According to Allen and Gale,[4] the asset prices merely reflect the availability of cash in the market.

The importance of the issue is increased by the globalization and deregulation of markets. In normal times, additional cross-asset, cross-market and cross-currency opportunities have exponentially developed the size of potential correlation matrices. In crisis times, one could think that the hunt for cash is made simpler due to the higher number of opportunities, but in reality the multiplication of investments have just made markets more shallow overall – if not completely illiquid in many cases. As a result, flights to quality, liquidity crunches and fire sales have been increasingly sudden and drove entire countries to the brink of bankruptcy, as in Asia in 1997, Russia in 1998 and Iceland in 2008.

If correlation shifts are by nature unpredictable, risk managers can try to detect regime boundaries, the inflexion point at which a market tilts into another regime. Since correlations are liquidity-driven, a good monitor would analyse a possible contagion effect whenever an isolated market shock occurs. For example, if a particular equity market crashes, the analysis should focus on the overall market leverage (margin trading, collateral) and on the funding sources (institutional, retail, foreign, other markets, etc.).

Correlation shifts in high-volatility markets are not only market crashes but can arise from rallies as well. In such cases they are driven by multiples, as an element of diversification. For example, when gold rallies and is perceived to be expensive, yet a risky bet, although still in uptrend, investors may resort to silver. At this point the correlation between both precious metals will be high. When both trends reach a peak and markets start to hover at the high price for some time in low volumes, then the variables are likely to diverge. One day one metal breaks downward, investors start cutting their losses or covering their long positions in emergency and may be forced to sell the other metal. Correlations will get tighter again, but they are usually asymmetric;

---

[4] F. Allen and D. Gale, Optimal financial crises, *Journal of Finance*, 53, 1998.

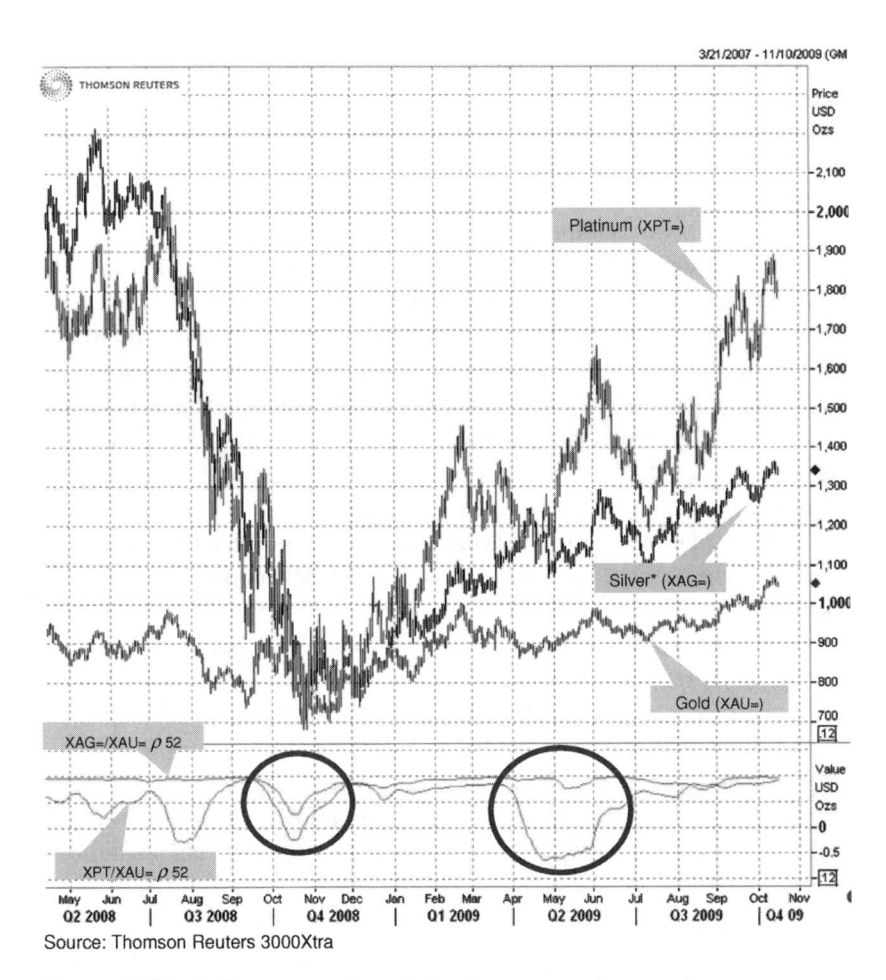

Figure 19.17 Daily moves and correlations between precious metals

they may not form in the same way, with the same implications and contagion effect on the way up as on the way down. Longin and Solnik[5] demonstrate that unexpected returns due to correlations (exceedances) are much more important when they are negative than positive (see Acharya and Schaefer).

The charts in Figure 19.17 exhibit daily moves in precious metals, platinum, gold and silver. The subcharts exhibit 52 period correlations between gold and platinum and gold and silver. The charts confirm

---
[5] F. Longin and B. Solnik, Extreme correlation of international equity markets, *Journal of Finance*, 2001.

the empirical evidence of important correlation drifts in times of trend reversal. However, it is clearly in times of fast correction downwards that the drifts are the most sudden and deeply pronounced. In times of steady growth, on the other hand, correlations strengthen and converge.

Our proposed methodology is to set a special earmark for all instruments and especially those that depend on correlations of any sort for their calculations as well as cross-currency instruments with volatility as input (as the cross-currency volatility is defined by the correlated volatility of each currency). In most cases the most severe liquidity shocks occur where the rise was the most dramatic and in spheres to which the most liquidity was driven. The market typically turns from excess liquidity to severe drought as leverage plays adversely, emotions are high and portfolios have overweighed those particular assets. It is therefore by monitoring liquidity concentrations and cross-asset, cross-market correlations during market rallies that the risk managers can better anticipate the tilting point and where the next bubble burst is most likely to turn into a liquidity crisis. Then, by observing the correlation shifts of the past, one can try to anticipate the correlation effects during the asset meltdown. This, to our knowledge, has never been done at an enterprise level. The disconnect is striking. Some traders at desk level may have this type of empirical hands-on approach while at mid-office or enterprise level correlations are only computed backward or implicitly modelled through stochastic simulations. Yet correlation estimations are so critical to hedging performance assessments, valuations and liquidity risk management.

From a purely statistical point of view one should be very careful with the covariance history selected to compute the coefficient of correlation. The most usual way is to choose a year of 252 trading days of history – an arbitrary choice that in itself influences conclusions significantly. In our proposed methodology the parameters should not be defined for technical or statistical convenience but based on real investment purposes, as discussed in Part 2 with respect to volatility calculations.

19.8 FUNDING STRATEGY IS A RISK PROFILE

Managing risks must depart from implementing uniformity as a strategy. In the particular case of liquidity risks such departure is absolutely compulsory. As an ultimate manifestation of operational risk, liquidity issues necessarily occur differently at each firm, depending on their

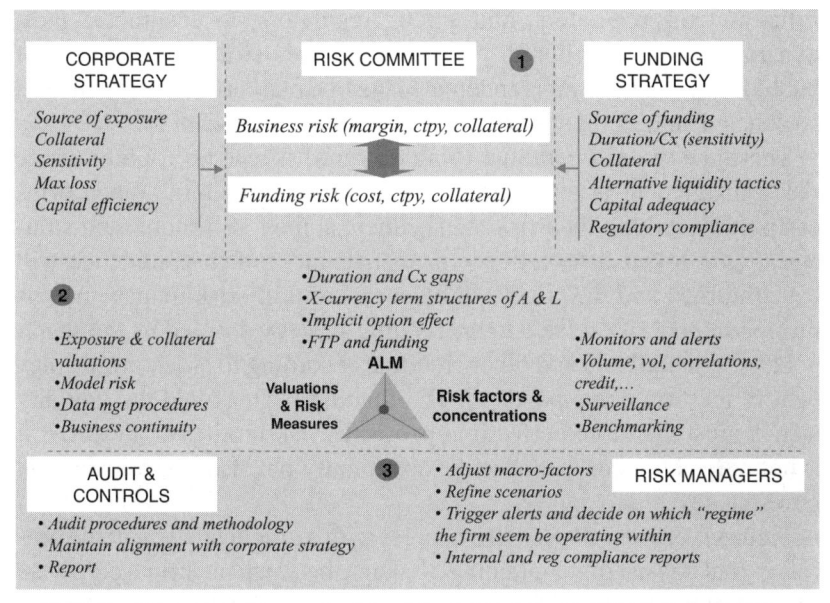

Managing and Mitigating Liquidity Risks

CORPORATE STRATEGY	RISK COMMITTEE ①	FUNDING STRATEGY
Source of exposure *Collateral* *Sensitivity* *Max loss* *Capital efficiency*	*Business risk (margin, ctpy, collateral)* *Funding risk (cost, ctpy, collateral)*	*Source of funding* *Duration/Cx (sensitivity)* *Collateral* *Alternative liquidity tactics* *Capital adequacy* *Regulatory compliance*

②

- *Exposure & collateral valuations*
- *Model risk*
- *Data mgt procedures*
- *Business continuity*

Valuations & Risk Measures

- *Duration and Cx gaps*
- *X-currency term structures of A & L*
- *Implicit option effect*
- *FTP and funding*

ALM

Risk factors & concentrations

- *Monitors and alerts*
- *Volume, vol, correlations, credit,...*
- *Surveillance*
- *Benchmarking*

AUDIT & CONTROLS	③	RISK MANAGERS
• Audit procedures and methodology • Maintain alignment with corporate strategy • Report	• Adjust macro-factors • Refine scenarios • Trigger alerts and decide on which "regime" the firm seem be operating within • Internal and reg compliance reports	

① The funding strategy mirrors the corporate strategy in terms of sought exposure (risk factors), sensitivity type (duration and convexity of assets and liabilities, acceptable leverage and maximum losses. Capital efficiency is a performance indicator, no longer the main purpose of enterprise.

② A balance between funding and business risk characteristics is maintained through a 3 pronged approach involving asset liability management (ALM), valuations and operational risk management and extensive market and sensitivity surveillance through sensors, monitors, alerts,

③ The Risk Committee monitors the sensitivity indicators and gaps in addition to sensor and alerts set up to detect in which type of markets or 'regime' the firm is operating. Alternative funding, collateral and liquidity tactics are pre-defined in case of regime changes.

Figure 19.18 Funding strategies and liquidity tactics to mirror the risk profile

business, customer base, preferred funding channels and their regulatory framework.

Liquidity risk prevention strategies require the firm to be agile enough to manage the unexpected rather than processes and model-based reporting. Managing liquidity risk consists of raising awareness, understanding and monitoring exposure, and analysing risk concentrations inside the company and outside with the rest of the market. Once the firm is in a position to benchmark its own exposure concentrations, it can design alternative courses of action and communicate the whole process internally and externally, to seek alignment with the risk policies and consensus agreements.

This takes more than a project implementation. It necessarily relies on a culture of risk management, established at all levels of the company's hierarchy. It requires continuous exchanges of information between the firms and the regulators, and among regulators, to ensure the most dynamic response to liquidity issues when they strike. The process of bubble *inflate-and-burst* is endemic to the free market economy in liberal societies. Bubbles do not happen to burst, they are meant to.

The industry will continue to morph until it reaches a point where risk management is repurposed into a corporate culture. When firms can proudly exhibit their risk management at the forefront of their strategies, as a token of excellence in management, then confidence will have returned and the crisis will be over. Liquidity risk management is the operational risk related to the funding strategy decided by the shareholders, bondholders and other creditors according to a risk profile they believe the firm corresponds to. The funding strategy and the liquidity tactics must therefore perfectly mirror such risk profiles at all times. It is not only about ensuring business continuity but also about ethics and governance.

Figure 19.18 summarizes the chapter with a graphical view of the processes that consist of maintaining a balance between the firm's corporate strategy and funding tactics.

Part 5
External Communications, Disclosure Policies and Transparency

Executive Summary

This part proposes to support the new culture of risk management with a culture of transparency. Through a communication policy focused on the values of risk management, financial institutions will lead their clients, partners, shareholders and regulators towards a next level of trust, achieved through transparency. This is a major departure from today's typical communication and public relation strategies, which tend to sell financial services like any other consumer product.

Of course, the information disclosed is not identical, depending on the audience. To the industry and the regulators, for example, the policy of communication should focus on the internal structures of risk, in particular all forms of exposure and liquidity concentrations and cross-currency gap analyses. In our proposed methodology, a particular effort is made to communicate details of valuation processes and explain how they reflect the risk policies of the firm. This particular aspect has been a weak link in the past, where sophisticated modelling was supported by questionable data. Similarly, high-level views of the macro-scenario used to describe adverse business conditions should be periodically communicated. With respect to innovation, we finally suggest that a side-effect analysis of financial instruments should be communicated, to enable the industry representatives and regulators to analyse their potential systemic effects.

Lenders of funds, collateral or bondholders are less interested in the potential impact of the risk management structures on the sector but even more on potential internal issues. A special emphasis should be made for them on disclosure of current balance sheet structures under scenarios. In other words, banks should explain how they finance which assets and how they intend to keep doing so in the eventuality that their worst scenarios would materialize.

Finally, the public, bank clients and fundholders deserve a special communication effort based on risk and transparency. The customers of financial institutions have been too often assimiliated into product consumers with respect to the communications they receive from banks and asset management companies. Whenever they asked for details about the banks' management they would be given shareholders' information. In the future, they will value accuracy and transparency rather than pure marketing. They will need to know rather than dream. Regulatory entanglements have created further opacity that banks and asset management companies can start to clear individually as a token of respect for their clients and to enhance their loyalty.

Later in this part we propose methods for transparency enhancement, in particular with respect to valuations of illiquid, exotic and structured (hard-to-value) products. The approach consists of breaking down complex products into parts where satisfactory levels of transparency can be maintained. This future proofing methodology ensures that such transparency can be maintained in spite of relentless product innovation.

Finally, we propose an innovative course of action and endeavour to enhance the transparency standards of the entire industry through new taxonomy and contributions bringing a risk perspective to prices.

An essential fact learnt from the 2007–2009 crisis is that risk should not be managed in isolation. We therefore propose interbank exchanges of exposure information, under a nonconfidential format, so that the entire sector can better evaluate the global risks of counterparties and the real value of collateral. Added to the improved taxonomy, we define a risk intelligence network that should be maintained by the industry and supported by the regulators.

The third pillar of the Basel framework (Basel 2) focused on the supervisory process and market discipline, essentially achieved through a transparent disclosure policy. Article 809 of the Basel Accord[1] (given below) summarizes the guiding principle:

> 809. The purpose of Pillar 3 – market discipline – is to complement the minimum capital requirements (Pillar 1) and the supervisory review process (Pillar 2). The Committee aims to encourage market discipline

---
[1] New Capital Accord, The Basel Committee's proposals of 16 January 2001.

by developing a set of disclosure requirements which will allow market participants to assess key pieces of information on the scope of application, capital, risk exposures, risk assessment processes, and hence the capital adequacy of the institution. The Committee believes that such disclosures have particular relevance under the Framework, where reliance on internal methodologies gives banks more discretion in assessing capital requirements.

The issue is that those guiding principles were never scrupulously followed. Of course there were disclosure policies and the websites of most Tier 1 banks are filled with risk management reports and remarks about the nature of their activities. When the bubble burst with the subprime crisis in 2007, the liquidity crunch of 2008 and the meltdown of 2009, the world discovered that large diversified financial institutions were not even aware internally of their total risk exposure and reliance on models with large operational risks. By setting up a system of incentives purely focused on a 'carrot and stick' approach, and as all the financial incentives were based on Pillar 1 (capital requirements) anyway, the Basel Committee turned itself into a rule book, departing from its coaching function to guide the industry towards sound risk management principles. Compliance to disclosure requirements was another regulatory to complete, no more.

The proposed framework now elevates transparency and communications to the level of a strategic corporate goal. The word communication replaces disclosure because it is really an exchange of information that needs to be set up in order to create a productive and reliable workflow. In the previous chapters we have explored in detail how to set up an internal information workflow for risk to be truly understood and proactively mitigated throughout the enterprise – no longer an obscure science confined to an ivory tower of quantitative analysis. What we ought to do now is to create a similar workflow from the inside to the outside of the firm and back. The goal is again to share the understanding of risk exposure and mitigations with the firm's shareholders, customers, partners and regulators. In the aftermath of the most serious post-war financial crisis, we see huge value in external communications of risk policies and mitigation methodologies, a low hanging fruit that could really contribute to restoring confidence to the markets.

20
External Communications

There is value in communicating the details of a risk management framework. Ironically, the more that is disclosed on how risk is managed, the less proprietary information would have to transpire.

Most bank communication messages (commercials and advertisements, for example) are either about stability or performance. Some would stress how long they have been in business – leading to an implicit assumption that they might be around for at least as long. Others declare themselves champions, either in bringing performance or for their capacity to operate smoothly. These messages, however, are seldom supported by anything else than nice pictures or scenes crafted by professional actors performing in studios set up for suggesting the proper feelings. Wouldn't it be better to explain how the firm expects to outperform the markets or the competition? Wouldn't it be more reassuring if they could explain what makes them feel so confident that they can weather all crises for another 100 years or more? This is not to suggest that bank TV commercials should become risk management lectures, but a new tone of communication, based on mutual understanding of a risk appetite, with a focus on respect for the trust of the customers, shareholders and bondholders have put in a particular bank or asset management company, could go a long way towards enhancing loyalty and performance.

In addition, transparency would pay for itself. A question that has not been raised in the previous chapters explaining how to implement a culture of risk management throughout the enterprise is the cost of the operation. Involving all people at each level of the hierarchy, taking time to discuss risk factors and scenarios through an iterative process, creating a new workflow of information involving IT, reviewing the integration of systems, data sources and models, setting up triggers, alarms and rehearsing the alternative process, notwithstanding all reporting and documentation, is by all means a costly exercise. Yet it is an endeavour with the highest level of strategic importance as it rebalances the very purposes of a firm, between capital efficiency and risk taking. So why not articulate it? Why not claim to the outside world, regulators, clients and shareholders that the firm operates under a culture of risk management that is by far more secure than any sort of expert predictive modelling or surveillance framework? If the firm manages to convince the outside world that risk management is now part of its DNA, then the public would have no doubt regarding the ability of the firm to adapt to change and thrive in most environments. How can this be achieved?

20.1 RISK, THE NEW MEDIA

A crisis represents change. New perceptions, new rationales instigate new behaviour. People think and act differently. The current crisis, started in 2007, is more likely to be remembered as part of history as the starting point of a journey towards a new macro-economic order. In the new order, risk management would have become more than a set of practices designed to accompany a corporation towards its economic objectives. Risk will become a media of communication.

Firms will use risk management to communicate their purposes, their philosophy, their skills and expertise, as well as details of their operations. However, firms will also use risk management as a media to receive information from the outside. As previously stated, the difference between disclosure and communication is that the latter is a two-way flow of information. Therefore, in the new order, risk is a language. It is used to receive instructions as much as giving feedback. It is used for benchmarking, performance measurements and forecasting.

Communicating on risk management, for example, could consist of providing answers to the following questions. What are the key risk factors the bank has chosen to expose itself to? How does it understand their sensitivity? What does it expect the maximum losses to be? Under which circumstances could that happen? How does the firm mitigate risks in order to remain within those boundaries? What makes the management confident that losses cannot exceed the maximum? How are risk responsibilities distributed? What type of training is performed? What are the skills of the key risk managers?

In 2008, for example, a new CEO was appointed at Merrill Lynch. Newspapers reported that one of the key criteria for the choice had been the risk management skills of this manager. The next step would have been to give details of his credentials. What were the past achievements of this person in terms of risk mitigation or for establishing risk frameworks, in which circumstances did he prove himself so particularly skilful, etc.?

Risk should also become a conduit of communications between the regulators and market participants. For the relationship to be more productive than it has been in recent years, there needs to be a continuous exchange of information across the industry, among the participants and with the regulators. Guidelines and controls are one-way communications. Other sectors of activities with a strong focus on risk management, such as the prevention of pandemics, wildfire fighting or the aviation industry, for example, have developed frameworks to gather risk intelligence and better predict issues before they occur. Regulators and participants continuously exchange intelligence to help identify in which 'regime' and overall level of adversity they operate, to analyse the potential side effects of products or action taken, to define the industry benchmarks, to educate resources and to inform the public.

The finance industry has yet to progress to such a level of interoperability to build the foundation of a robust communication framework with the regulators. In Part 6, we examine in detail which type of information interchange would be possible and most profitable.

20.2 DISCLOSURE POLICIES

The risk information a firm needs to disclose obviously depends on the audience it is intended for. Sorted by order of decreasing granularity and details, there are three different groups to which information needs to be directed: the regulators and industry representatives, the shareholders and bondholders, and the public.

20.2.1 Communications directed at regulators and industry representatives

The type of information considered here should not be confused with regulatory disclosures, such as capital adequacy ratios, for example, which are mandatory and covered by the regulators themselves. The proposed approach is to look for risk intelligence; in essence, it is made of any type of information that describes the culture of risk management of the firm as it has been implemented.

20.2.1.1 Risk management structures

The first important element of the risk culture is clearly its foundations. Not only should the distribution of responsibilities and the accountability of each manager be explained but also the adequacy of the risk policies should be highlighted.

For example, a firm particularly averse to risk concentrations could decide that its overall financial exposure to a single macro-risk factor should never exceed 5 % of its total sensitivity and maximum loss. In such a case, the distribution of responsibilities should correspond to the aim for diversification. The information feedback should favour the distributed sensitivity and methods of computation. The stress tests and catastrophic scenarios must focus on circumstances where the exposure would unexpectedly reconcentrate due to spontaneous correlation build-up, for example.

On the contrary, a firm could have developed a culture in which a small number of executives are accountable for substantial levels of exposure, combining risk factors together. Concentration of responsibilities is not necessarily riskier than wide spreading. It is merely a management choice. What is important, however, is that the rest of the framework remains aligned with those choices. In the latter case, where accountability is concentrated on a reduced number of nodes, special emphasis must be made on transparency, model risk and business continuity, for example.

Figure 20.1 explains the impact of these choices.

20.2.1.2 *Exposure concentrations and portfolio effects*

Once the skeleton of the corporate culture has been exposed, the second important aspect to disclose in order to demonstrate a good command of risk controls is a snapshot of risk concentrations and of the potential portfolio effects.

The former is essential to managing risk and the management of concentrations has been extensively discussed in Part 4 especially. The important aspect at the stage of external communications is to be able to demonstrate the adequacy of the concentrations to the risk and business policies. In hindsight of the US real estate bubble burst, for example, a number of European banks found themselves exposed to either subprime mortgage or collateralized securities although they had absolutely no reason to seek this type of exposure in the first place, other than a search for easy profits and concerns about being outperformed by their competitors. This type of misalignment with the shareholders' expectations must be made impossible by the new approach to risk and transparency.

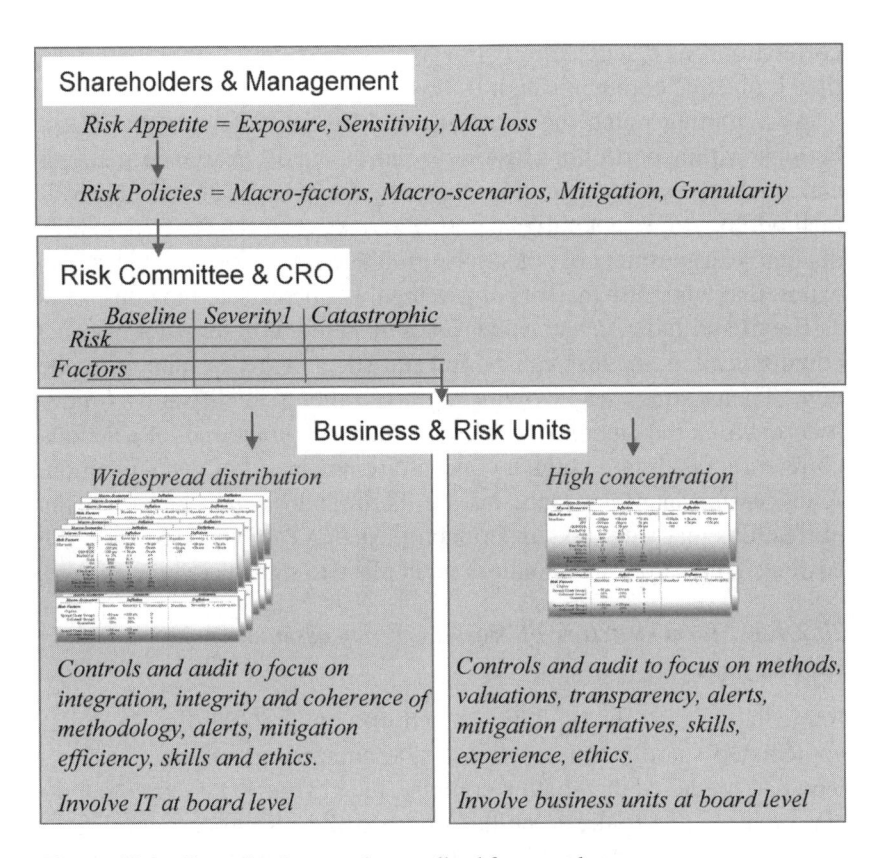

Figure 20.1 Centralized versus decentralized frameworks

To achieve a dynamic picture of risk concentrations, periodic reporting must emphasize concentration on risk factors and the changes over the period. Ideally, some industry benchmark would have been created by industry groups or regulators so that each firm could better assess their individual exposure to the bubble effect. In the absence of such a benchmark, firms will have to resort to individual assessments.

Dynamically monitoring concentrations involves a special focus on portfolio effects. Departments or divisions can be individually diversified but exposed to the same factor of sensitivity, for example if equity desks and fixed income desks are exposed to the same issuer. This type of concentration has been monitored in our proposed framework by the integration and aggregation of sensitivities, explained in Part 1. What is more difficult to predict is whether two or more independent risk factors can end up unexpectedly dependent due to some spontaneous correlations, as discussed in Part 4. If this secondary risk is important, then it must be communicated.

As a starting point, the firm can disclose the existing value distributions within portfolios, historic volatility and covariance matrices and stochastic simulations. This theoretical approach, close to the VaR methodology, does not mitigate portfolio risks yet it can be the base for a qualitative assessment of potential correlation risks. For example, a firm exposed to emerging markets of presumably uncorrelated regions, such as Brazil and India, can consider itself diversified. In terms of external communication, the firm can exhibit statistical evidence supporting the view. Then a stress test involving a global flight to quality and a liquidity crunch on the emerging markets could explain the risk of a sudden correlation resulting in higher concentrations instead of diversification. A discussion can take place on the likelihood of such an event, the mitigations that would be undertaken in such a case and especially the advanced indicators and monitors set in place to signal a regime change.

20.2.1.3 Term structure of cross-currency asset and liability gaps

Immediately after the liquidity crunch of autumn 2008, the US dollar appreciated sharply and steadily, to the amazement of some analysts who had predicted that, on the contrary, the US currency should depreciate sharply due to the combined effect of the current account deficit, monetary easing and lack of confidence. A few weeks later, the Bank of International Settlements (BIS) published statistics that indirectly explained the phenomenon.[1] It appears that, during the previous years of fast growth, the strategies that were commonly funded through the international banking network either consisted of alternative investments, financing emerging markets or securitized US real estate. In other words, the most usual strategies consisted of borrowing local currencies and lending US dollars. So when the interbank market turned dry, everyone found themselves short of dollars, especially when they had to unwind some exposure.

This type of imbalance was a surprise to the regulators, leading the Bank of England to express concern, as reported in the FSA consultation paper 08/22.[2] What the world actually discovered was a new

---

[1] *BIS Quarterly Review*, March 2009.
[2] FSA CP 08/22, *Strengthing Liquidity Standards*, Financial Services Authority, December 2008.

type of risk created by both the idiosyncratic imbalances within the term structures of cross-currency asset and liabilities and the systematic uniformity of cross-border strategies. The cross-currency term structures of asset and liability is therefore a piece of information that banks should dynamically communicate to their shareholders, their peers and their regulators. Regulators should communicate back the industry's concentrations.

20.2.1.4 *Economic capital and liquidity provision*

Although we did not mention it as a first item, economic and regulatory capital reports remain a necessity. In the proposed methodology, however, capital allocations are a very important tool for the risk management framework, but no longer the most essential one. Since the firm focuses on risk factor sensitivity rather than expected losses, the areas of risks can better be isolated and origin of losses they might potentially record can be more precisely located. Since the responsibility of mitigating risks has been distributed to business managers and division risk managers, liquidity provisions can be built locally and more accurately according to their loss provisions. Since the divisions have grown more agile in adapting their scenarios to external changes in the business environment and keep monitoring sensitivity alerts and triggering procedures under supervision of risk managers and the audit, they contain their losses within their own department, thus avoiding contagion spreading across divisions through failure to react timely enough. In traditional risk frameworks, each division is merely accountable for supplying the enterprise risk divisions with the necessary information to compute risk. Managers of the trading books or of loan collateral are involved in hedging but are sketchy in providing the resources potentially to mop up the damages resulting from unexpected losses. By contrast, a huge machinery independently gathers exposure and computes risk through predictive modelling based on stochastic distributions. When risk figures are available, they would need to drill down back to the origin of the risk and at first back-engineer the excessive exposure or sensitivity that caused the models to react. Obviously the whole process is much less agile than the proposed one and only reactive. It suffers especially from a huge disconnect between the day-to-day management of positions and hedges, and the ivory tower style of enterprise-wide modelling of risk and economic capital. It is this gap that our methodology proposes to narrow until there is an immediate reactivity between sensitivity drift and risk mitigation action. What must be communicated externally is the evidence that this gap has been made as narrow as possible. In external communications, the structures of the risk management framework should be described before the risk-weighted economic capital.

As a result, there is no longer a clear separation between economic capital requirements and the provision of liquidity to fund assets and positions regardless of duration. In the traditional approach, the disconnect described above and the obsessive focus on regulatory requirements resulted in a dramatic undercapitalization of most financial institutions. In the wake of the 2008–2009 liquidity crunch, regulators started to work on new requirements, such as liquidity buffers, considering liquidity risk as an additional standalone risk that had been overlooked in the past. It will take an excessively long time for them to define the liquidity buffer requirement and endless discussions as to how to build and maintain those buffers or which instrument to use. The reason is that no single firm has the same liquidity needs or definition of liquidity risk, alongside the next one.

In our proposed methodology the provision of liquidity to address potential losses, whichever part of the balance sheet they may be funded from, remains within the business divisions. The risk management departments coach and direct the process of preparing hedges for expected drawdowns and reserves for potential losses. They work with the Finance Department to gather the figures and determine Tier 2 capital versus liquidity arrangements by painting the aggregated picture of risk sensitivities based on duration and sensitivity, as described in Part 4. There is no longer any dogmatic view on how to allocate risk-weighted capital to exposure. The tactics are instead finely crafted to the very nature of exposure sensitivity and in the context of scenarios defined by the persons directly responsible. The granularity of capital requirements and liquidity buffer computations has been refined to the very levels where risk is created and managed. The culture of risk management is now fully active and deeply rooted in the day-to-day management of the firm's balance sheet.

In terms of external communication, the aggregated amounts allocated as economic capital and set aside for liquidity management based on expected and unexpected losses can be described next to the regulatory capital reports, which will now be used as benchmarks.

20.2.1.5 *Accounting methodology*

As discussed in Part 2 and Part 4, the accounting methodologies have an enormous impact on the valuations and assessment of risks and by repercussion on liquidity provisions. Since the proposed methodology suggests computing capital and liquidity buffers at the most refined granularity, the accounting methodologies should be reported as well so that additional refinement results in more transparency.

In Part 4 we have suggested that financial instruments and positions should be marked to value at frequencies that depend on the investment timeframe, thus reflecting the inherent liquidity and volatility status of the markets where they are traded or negotiated. It is therefore necessary to communicate details of these choices to the regulators and the partners of the banks and asset management companies who hold the portfolios.

The choices must also reflect the risk policies and the risk profile of the firm. For example, if a hedge fund or alternative investment fund holds arbitrage positions that are typically held for a few days or weeks, then the mark-to-value should be as frequent as possible. The positions will be disclosed as part of the usual compliance reporting in terms of assets under management and concentrations. We propose to add notions of the intended holding period and details of mark-to-value rules aligned with the strategy. The sources of information should also be disclosed, in particular contributed prices versus calculated positions. In the case of OTC valuations, disclosures should be given on whether there was any third party involved and if not as much detail as possible should be made known on valuation methodologies, algorithms, curves, etc.

For banks and any financial institution involved in mortgage loans, special attention should be provided to the valuations of collateral and how it fits the risk profile of the company. Mortgages and mortgage collateral valuation frequency should not depend on the intended duration of the transactions but on the duration of financing instruments. For example, if a bank funds 10 year collateralized loans with 3 month Libor rates, then the collateral and the credit-adjusted loan should be marked to value every 3 months.

20.2.1.6 Macro-scenarios

As stressed throughout Part 1 and Part 2, our proposed methodology relies extensively on scenarios, in particular for the purpose of stress testing and the preparation of potentially catastrophic developments or tail events. The reason emphasizes not on the fact that people's common sense is usually more accurate than models, but rather the fact that involving business managers in the definition of tail risk and maximum loss is the only way to make them feel responsible and accountable for the risks they create and manage. As explained, the combined views of all business and risk managers, their aggregated monograph of what they call catastrophe, is the living picture of the risk appetite of the company. It is their actual risk appetite, demonstrated day in and day out through their filed activities. As such it can be reconciled with the initial risk appetite desired and expressed by the shareholders and controlled by the regulators. The macro-scenarios of the firm, the spirit with which they are designed and the way they are used, are therefore critical information to communicate to the outside when the firm wants to describe its corporate risk culture. A description of the risk factors, rationale for their choice, scenarios considered to be baseline, high severity and catastrophe, are all outlines of the risk profile of the firm.

An important aspect of this communication is that it is not static but changes with time, depending on the external market conditions and on the internal pressure to which the company is subject. To some extent it also depends on the persons involved. In other words, the macro-scenarios are a real, dynamic reflection of the company's risk profile. They evolve with it and adapt as a part of its 'risk-DNA'.

20.2.1.7 Side effects, systematic and systemic impacts

Some industries, medication manufacturing, oil exploration, motoring technology, for example, are required to study the potential side effects of their products or services before being allowed to market them. Their innovations must be documented in terms of the purposes they are designed to serve and under which conditions they could become harmful. Before such disclosure becomes mandatory in the finance industry, the financial institutions themselves could endeavour to proceed with this type of analysis.

The analysis can be carried out at two different levels. First, the financial products, in particular the innovations, can be documented in terms of their purposes, market segment targets, cash flow and risk profiles. Second, the mitigation strategies can be envisaged in the case of tail events and under extreme market conditions.

In terms of financial products, most banks have already set up detailed explanations of retail structured products in particular, such as capital protected notes, reverse convertibles or the myriads of leveraged equity products enhancing the holders' market exposure under specific conditions. Although the information is certainly useful to product holders and distributors, there is little the regulators or the industry representatives can do truly to assess the overall impact the products might have on the industry, since it is the combined effect of structured products from multiple issuers that should be studied in terms of the externalities they might create.

For this reason, we suggest in Part 6 the creation of a nomenclature of structured products and multilegged instruments so that they can quickly be sorted independently of their commercial names and bespoke characteristics.

The second type of impact that should be reported and aggregated by industry representatives and regulators is the type of liquidity arrangement, position unwinding, cross-currency transactions or borrowing the bank could be led to undertake should some of its stress scenarios materialize. Since the bank has disclosed its macro-scenarios, with special emphasis on high-severity and catastrophic ones, it can give high-level views of its risk mitigation and contingency plans in case of tail events. Such information aggregated at the industry level would be a precious tool for the regulators in order to better understand externalities and prevent the propagation of tail events.

The confidential aspect of this is obvious. No bank, nor hedge fund, nor portfolio manager would be willing to unveil what it would trade and when or what risk was being arbitraged immediately. Here, as with details of financial products, the idea is not to disclose proprietary information. A generic description of a course of action is enough for the regulators to be able to measure the systematic and systemic impact of it. For example, a scenario can be described with a 'tail of 7 sigmas' on a currency. A firm need not disclose its position, neither amount nor direction, but it can indicate that in the unlikely occurrence of this particular event it might engage in FX swaps rather than interbank loans, for example. This piece of information, although meaningless to most and remaining only disclosed to regulatory authorities, can be important for the industry to aggregate with other firms of the sector. With a general view of what level seems to constitute an extreme market development for a majority of participants and an understanding of their most likely course of action should the markets turn to extreme volatility, the industry and the regulators would be in a better position to anticipate liquidity shocks and asset shocks.

20.2.2 Communications directed at shareholders and funding partners

The granularity of details communicated may be identical, as above, with the reports for peers and regulators, but the purpose and the spirit are really different. Previously, it was about communicating to what extent the firm complied with regulatory requirements and how to position it with respect to its peers within its industry. What shareholders and funders want to know is whether their capital is managed in respect of the risk mandate they have defined.

20.2.2.1 Actual versus observed risk appetite

It can be shown from the results above that thanks to the proposed methodology a firm would be in a position periodically to compare and reconcile its expected risk appetite with its actual risk profile. The more often this reconciliation can be communicated the more transparent the firm shall appear. Therefore the best possible strategy in a case of mismatch is to disclose the gaps, reveal their sources and describe what is being undertaken to address them, a time schedule for readjustment, milestones and controls.

The issue of compensations, which seems to be so acute according to news headlines, has not been extensively discussed in previous chapters, mainly because this issue is primarily a consequence of misaligning the risk appetite of the firm with its actual pace of operations. If some senior managers and traders have been 'misincentivized' it is essentially because the prime value of the corporate culture was solely capital efficiency. Shareholders who now discover that the sole pursuit of a return on equity has led them into markets or regions characterized by risks they had very little control over are actually realizing the mismatch and the lack of corporate policies defining the boundaries of risks.

Most embezzlements or abuses of the past, such as at Barings, Allied Irish or Société Générale, present the same base ingredients leading to disaster. At some point, the rogue traders were all very successful, leading their managers to close their eyes to some of their practices as long as fast returns kept pouring in. It is not necessarily about greed as in most cases the rogue traders did not steal anything and only indirectly benefited from the scheme. It is an operational failure that comes from the mismatch between the values rewarded and the values that should have normally resulted from balanced and clearly defined risk policies.

The manner in which adequacy is reported is first carried out through a description of the risk factors and macro-scenarios and their aggregation, as previously explained for disclosure to peers and regulators. In other words, the firm explains the sources of risks (risk factors) it chooses to expose itself to. Once the factors are clearly outlined, then the sensitivity can be discussed, leading to sensitivity limits and current limit utilization. Through this type of report, the external observers can immediately see the factors of sensitivity, appraise the limit levels and assess whether the firm remains within the defined boundaries or not. A very important piece of information at this stage is an audited history of limit utilization, so that the firm cannot drift away between periodic reports.

The proposed approach is a significant departure from the traditional one, where risks are presented under a regulatory inspired logic, regardless of the expectations of the shareholders. The description of risks is generally very short and immediately leads to VaR figures for market and credit risks. Special risks related to off-balance-sheet exposure, hedge funds, leveraged exposure and OTC exposure are highlighted. There is little room for specific disclosures or details based on the known expectations of the shareholders of a particular firm. In our new methodology, we instead approach by way of risk factors. Whether it is credit or market risks that is the main cause of concern is less important to nonspecialists than to know what the firm can lose due to its exposure to a particular risk factor. Therefore the content of stress scenarios is more important than the sophistication of predictive modelling.

20.2.2.2 *Capital adequacy and balance sheet structure*

The second most important piece of information for the shareholders is whether the firm is properly structured to weather the risk it is set to face. Economic and regulatory capital provide important information but they are no longer sufficient after the events of 2008 proved that a Cooke ratio was a very thin protection against tail risk. In addition to Tier 1 and Tier 2 capital, the entire structure of the balance sheet should be explained in terms of what types of risk events it can sustain. Most importantly, the firm should be in a position to explain how the balance sheet structure fits the risk profile of the company and the expressed risk appetite of the shareholders. For example, a firm may be poised to engage in businesses with leverage exposure, funded exclusively with short-term liabilities. The shareholders must then understand at which level of tail event the firm may cease to exist and validate their strategic choice. On the other hand, a firm with a prudent, risk-averse strategy may need to understand how its commercial margins and its balance sheets are immunized against market shocks on either side of the balance sheet. Clearly this assurance will be conditional on a range of market conditions that the shareholders need to accept. Defining those boundaries inevitably drives the firm to assess liquidity risk management and alternative tactics under stress scenarios.

20.2.2.3 Stress test capital adequacy and liquidity management

Traditional risk reports feature details of stress tests in terms of VaR and capital adequacy. In our proposed methodology, we suggest providing all details about the scenarios – how they impact the risk factors and the extreme sensitivity shocks they create. Plans for alternative liquidity risk management should be disclosed in detail as well, together with their own risk and operational uncertainty. The goal is not to pretend that any possible development in the Universe is known and can possibly be addressed. The aim is for the shareholders to understand the exact level of risk they take, what level of capital is required to keep the company afloat in times of adverse market conditions and what type of tactics they believe can be used in case of emergency.

The communication should therefore focus on the potential impact of the scenarios on multiple external factors. We have seen in Part 4 on liquidity risk management how externalities and systematic risk can potentially impact the firm from several factors at a time – say a run on deposit, collateral meltdown, haircut requirement and rising credit spread. This type of multivariate scenario can be defined as a 'regime' and the course of action that it would trigger can be described to the shareholders, seeking their feedback. The corporate culture of risk management now extends outside the firm's operations as the shareholders and funding partners are now involved in the discussion, progressively led to share the same culture.

20.2.3 Communications directed at the public

The public can be defined as the customers of a bank, the investors of a fund and all depositors of any type of collective investment schemes. We have dissociated them on purpose from the shareholders, who we believe require and deserve special attention. The public also involves the press and all media, which again have been dissociated from financial analysts for whom communications can be more focused on technical and economic issues.

What the public wants to know, in terms of risk management, is how safe a bank is or what the actual risk profile of a fund is. The public is also entitled to know the true pay-off profile of the products they hold, the legal frameworks in which they are actually engaged and how and when position valuations are carried out.

Communication services and public relations so far have sold financial services like any other products or services, by highlighting benefits and conveying images and feelings that lead to a belief that the institutions are safe and sound without directly stating so or elaborating on why they would be. There are many disclaimers typically attached in small print, but seldom any contraindication or any details of what the legal implications might be.

In the post-crisis era, financial institutions will realize that there are merits in transparency. Communications should become much more factual and descriptive of risks inherent to financial institutions. Business resilience should no longer be inferred but explained, if not demonstrated. Without going into too much detail, a bank of a fund manager can clearly state what are the guarantees in case of bankruptcy, the main risk factors the bank typically seek exposure to and, most importantly, some outline of the risk management framework and corporate governance ethics.

With asset management companies, there is even more room for transparency enhancements. First, many funds are sold in one country and managed from another, while the custody is carried out in yet a third legal environment. Do investors know where to appeal in cases of failure, mismanagement or embezzlement? Moreover, valuations have come under scrutiny in the wake of the Bernard Madoff case. Following the rush on alternative investment funds between 2003 and 2007, which resulted in the creation of hundreds of funds of funds or alternative investment portfolios within institutional investors' holdings, it appeared that regulated funds could in some cases hold unregulated assets. In some cases there was total opacity in terms of positions and valuations, and it may not always be possible to even know within which legal framework the positions are being evaluated.

The European regulation UCITS III[3] created more opacity by allowing funds to use OTC derivatives for investment purposes without clearly defining valuation and accounting rules. There is by definition an infinite variety of OTC instruments; therefore they seldom trade in liquidity levels allowing for screen-based prices to be used for

---

[3] The EU Directive UCITS (Undertaking for Collective Investment in Transferable Securities) are freely marketable within the EU. Directive 2001/107/EC is the Management Directive and Directive 2001/108/EC is the Product Directive of the European Parliament and the Council.

mark-to-market, as could be done with equity prices or foreign exchange contracts, for example. Thus, when the regulation requires appropriate risk management frameworks to be put in place as a condition for derivatives trading, without specifying precise requirements for valuations or even categorization of financial instruments, it hands over a blank cheque.

Obtaining transparent revaluation methodologies of OTC derivatives across the industry would involve an in-depth analysis of the instruments and categorizing them by sensitivity components. Since it is not possible to rule on valuation methodologies for each product based on models, assumptions and interpolations, it is necessary to dismantle them by category of exposure. For example, instruments can be classified according to their exposure to short rates, long rates, issuer credit, optionality, convertibility, capital protection, duration and more. We develop this suggestion in depth in Part 6, where we suggest possible ways forward for the regulators and the market participants to establish a constructive dialogue. When available, the level of exposure of each instrument by risk category would be among the key elements to be communicated to investors.

The European regulation MIFID,[4] by trying to protect investors with mandatory tests of investment suitability and appropriateness to be carried out by financial advisers, has actually exposed small investors further. While the tests can realistically be performed for high net worth individuals, there is no economic rationale to proceed with those tests for each and every client of a securities house or a broker. As a result, most of them asked their client to sign for the 'execution only' type of service – another MIFID arrangement – which waives all commitments to any sort of advisory service.

20.2.4 Public relations and disclosure policies

Whatever the audience might be – the industry, the regulators, the shareholders, bondholders and funding partners, customers and media – the financial industry needs to build a dialogue. A study of other sectors where managing risk is part of a core culture – pandemics, wildfire fighting, communications, aviation, just to name a few – shows that a commonality exists of a constructive exchange of information between

---

[4] MIFID Directive 2004/39 EC, the European Parliament and the Council, Article 47(2) TEC, Journal L145, 30 April 2004, pp. 1–44.

all participants, be it the regulators, the public or the market participants as an industrial group. Those sectors, as many others, are able to recognize different regimes of operation and communicate proprietary information to each other when a state of emergency requires it. They are able to build risk maps, a body of knowledge for further refinements in training and education. In brief, they have established a culture that they allow to evolve and adapt over time.

The finance industry, through a spectacular effort of transparency and communications, will need to learn to exchange information and communicate in a constructive way. The very first institutions who pioneer this type of communication will receive windfall profits for their audacious, refreshing and honest approach. This document will discuss later in Part 6 what type of information interchange it is possible to create between the industry and the regulators to enhance transparency in order to restore confidence. In other words, it is about creating a culture of risk management across the industry, using the same core principles that we have used for the corporate strategy.

Before reaching this point, it is necessary to redefine transparency.

21
Enhancing Transparency

'Sunlight is said to be the best of disinfectants; electric light the most efficient policeman' (Louis D. Brandeis, *Other People's Money and How the Bankers Use It*, 1914). Since the issue has been known for so long in the finance industry, how did it manage to remain the key factor of most crises, scandals and mismanagement and remain a key issue in the 21st century? Transparency (or lack of it) is the essence of the crisis that started in 2007. The rules are in place and virtually every single regulatory document, code of conduct, best practice guidelines from industry associations, corporate policies or company ethics statement promote transparency as a core value, a key ingredient for the success of the entire structure. Institutionally, from the International Financial Reporting Standards (IFRS) promulgated by the International Accounting Standards Board (IASB) to the rule books of the Financial Services Authority (FSA) or the Securities Exchange Commission (SEC), this preliminary condition will permeate throughout the industry with the ultimate goal of achieving transparency.

This particular issue is complicated by the fact that it strikes in various ways and from all angles. In reality, transparency is never a target definitively attained but a continuous effort to maintain enough intelligence within operations in order to describe them as they occur throughout processes. Transparency is the essential ingredient of confidence, which needs to permeate processes, prices, methodologies, corporate cultures, regulatory requirements, industry and national statistics. There are several aspects where the issue of transparency needs to be reviewed within the finance industry, specifically prices and valuations, internal processes and procedures, corporate governance and external communications, and intraprofession information exchanges.

21.1 PRICES AND VALUATIONS TRANSPARENCY

Is financial innovation the enemy of transparency? Ground-breaking innovation is precisely about exploring uncharted territories. It does make transparency a primary goal. Financial innovation often results from bespoke engineering for specific clients. Both the client exposure and the financial structure are highly confidential in most cases. Moreover, financial innovation leads to ever-increasing diversification. The multiplication of derivatives, structures, markets, execution venues and even geographies has been remarkable over the past decades, making the traditional definition and approach to transparency simply obsolete. Market price transparency has been defined in the 1960s and 1970s through connectivity implemented by data aggregators and distributors such as Thomson Reuters, Telerate or Bridge. The view was that having several brokers or exchange venues contributing their prices as frequently as possible would provide a fair value that was observable and recordable of the trading conditions for each individual instrument.

While this approach had been satisfactory enough to allow most of the financial theories, in particular the efficient market hypothesis (EMH), to thrive, it had reached clear limitations as soon as the 1980s. Clearly the above definition of price transparency is based on market liquidity. When securities multiplied, when trading exchanges mushroomed all across Europe and with OTC derivatives exchanges further stretching liquidity, it has not been possible to get enough evidence on price to claim that prices were transparent. Transparent prices are not to be confused with market depth or fair value. Price transparency is about being able to recalculate a price, recompute a valuation or backtrack all elements and contributions that have led to a particular figure.

When exchange-traded option prices are reported, for example, there is no transparency about the date and time at which the underlying prices have been traded. If the computation is based on a mid-price (average between bid and ask) based on the last known spread of an illiquid small capitalization that may not have traded in days, then the resulting option value is absolutely meaningless. What is even worse in terms of transparency is that even if there is a price it cannot be explained. When prices are evaluated using models, themselves based on curves, in turn based on interpolations and assumptions, then transparency is about recreating this long chain of transformations, not gathering prices produced by the models. Another issue is the range of available items. If it were at all possible to provide transparency for the prices of swaptions, for example, then it would not be possible to get quotes for all strikes and tenors, pay-off profiles and barriers, and special termination clauses, and in several currencies too.

To be able to maintain transparency across the ever-increasing range of financial products, a different approach is necessary. It may be

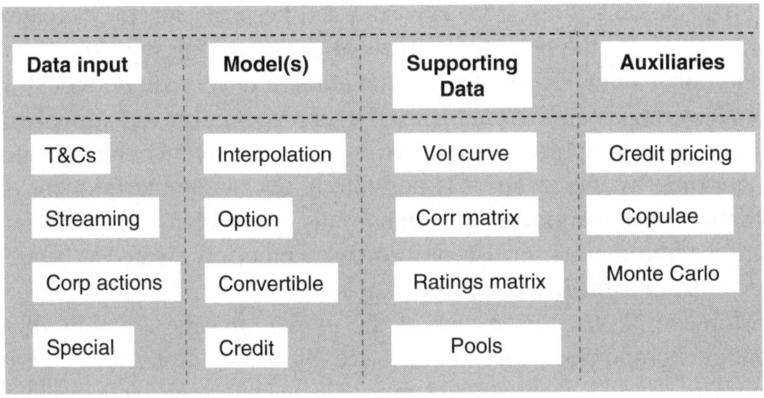

Data input	Model(s)	Supporting Data	Auxiliaries
T&Cs	Interpolation	Vol curve	Credit pricing
Streaming	Option	Corr matrix	Copulae
Corp actions	Convertible	Ratings matrix	Monte Carlo
Special	Credit	Pools	

Figure 21.1 Price mapping components

impossible to track all products available but it is possible to monitor the 'assembly lines'. Figure 21.1 maps the various components of most financial derivatives. They are all composed of an underlying instrument itself described by terms and conditions (T&Cs), corporate actions and in most cases some price input. Until this point transparency is possible. Then derivatives are either derived from models, such as options and convertibles, or from curves, such as interest rates swaps. When they are derived from models, the models are fed with underlying input or again with interpolated data such as curves, surfaces and matrices. Providing transparency at this stage consists of documenting what product is priced with what model, the curves in use, the values of variables utilized and the interpolation methodologies of the curves. Finally, complex or structured derivatives may use a nonexhaustive list of data such as stochastic simulations for Asian options, Gaussian copulae for credit structures and more. Here again, transparency lies in the quality and history of data supply and in documenting the pricing processes with details of data in use.

By breaking down financial derivatives into series of components for which it is possible to reach satisfactory levels of transparency, the entire financial industry would complete a giant leap towards restoring confidence and creating guidelines that do not damp the innovative spirit.

Another approach, currently discussed as a remedy to the confidence crisis, is to clear and settle OTC transactions through risk-free clearing houses. The view is that a clearing house should first of all be riskfree and that when prices are no longer discretionary within biparty transactions then they will be transparent. Both statements are dangerous sophisms.

First, clearing houses are as strong as the provision they create to compensate for the potential default of their clearing members. Since the notional amount currently in circulation of only credit default swaps (CDS) is roughly equivalent to the GDP of planet Earth, a clearing house of unheard-of proportions would be necessary. To reduce the risk borne at any time by the group, it is possible to accelerate the frequency of settlement and margining operations. This implies a massive standardization of the contracts in use, as those were precisely created as bespoke products tailor-made for specific exposure.

Moreover, given the origins of the market and the amounts of astronomic proportions that characterize the transactions, the clearing members would largely be the largest Tier 1 banks and securities companies with a vested interest in this market and exceptionally strong financial backbones to sustain the volumes. As their balance sheets are infamously stretched for the foreseeable future, government guarantees would certainly be necessary to instil the level of confidence that an undertaking of this magnitude requires.

Finally, what brought about the success of the world's oldest and strongest clearing houses, such as the one of the Chicago Mercantile Exchange (CME), is that products used for settlement are highly fungible. They can easily be swapped, exchanged or divided. The fundamental arbitrage rules are respected at all times, ensuring that the fair value of any instrument is the underlying plus a transparent cost of carry. It is unclear how this agility can even be approached with contracts such as CDS, even in their plain vanilla configuration.

In other words, through a laudable intention to bring transparency to the derivative markets, the regulators and the industry representatives may create an unheard-of risk concentration underwritten by governments with taxpayers' money again. Not only would the opacity of prices remain but the market would have to be substantially downsized and banned from further innovation to reach the required instrument standardization. In addition, systemic risks of epic proportions may arise from such concentration.

21.2 TRANSPARENCY OF INTERNAL PROCESSES AND PROCEDURES

The transparency of all processes linked to risk management is as important as figures and performance. Transparency had been one of the drivers in traditional risk management frameworks for modelling all sources of exposure, automating data management and risk computation, all straight through until the final reports of performance and capital allocation. The view is that if a process is automated and controlled electronically, then it is efficient and auditable – and hence transparent. The reality has been very different as the combination of financial modelling and electronic processes created entire spheres of a technocratic elite within corporations whose activities were unknown to most – even CROs and CEOs in some cases. Some firms might have almost split quantitative and qualitative risk management apart. Audit and controls would play their role of internal surveillance and integrity checks, but again that remains a remote concern to most people. Such separation of risk management and business activities has never shocked anyone. On the contrary, it was sealed in the principle of independence of risk functions. While the concept appears to be sound at first sight, the independent groups progressively learn to live and evolve separately until one day they end up with obvious cultural gaps. It is only when it is too late and when the unthinkable appears through embezzlement or massive failure that all entities are forced to communicate again and discover that risk processes had been mismanaged behind curtains of technology and opaque processes.

Our proposed methodology builds on an entire culture of transparency and communications. By involving the largest possible population into all aspects of risk management, we give transparency a chance to prevail on discrete, individual approaches. Processes are transparent when they are known and understood, when they can be traced, audited and explained. Processes will remain transparent if they are allowed to evolve with the firm and adapt to changing market conditions, staff turnover, mergers and acquisitions. Any crystallized process is obsolete from the moment of its creation. Electronically controlling the process does not make it more transparent but will sadly confine it to an even smaller group that understands both the process and the technology and access to related information.

Internal transparency is a prerequisite to external transparency. If we define internal transparency as the availability of clear, reliable, audited information throughout, then it is a mandatory condition to preparing concise and accurate information for an external audience. However, making information available is far from a transparent practice. On the contrary, information 'white noise' creates opacity. Therefore information must be shared and understood by all before being aggregated and communicated. It requires more than processes and rules to achieve this but an entire culture.

The proposed methodology therefore promotes the concepts of internal and external process transparency to the level of a corporate culture. In Part 3 we have proposed an enterprise-wide information workflow based on risk factors, exposure and mitigation in order to make the firm as agile as possible and minimize operational risks. As explained, it drives towards a 'risk bus', whether electronically or manually operated, where risk-based information gets a chance to be reconciled, checked and audited. This was to provide efficiency. Allowing internal and external recipients to freely use such information will foster transparency.

International organizations fighting corruption know as a guiding principle that transparency comes from 'voice and participation'.[1] As such, the culture of responsibility and participation we propose to build throughout the enterprise is much more important than the accuracy of predictive modelling. Being collectively transparent does not mean watching over shoulders and denouncing each other, but making sure that each person, department or division understands what the rest of the firm is doing and why. In our proposed methodology, each business manager responsible for activities that expose the firm to some risks is also responsible for the mitigation and reporting of risks as well as the internal transparency of the process.

For the firm to be transparent to the outside world in terms of its corporate governance rules and risk management processes, it needs to aggregate internally the information relevant to the key risk factors it has chosen to focus on and then communicate the reasons for these choices – figures with details of valuation methodology, control processes, depth or audit and history available, and all additional information that would add to the reliability of the disclosed information. The Risk Bus defined in Part 3 is key to extract this information. As it conveys components of risk calculations, such as haircut ratios of counterparties, for example sensitivity figures or credit spreads, it is always possible to know where a piece of information originates from and where it was used. It forms an enterprise-wide repository of risk intelligence, which is the foundation of transparency. Figure 21.2 highlights the process with some examples.

---

[1] Tara Vishwanath and Daniel Kaufmann, Towards transparency in finance and governance, The World Bank Draft, 6 September 1999.

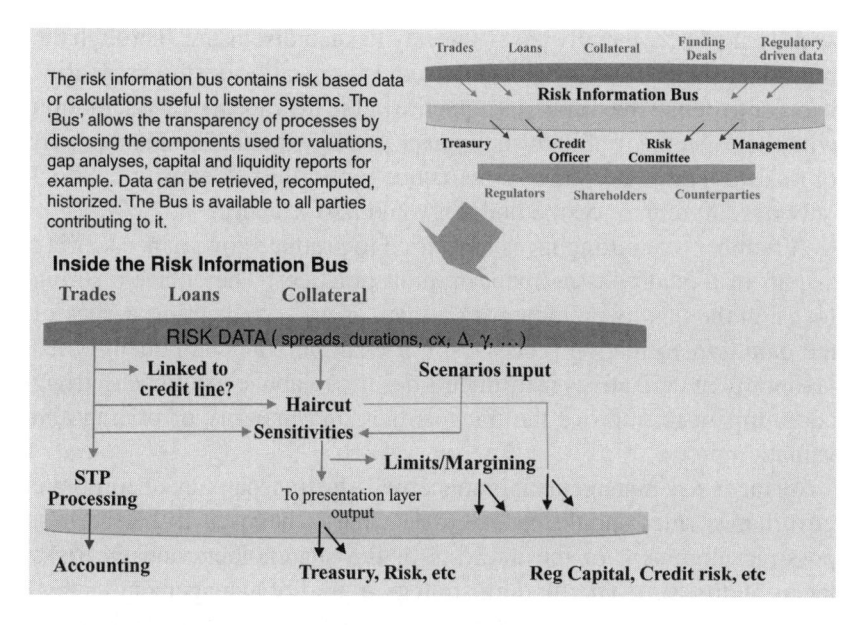

Figure 21.2 New age risk control and reporting framework

21.3 TRANSPARENCY OF CORPORATE GOVERNANCE RULES AND EXTERNAL COMMUNICATIONS

All listed companies and most unlisted corporations have a written code of ethics, some steering committees dedicated to corporate governance and detailed language about their code of practice. In most cases it is a pure communication exercise, an add-on to PR assignments, but the reality is totally detached from all this.

In large diversified groups especially, the roaring years leading to 2007 have seen a total disconnection between profit-generating activities, risk assessment and reports, strategic thinking and regulatory compliance. Rules such as the Sarbane Oxley Act of 2002 have attempted to change this but, again, the Act is a set of rules. Once compliance is technically ensured, there is no guarantee that the corporate governance rules will truly abide to that spirit. The only way is to align corporate governance with the corporate culture.

As a token of best practice, corporate governance rules related to risk policies should be disclosed with all supporting information as evidence of how the rules are enforced. The implementation of the new framework as described above really paves the way to such disclosure. Through the reporting of sensitivity by risk factors, the aggregation of stress scenarios in order to depict the actual risk appetite of the firm and the reconciliation with the expected profile formally expressed by the shareholders as part of risk policies, a corporate governance report on risk exposure would only need to remark on methodology and performance.

A number of auditing firms have tried to produce governance scoring as part of a quality assessment of audit practices. They place a strong focus on the quality and integrity of data as well as the transparency of the data transformation processes. For example, the component-based taxonomy of derivatives instruments described above would be a strong commitment to improve the transparency and integrity of pricing and valuation processes.

As far as risk management is concerned, the transparency of corporate governance rules should be based on what is believed to be the best possible alignment of the interests of the shareholders and the risks faced by the firm. The funding strategy, liquidity management tactics, risk mitigation tools and all key processes should be reviewed in this spirit.

22
Information Exchange for Risk Intelligence

The ultimate achievement in transparency is to be able to communicate risk-based information better among firms to harness exposure, detect rogue behaviour on the market and anticipate tail events.

There are many examples where cooperation and information sharing would help to prevent huge losses. Being transparent does not mean disclosure of proprietary information. Although most of the undertakings we explore below would involve the intervention of an unbiased neutral third party, it seems always possible to communicate through indices or ratios and keep information anonymous.

We propose in Part 6 a number of potential regulatory-driven possibilities to improve the overall efficiency and transparency of the financial markets. In this chapter, we only focus on what the industry or simply professional groups of economic interests can do themselves.

There have been calls for surveillance systems that would provide a potential lender with a view of the overall credit exposure of a counterparty. Prime brokers, for example, who finance hedge funds operating through several prime brokerage firms, would like to know the global exposure of their client for an accurate assessment of leverage ratios. Similarly, some national and regional European banking groups have expressed their need for a scheme that would provide them with a view of the total counterparty exposure each of their customer has not only with themselves but with their peers as well. Quarterly statements and balance sheet analyses are no longer dynamic enough in today's highly volatile business environment.

22.1 PROPOSAL FOR A GLOBAL CREDIT AND COLLATERAL EXPOSURE SURVEILLANCE SCHEME

The global focus on transparency and counterparty risk issues leads banks to think of a system for assessing the total exposure of their clients to all financial institutions, in order to measure their own marginal exposure to those clients better. The task is complicated by confidentiality issues. It is commercially and legally difficult for a bank to disclose and maintain information about their clients to their competitors. Technical complexities also arise from the necessity to combine trading and banking book exposures with trading and nontrading collateral that also involves intangible guarantees or covenants.

An unbiased independent risk aggregator can set up and maintain an anonymous repository of exposure, collateral and credit-related information for a selection of counterparties on behalf of a group of banks. An interactive real-time credit enquiry system will allow each participant to obtain system-wide exposure views for clients and measure the marginal impact of the deals or credit lines considered.

For the participating banks, the benefits are clear. They would better manage the risks or opportunities arising from clients' activities. For the banks' clients, corporates or fund managers, it is a demonstration of best practice and of their endeavour to enhance their own transparency. Regulators should be supportive of the scheme, which brings transparency, confidence and control on both sides. The main foundation of such a set-up is a membership charter establishing the rules of engagement, the responsibilities and accountabilities of each group: lenders, debtors, custodians and the independent risk aggregator.

The group of banks must select a number of customers who will accept an enhanced level of scrutiny and agree on a granularity of information provided. The banks will be able to optimize their credit lines, in exchange for which they would disclose their own customer exposure information. The accuracy of the information they provide and receive is absolutely critical. Information must be available on request at all times. The risk aggregator must commit to keep customers' information anonymous to the other banks.

Corporates and fund managers who chose to participate in the scheme obtain a higher level of confidence from their funding entities. The constraints of establishing this new bond with the financial community allows them to optimize their funding strategy and rely on a solid relationship. Amendments to their legal documents with the banks will be necessary to ensure the confidentiality of information provided and establish boundaries for using it. Working within the scheme does not preclude working outside of it. The credit lines within will be based on collateral within. Participants also commit to disclose additional exposure without the scheme.

Custodians need to participate in the scheme to provide collateral information and collateral value reconciliations. Through their participation they ensure themselves of privileged access to a community with an intense business relationship relying on trust and transparency.

The third party independent risk aggregator must commit to maintain accuracy, integrity and business continuity. In particular, the aggregator 'anonymizes' the information so that a bank would know the overall exposure of a client to all participants of the scheme without knowing the exposure to any of them.

In addition, the aggregator can provide an interactive inquiry and credit authorization system with the most accurate and up-to-date credit information and with real-time alerts based on credit events. Pledged collateral must be documented. Banks would provide for each client the sources and details of custodians who will provide the collateral type and value daily, weekly or monthly depending on the type of collateral. The aggregator keeps records of instruments pledged as collateral and of their value. Participants commit to inform the aggregator of the value of all other exposure they hold in books or in collateral.

A data aggregator can keep records of all counterparty data and monitor credit events to trigger alerts where applicable. On alert, it is possible automatically to freeze all limits to a particular issuer or counterparty.

Figure 22.1 describes the data-gathering workflow and the role of each group.

Once the multiparty aggregated information database is operational, the conditions are in place for an unmatched level of trust and transparency to support business and project management. In case of a credit event (default, downgrade, delayed payment) or in case of unusual changes in the spread value or volatility, the system can be set up to trigger alerts. These alerts can be simple messages sent through emails, the short message service (SMS) or instant messages.

22.2 PROPOSAL FOR A TAXONOMY OF PATH-DEPENDENT DERIVATIVES AND RETAIL STRUCTURED PRODUCTS

As proposed earlier with the breakdown of all opaque instruments in components where transparency is possible, the aim of the present proposal is to develop strings of generic expressions that can quickly describe the nature of complex financial products in terms of the type of risks to which they expose their holders. It is not about assessing

Figure 22.1

Banks contribute counterparty data
1-Limit allocations
2-Collateral value ❶
3-Leverage ratios
4-Max concentration

Risk Aggregator ❸
o *Mark positions and collateral to market*
o *Aggregates banking and trading books*
o *Receives collateral values from custodians*

Collateralized Exposure Datastore

❹

Custodians contribute collateral
1-Asset % allocations ❷
2-Leveraged exposure
3-Pledged collateral
4-Exposure to specific risk factors

Data Aggregator
o *Obtain credit events (downgrade, default)*
o *Aggregate credit news on counterparty*
o *Trigger alerts*

❶
Each bank contributes counterparty group exposures for a selection of clients with an agreed upon level of granularity
1-Total limit allocation
2-Ctpy exposure by asset class, currency, sector, time band
3-Collateral value, class, currency, duration
4-Max leverage (if applicable)

❸
The Risk Aggregator compiles and anonymizes the data, produces and publishes overall exposure views with changes and term structure

❷
Custodians contribute collateral and collateral value under agreed upon categories
1-Trading collateral (securities, commodities, ETFs)
2-Tangible non-trading assets
3-Intangible collateral (guarantees, covenants)

❹
The Data Aggregator monitors credit events, credit related news and data and trigger alerts automatically, with potential limit freeze if applicable

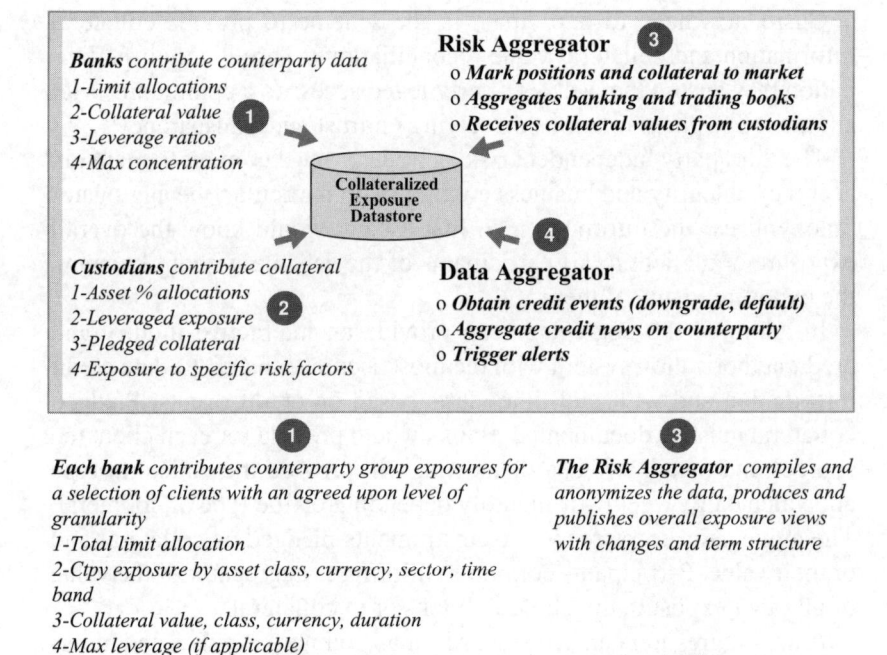

Figure 22.1 Building a system-wide net collaterialized credit exposure repository

whether a product is risky or not but to categorize it so that one can know what types of sensitivity the product is exposed to.

The second important goal of the new classification is to include countless OTC and structured products to existing taxonomies. Too often, products are called by commercial names, making them more difficult to record in back-office and settlement systems or to the warehouse in databases. The pace of innovation and diversity is such that even a gigantic catalogue of all products would be quickly obsolete. It is possible, however, to describe the products so that one can quickly categorize them and allocate them to the proper back-office and risk management channels for prompt clearing and better transparency.

The proposed taxonomy in Figure 22.2 describes the products in terms of market and legal risks.

Market	Duration class	Short/Medium/Long/Extended
	Coupon	Fixed/Variable/Minimum guaranteed
	Participation	Multiple/Full/Partial/Variable
	Principal protection	None/Partial/Full
	Convertibility	Auto/Dynamic/Periodic/Synthetic
	Path dependence	Callable/Auto/Barriers
Legal	Supervisory body	Bank/Securities/Exchange/Others
	Regulatory region	EU/US/Other OECD/Others

Figure 22.2 Products in terms of market and legal risks

In each category, a single term must be selected. Terms are mutually exclusive.

The first group, Market, categorizes the type of market risk one might expect and the type of back-office processing likely to follow a deal execution. The aims are to accelerate the allocation of products to the portfolios and to the proper processing channels and to allow for combinations of OTC and structured products with other products that might be processed straight through and electronically.

The second group, Legal, indicates the set of rules the instrument is expected to depend on and the regulatory region it normally emanates from. This is expected to help auditors verify valuations and valuation processes and to avoid unregulated products finding their way within the regulated portfolio.

22.3 RISK INTELLIGENCE RATINGS

Through better pricing and more transparent information, all market participants, including investors, companies and ultimately the markets, could better assess their risks and returns. The multiplication of financial instruments and pricing sources and the fragmentation of liquidity pools have created more opacity than market efficiency. Whether they appear on screens or not, prices and valuations are only valid for the market depth and liquidity they represent. As a result, valuations must be seen in perspective. Prices need to be qualified based on liquidity and transparency.

Issues related to valuations have had a deep impact on risk management and market liquidity during the crisis. Market participants voiced concerns that some valuations had triggered margin calls and haircut adjustments or hit path-dependent instruments unnecessarily. However, pricing the same instrument differently depending on its use would obviously not be realistic and would certainly not make the markets more transparent.

We propose to create 'risk classes' in order to qualify the reliability and transparency of all market quotes, which will also allow instruments to be sorted according to their level of transparency or 'valuation risks'. Then, the valuation risk classes can be used to adjust the pricing frequency of instruments to best suit their levels of transparency and market liquidity.

22.3.1 Valuation risk ratings

The so-called 'hard to value' instruments greatly depend on the underlying assumptions and on the models they are based on. The emergence of new markets, sometimes based on unregulated sectors or simply within different legal frameworks, also calls for a different approach on prices. In other words, the financial markets have reached a new definition of 'efficiency'. Price contributions need some context and perspective to help assess the valuation risk they bear. By attaching 'risk ratings' of four different classes to each price contributed by market participants, the industry would bring perspective to prices and valuations.

The financial instrument allocated to customer portfolios would subsequently be described in terms of the risk factors that may impact their value, their pricing frequency and methodology and the level of transparency that it is possible to achieve. Financial instruments can therefore be sorted by 'risk classes', in addition to asset classes or execution networks. The risk classes are defined depending on volatility, depth/liquidity, the availability and accuracy of news and data referring to the instrument (see Figure 22.3).

22.3.2 Risk-based pricing frequency

The general view is that each instrument allocated to a client portfolio or a fund or pledged as collateral should be marked to value at an agreed

Price	Risk class	Rating
	A: Depth/Liquidity	0 to 5
	B: Quotation frequency	0 to 5
	C: Typical slippage	0 to 5
	D: Spread/Price volatility	0 to 5
	E: News/Data availability	0 to 5

Figure 22.3 Chart of the valuation risk classes

upon frequency depending on the investment timeframe. A hedge fund holding some securities for a few days, for example, should not use the same mark-to-value rules as a closed-end fund holding it for several years. However, pursuing this logic would quickly lead to extreme situations, such as securities pledged as collateral priced differently from those in the portfolio they are held for, or if OTC products were valued with different models depending on declared purposes.

Since it is not possible to price similar assets differently depending on investment horizons and risk policies, we suggest adapting the valuation frequency to the valuation risk classes defined above. Thanks to this classification, the choice of instrument by the portfolio managers reflects the risk policies. This also simplifies the task of the market regulators who can refine their policies based on the risk ratings of instruments, as it is already done with counterparties, for example.

Figure 22.4 describes the process and the build-up of consensus-based valuations obtained through consultations between the market, the regulators and the providers of financial data and information.

Some instruments can be directly marked to market due to their liquidity, market depth and duration regardless of the timeframe and

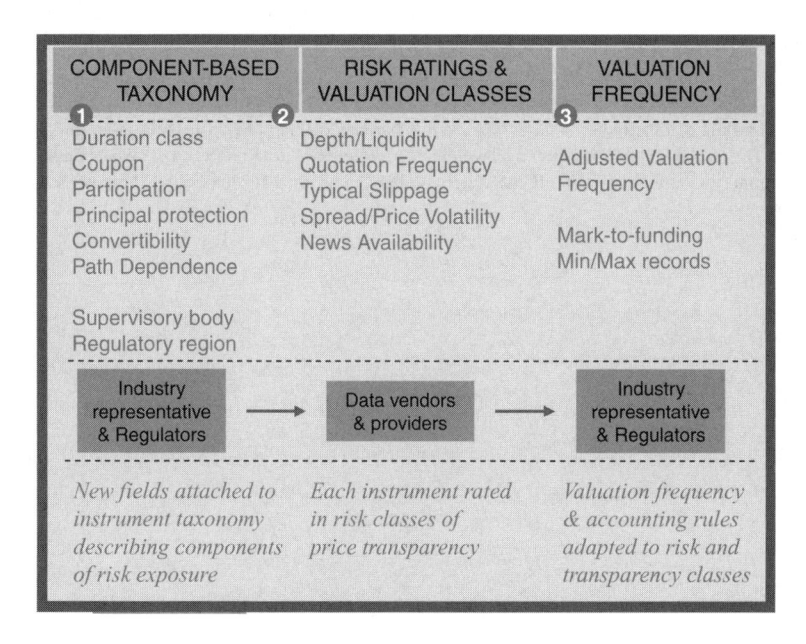

COMPONENT-BASED TAXONOMY	RISK RATINGS & VALUATION CLASSES	VALUATION FREQUENCY
❶	❷	❸
Duration class Coupon Participation Principal protection Convertibility Path Dependence	Depth/Liquidity Quotation Frequency Typical Slippage Spread/Price Volatility News Availability	Adjusted Valuation Frequency Mark-to-funding Min/Max records
Supervisory body Regulatory region		
Industry representative & Regulators →	Data vendors & providers →	Industry representative & Regulators
New fields attached to instrument taxonomy describing components of risk exposure	*Each instrument rated in risk classes of price transparency*	*Valuation frequency & accounting rules adapted to risk and transparency classes*

Figure 22.4 Providing risk intelligence for transparency

risk policies of the instrument holders. Some others, the prices of which can vary considerably based on external factors, would be better evaluated through the 'mark-to-funding' approach.[1] Finally, some assets may rarely quote and little information about them or their issuers ever transpires due to the legal frameworks they operate within. In such cases, data vendors can historize minimum and maximum quotes, leaving each operator the freedom to price themselves within a bracket according to their policies.

The proposal consists of adding risk characteristics to the taxonomy of financial instruments, followed by gathering a consensus opinion with respect to the transparency and market depth behind each valuation. Finally, the pricing and mark-to-value frequencies and methodology can be adapted to the risk, sensitivity, transparency and liquidity of instruments.

One key benefit of the proposal is to encompass all financial instruments that exist or will exist in the future, regardless of asset classes, exchange venues, complexity or nature. At the same time, the methodology is a true consensus-building process between the main professional groups of the finance industry, banks, buy-side, information providers, execution venues and regulators. Data vendors and media, as neutral players, are useful in aggregating the sentiment expressed by market participants.

---

[1] Markus Brunnermeier, Andrew Crockett, Charles Goodhart, Avinash D. Persaud and Hyun Shin, *The Fundamental Principles of Financial Regulation*, Geneva Reports on the World Economy, Preliminary Conference Draft, ICMB International Center for Monetary anad Banking Studies, 2009.

Part 6
The Regulatory Upheaval of the 2010s[1]

Executive Summary

Building on the recommendations for an industry-wide culture of transparency, this part proposes ways forward for the regulators to address issues related to idiosyncratic, systematic and systemic risks.

The baseline is to acknowledge that the very principles underlying the current regulatory frameworks are no longer suitable for the size and main characteristics of the economy. The foreign currency 'balance sheet' of the G7 banking systems grew ten times over by the time Basel 2 was discussed and implemented in a few countries only. Moreover, Basel 2 set the example for other industries to follow, which they did, while many bridges were simultaneously built between asset classes and industries as a result of repealing the Glass–Steagall Act of 1932. The regulatory entanglements resulting from these parallel endeavours have created a web of complex and opaque rules, which in a best case scenario will be revealed as unproductive but could as well lead to chaos if the markets are again seized by panic.

We propose to extend the very principles of the corporate risk management culture to the financial sector as they can be leveraged by regulators to foster an adaptive and agile macro-prudential oversight system. As usual, our philosophy hinges on transparency and dynamic exchanges of information.

With regard to idiosyncratic risks, a crucially missing link is a concentration benchmark that would let any firm assess their own concentration risks against those of the sectors they operate within. The regulators would in turn monitor the creation and inflation of 'asset

---

[1] This part refers to and elaborates on an unpublished White Paper by Philippe Carrel, 'Journey to a new regulatory model'.

bubbles' before they burst. The production of such a benchmark would be based on industry contributions to a central aggregator who would receive, anonymize and categorize the data and produce an industry monograph of asset concentrations. A similar undertaking can be set up for the term structures of asset and liabilities in foreign currencies.

Systematic risk also depends to a large extent to industry insights on concentrations and opacity. Asset bubbles are typically known at industry level but little is done to prepare the sector for their bursting or to control their growth. We propose sets of industry-wide communication schemes leading to variable capital adequacy ratios, more likely to scale with the volumes and volatility of today's markets. Most importantly, we recommend departing from a capital-only approach to risk and from assessments purely based on market-based information.

With respect to systemic issues, there is a contradiction between the creation of standardized norms and the management of risks. Diversity mitigates risks. Uniformity concentrates them further. The creation of standard capital ratios and the uniformity of methodologies to compute them and of the tactics designed to address the issues that might arise creates systemic risk every step of the way. In addition, the consultative process usually adopted by regulators to design and implement new language and implement decisions is ridiculously unsynchronized with the pace of the financial markets. It took 10 years to discuss and refine the mere guidelines of Basel 2 while in 5 years the credit default swap (CDS) outstanding notional grew to equate to the GDP of the planet. It is not the duty of the sole regulators to address this issue. The entire industry, including buy-side and sell-side participants, their representatives, policy makers and even third parties, such as consultants and data vendors, should participate and contribute to the regulatory effort. We propose in particular dynamic exchanges of information related to risk exposure, sensitivity, capital structure and the investment timeframe. It is especially important that the information contributions, scenario building and simulations are carried out across industries. In the absence of a formal language to specify the boundaries of cross-market engineering and regulatory assignments clearly, the industry will be left to consider the potential impact of systemic risks on the entire finance industry and on the economy by repercussion. This is likely to lead to downsizing the largest diversified conglomerates.

23
The Great Unwind

A growing economy inevitably generates imbalances. In times of growth they are called opportunities. When the cycle reverses, they are described as excesses, disorderly practices or asset bubbles. The role of regulators is not to distinguish the 'good from evil' or to police the system. Regulators should observe good practice, format it and translate it into models understandable and implementable by all, in the context of their specific national, legal and cultural environments.

23.1 REGULATORY RESHUFFLE

Legislators and regulators inherited from the 2007–2008 crisis a unique opportunity to correct the distortions and to shape the future of the world financial system. The reforms need to restore confidence in the system as a whole, while maintaining market innovation, so that credit is available to businesses and individuals and global growth can resume. At the same time, regulations need to move beyond simply preventing a reoccurrence of historical events, by providing the ability to identify and resolve future issues.

Around the world, the regulators' main challenges are to:

- define regulatory boundaries for the financial institutions to operate and control their risks while allowing enough freedom for them to prosper and innovate;
- ensure the diversity of hedging strategies and techniques to control systematic risks and maintain enough independence between business sectors to prevent systemic risks in the future;
- federate regulators' efforts around the world to ensure a coherent yet diversified approach to impede durably systemic risks challenging growth and globalization.

The proposals from the US Treasury,[1] the EU undertakings based on the de Larosiere report[2] and the UK Banking Act 2009 seem to converge on addressing one key issue of the 2007–2008 crash: tail risks are not necessarily idiosyncratic in nature and may quickly impact entire sectors and even spread into systems. In other words, a sum of individually safe banks within a system does not alone ensure that the system itself is safe. Unlike in other sectors, banks' failures (especially the large ones) tend to impact the rest of the sector and even the economy through 'externalities'.[3] That is the key learning of 2007–2008 and it is the one issue regulators and policy makers are currently committed to address.

The situation arose because market participants have come to rely on each other for their funding operations and because the rest of the economy relies on banks for their day-to-day operations. In search of efficiency, the whole world ended up investing long and funding short for various and specific reasons. This massive dependence on leveraged finance is far beyond all points of no return. This changes the rules of the economic game as if the entire world economy had inherited the financial structure of a hedge fund. The finance sector is no longer an important organ within the body; it is the heart pumping blood through it.

This deeply changes the nature and definitions of risks.

23.1.1 How risks have evolved

High-profile failures of the 1990s came through individual firms. As a result, the regulatory requirements have traditionally focused on company-specific, idiosyncratic, risks. They were usually defined as market, credit and operational risks, with side remarks on liquidity, legal or reputational risks. These types of risk still exist but we will show in this chapter that such classification is no longer relevant with respect to risk management and that risk should now be recategorized as idiosyncratic, systematic and systemic. Notably, the definition of such risks has changed since 1990s.

---

[1] *Financial Regulatory Reform, A New Foundation: Rebuilding Financial Supervision and Reform*, Department of the US Treasury, 17 June 2009.

[2] Report by the High Level Group on Financial Supervision in the EU, Chaired by Jacques de Larosiere, Brussels, 25 February 2009.

[3] Markus Brunnermeier, Andrew Crockett, Charles Goodhart, Avinash D. Persaud and Hyun Shin, *The Fundamental Principles of Financial Regulation*, Geneva Reports on the World Economy. Preliminary Conference Draft, ICMB International Center for Monetary and Banking Studies, 2009.

In specific cases such as Continental Illinois, LTCM or Enron, the regulatory authorities involved to counterbalance the effects of the failure successfully confined them to the near environment of the failing entity. Some crises, though, threatened to spill over, in particular the emerging market crisis of 1997–1998 and the Internet bubble burst of 2000–2001. Those crises were systematic to the extent that they impacted on entire sectors or regions, but were not systemic since the regulatory authorities managed again to control the chain reactions with their traditional weapons of interest rates, refinancing facilities and updated supervisory structures.

The distinct difference between 1998 and 2008 is that the globalization of financial activities has become a reality but the regulatory structures and legal frameworks haven't. Some portfolio managers lost huge asset value in 1998 when emerging market securities crashed. Some lenders had to mop up defaults and cope with vanishing collateral values. Losses went spiralling but remained within their silos.

The bridges thrown between the banking and asset management worlds since repealing the Glass–Steagall Act in 1999, the interdependence of equity and debt valuations linked by uniform credit assessment models and the regulatory entanglements that allowed leveraged strategies to spread and corrupt systems have created a new world where, in the case of a major economic downturn, there will be no quality to fly to.

Feeling incapable of controlling risks and facing considerable economic and political pressure, the policy makers have no choice but to deleverage the economy. They have tasked the regulators to accompany the unwinding, but the world economy might be well past a point of no return.

The charts in Figure 23.1, extracted from the BIS quarterly review Q109, illustrate the magnitude of the issue. The shapes of the charts perfectly describe 20 years of growth and globalization of the economy from the fall of the Berlin Wall until 2009. The economic contraction started in August 2007 is also visible, but it appears as a tiny inflexion on the charts, relative to the growth of the decade.

If the 'tiny' compression of activities visible on the charts since mid-2007 corresponds to the harsh reality of the global recession experienced since 2008, how then will it be possible to unwind such leverage without creating a deep, long depression of exceptional severity and political unsustainability? Realistically, we should expect governments to become increasingly interventionist. Moreover, the figures in trillions of

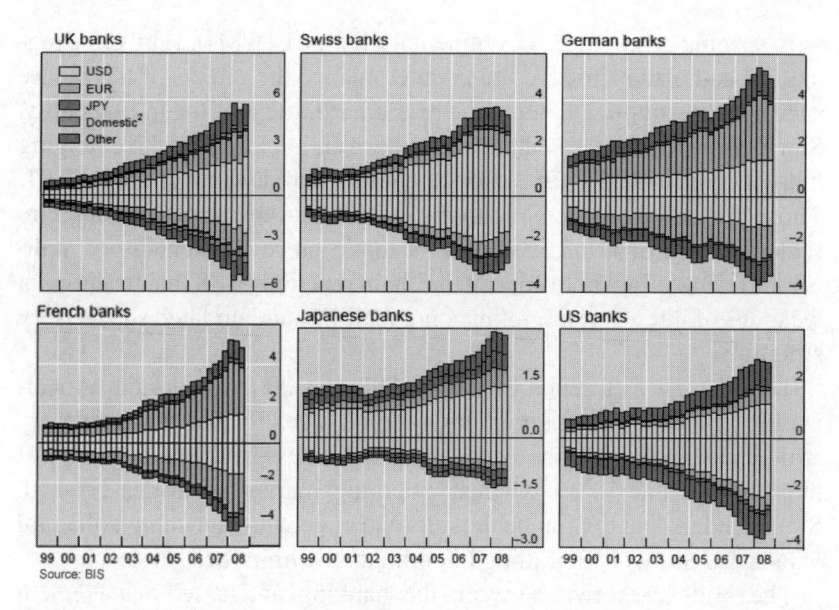

Figure 23.1 Gross foreign assets (top) and liabilities (bottom) of bank systems (in US$ bn 000s) (Taken from a larger BIS chart from the *BIS Quarterly Review*, March 2009)

US$ exceed by far those of the GDP of the countries involved – except the US and Japan. How could governments provide enough liquidity and incentives to counterbalance the effects of a durable contraction of credit activities of this magnitude? It will be fiscally unsustainable.

In other words, there is no coming back to level of risks that, as in the past, could possibly be contained by capital allocation or bailed out by regulatory authorities. The only component of the growth/risk equation that can be realistically deleveraged is the emotion and discomfort that accompany the notions of risk. Learning to live with the risks we generate to ourselves and to others is the only sustainable way forward. The culture of risk management needs to pervade all sectors and regulatory systems of the financial industry.

Yet the current plans for regulatory upheavals focus on structures rather than on a culture of risk management. It is perceived that preventing spillover effects will eradicate systemic risks, thus bringing back the overall exposure of the system to the risks related to individual firms or to a sector. However, if the world has changed, if the firms and their businesses have evolved, so did the risks and the nature of those risks.

23.1.2 From risk regulation to regulatory risks

The raging debate between regulators, policy makers, market participants and their expert advisers is no longer to discuss whether individual firms' risks externalize and impact the entire sector and system, but about finding the right balance between micro-prudential and macro-prudential supervisory structures. Among supporters of emphasizing the latter, a second debate brings forward the procyclical effects of the current capital regime that led firms to cut credit lines to those who were most in need. Should the new measures be procyclical and allow for higher leverage when balance sheets are larger or should they be countercyclical and require more provisioning in good times in preparation for the bad times? A consensus seems to be growing in favour of the latter, as it is feared that high levels of leverage contribute to asset bubbles in times of economic growth and to the subsequent liquidity holes.

The macro-prudential regulations proposed are designed to monitor leverage ratios, balance sheet structure mismatches and the associated concentrations of the large institutions that seem to pose systemic risk. The regulators will be empowered to take preventive action and act specifically against asset bubbles before they burst. The remaining questions essentially relate to who should be in charge of defining those rules and trigger the macro-prudential course of action.

Figure 23.2 illustrates the new measures proposed by the US Administration. The essential changes are the additional powers given to the Federal Reserve, as a 'super-regulator'. The EU presents different plans yet very much derived from the same principles, all inspired from the resolutions of the G20 meetings in April 2009.

It is beyond the purpose of this book to discuss the efficiency or the appropriateness of the undertakings. Yet one can observe that the regulators could create a new notion of 'regulatory risks' for themselves if they concentrate the fate of the entire systems in the hands of a few super-regulators, falling short of implementing a system-wide culture.

Risks arise from the unexpected – tail events, internal imbalances, counterparty failures, market crises, systemic risks or from the combined effects of those shocks. They can't be hedged with a process but through a culture of risk management aiming to routinize the unexpected. The role of regulators in this respect is to drive firms to develop rules of corporate governance and risk management tactics deeply rooted within their corporate culture, as an immune system. Risk management

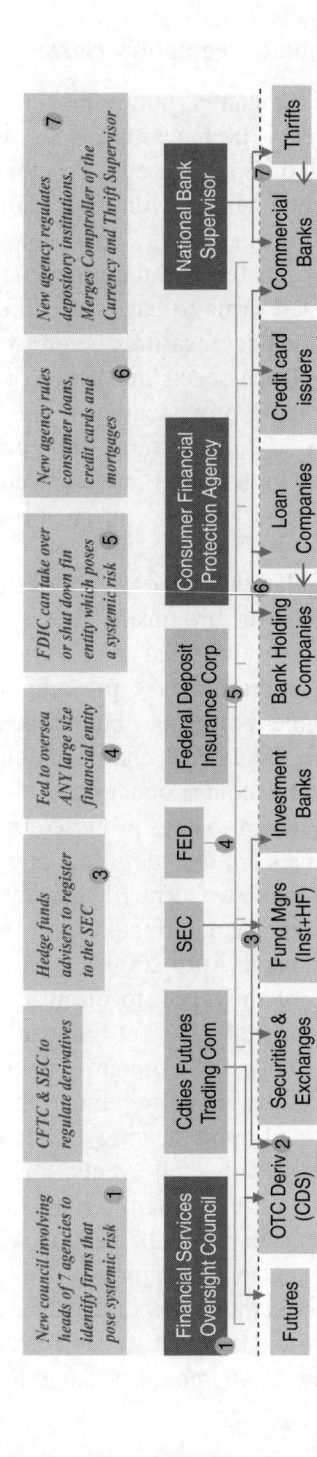

Figure 23.2 US regulatory system overhaul

Source: US Treasury, Herald Tribune, Thomson Reuters

strategies and mitigation tactics should not be standardized but, on the contrary, remain as diverse as possible, yet within the spirit inspired by the regulators.

If we accept the definition of systemic risk as the danger that the whole system could collapse under the weight of massive inefficiencies in managing systematic risks and their interactions, then we can say that, in a decade, the financial system has built its own chronicle of a foretold disaster every step of the regulatory way. There has been extensive debate on the causes and origins of systemic risks in the run-up to the new regulatory proposals. In reality the systemic crisis stems from many vicious circles that all played out simultaneously and triggered or amplified each other. From the chain reaction following the subprime crisis to the credit crunch triggered by Lehman's failure, each vicious circle was cause and consequence of the next one, sparing no segment of the economy, including corporate clients, rating agencies, hedge funds and even information networks.

The similarities we can notice in each of the vicious circles were in each case a heavy reliance on models and a generalized culture of uniformity:

1. **Reliance on models.** Growth and competition led to innovation, which led to complexity and reliance on models for pricing, trading, reporting and accounting purposes. The complexity of the structures of universal banks also led to modelling exposure, risk profiles, capital allocations and credit assessments. There are no good or bad models. Models are as appropriate as the sets of business scenarios they have been calibrated for. Popular models used in finance rely on calibrations generally carried out with linear variables. They typically assume well-accepted notions such as the efficient market theory, Brownian motion, mean returns and probability density functions leaning towards normality. The problem is that the multiplication of pricing and risk management models across products and sectors and their interdependence may overlook the integrity of the sets of assumptions, creating compatibility issues, especially in times of tail events.
2. **Culture of uniformity.** The other issue is a widespread culture of uniformity, which led most institutions to pursue similar strategies with similar offerings based on similar models. Three ratings agencies, two copula pricing models and a handful of market makers have been the main engineers of OTC markets reaching a combined

notional value equivalent to the GDP of the planet. Not only are pricing and valuations based on similar models but the same approaches are used and recommended by the regulators for revaluations, risk measurement, performance reports, credit limits and netting rules, as well as regulatory capital requirements.
3. **Regulatory entanglements.** The combined evolution of the regulatory frameworks of the banking, asset management, insurance and brokerage systems let the entire financial system become greatly exposed to misconceptions from the regulators and policy makers, arbitrage from the market participants or simply incompatibilities within the framework under adverse market conditions. It is a new type of systemic–operational risk that cannot be ignored.

Regulatory entanglements against a backdrop of deregulation and the subsequent arbitrages create layers of opacity that can disrupt or bias the normal flows of funds. They are real threats to the systems that they were initially designed to protect. For example, Basel 2 indirectly encouraged securitization as credit transferred to SIVs would alleviate balance sheets and reduce capital requirements. Since the industry was no longer ruled by the Glass–Steagall Act, the securitized credit exposure moved freely into the securities world. There, UCITS III opened the gate for those instruments to reach regulated institutional funds, which were permitted to use derivatives as investment vehicles. Structured finance ended up pouring illiquid and opaquely priced collateralized assets into a world of perfectly regulated risk-averse pension funds.

Operating off-balance sheet, financial engineers can turn any collateralized asset into an obligation using discretionary methods. While FAS 157[4] 'fair-value' accounting rules give a false sense of precision, it tolerates marking to models and indirectly encourages the maintainance of a level of opacity around some products.

The MIFID has fragmented liquidity pools, which led large investment banks into the execution business. As they can also operate proprietary desks and front positions against the very hedge funds they finance, they can now simultaneously own the execution venue, make the market, execute deals as brokers, act as systematic internalizers and hold positions – all potential sources of conflict of interests.

---

[4] Statement 157, Fair value measurement, The Financial Accounting Standards Board, issued September 2006.

Our purpose is not to diagnose the benefits and deficiencies of the regulatory rules but to understand how their combinations might be responsible for some of the systematic and systemic risks and how regulators can address this problem. There are two different sources of issues.

First, there are cases where the uniformity of the guidelines and of the rules enacted led to systemic risk every step of the way. Somehow policy makers have lost one core principle – that balancing risks always requires diversity. Uniformity of the approaches only concentrates them further. Requiring or simply encouraging entire segments of an industry to use similar models under similar circumstances for similar purposes inevitably creates concentrations that will turn to liquidity holes when tail risks occur. Those are even more difficult to detect because the risk is at its highest when liquidity is in excess.

Second, while each set of rules serves the good intention to make markets fairer and safer, none of them overarch the entire framework in which the financial systems interoperate nowadays. Alan Greenspan himself wrote: 'The essential problem is that our models – both risk models and econometric models – as complex as they have become, are still too simple to capture the full array of governing variables that drive global economic reality' (*Financial Times*, 17 March 2008).

Regulators and policy makers officially endeavour to address this type of issue and call for an international regulatory body, a regulator of regulators. In our view, all efforts should be driven to integrating and simplifying the sets of rules relevant to the banking sectors, buy-side and insurance sectors, hedge funds, execution venues and information providers such as rating agencies, risk aggregators, fund administrators, custodians and external auditors.

Agile methods based on individual views, such as scenario-based approaches, less reliance on models and recognizing idiosyncratic versus market-based issues will progressively implement a culture of risk management within the firms and the systems. In particular, efforts to prevent liquidity issues should encourage diversity or risk having the opposite effects from what was originally intended. Regulations that would too narrowly define the elements used for liquidity counterbalancing purposes could create severe liquidity holes when tail events strike in the future.

24
Propositions for a Regulatory Upheaval

In parallel with current undertakings to find an appropriate balance of micro-prudential versus macro-prudential regulations, we believe that it is essential that the financial industry adopts a very dynamic approach to risk management and reconnects at the macro-economic level with some of the fundamental principles of risk management, given below:

- Managing risk is managing information. In a fast-growing global economy characterized by innovation, information and sources of information multiply exponentially. Extracting true reflections of exposure out of the white noise is essential to building dynamic and adaptive risk management frameworks.
- Asset bubbles are endemic to free market operations in liberal economies. In other words, new bubbles will arise that are bound to burst again.
- Only diversity mitigates risk, whereas uniformity in tactics, strategies and models only concentrates them.
- The consequences of idiosyncratic tail risks may externalize to the rest of the sector and beyond, creating other tail events and potentially an uncontrollable chain reaction.

The previous regulatory frameworks were not inefficient but relied on assumptions inherited from ageing market structures, mostly inherited from the remedies of the previous crises. Our set of propositions aims to improve transparency and define information flows in order to address the challenges raised by today's market and adapt to the future. Further, the goal is to create agility and transparency on the exchange of information and to foster a culture of risk management through diversity, education and a sense of responsibility.

24.1 PROPOSITIONS RELATING TO IDIOSYNCRATIC RISKS

In response to the crisis, market regulators and participants have embarked on programmes to enhance risk management and corporate governance rules. Banks and asset management companies are trying to enhance transparency at every level of their organizations, while the regulators face the daunting task of implementing stricter rules without impeding innovation or business growth.

The task is complicated by the incredible diversity of financial instruments that result from fast pace innovation, by the difficulties of valuation of complex or illiquid products and by the lack of substance behind some of the valuations. The multiplication of economically active regions, the emergence of new markets and the fragmentation of liquidity pools compound the issue. As a result, the financial industry seeks a new definition of transparency.

It is essential that the financial industry establishes a culture of transparency to support a dynamic approach to risk management, to restore confidence and to open new perspectives to the regulators. We recommend a new approach to risk management to reconnect with some of the fundamental principles of risk management, by privileging consensus-based estimations versus modelling and enabling fast dynamic reporting of exposure and sensitivity. The aim is to be able to synthesize activities without creating uniformity.

The proposed steps are:

- Develop an enhanced taxonomy and nomenclature of all financial instruments so that they can be identified by the types of credit, market, valuation, liquidity and legal risks to which they expose holders.
- Attach 'price quality ratings' to each quotation submitted to the markets. With the support of regulators and contributions from market participants, they allow for assessments of market depth, price transparency, reliability and legal risk hindsight behind every price.
- Implement new reporting frameworks embedding the enhanced taxonomy and the new risk classes, to qualify portfolios better in terms of risk exposure and price transparency.

Our set of propositions aims to improve transparency and information flows in order to address the challenges raised by today's market and adapt to the future with the vision to privilege agility, transparency and the exchange of information and to foster a culture of risk management through diversity, education and a sense of responsibility.

24.1.1 Risk concentration benchmarks

Immune systems within live organisms rely on information exchange. Sensors transmit some facts (changes of external conditions) and emotions (risks) to the brain, which reacts by instantly conveying orders to multiple systems in order to trigger a coordinated course of action. Extreme situations may generate different reactions and externalities may eventually threaten the entire living body. The brain acts out of DNA and pre-established processes built in memory.

Similarly, the risk management culture of the 21st century will come to life when a workflow of risk-based information will constantly feed the regulators' databanks with facts and changes of risk factors, system-wide exposure and mitigation tools. The regulators can in turn aggregate industry monographs and communicate them back to the firms for them to benchmark their risk exposure and especially their risk concentrations.

We propose a new risk concentration information exchange based on the following workflow:

- All financial institutions should report their asset allocation concentrations as cumulative shares of total assets and liabilities to a central independent entity aggregating all figures and publishing industry monographs.
- Concentrations are disclosed as concentration indices to avoid unveiling proprietary or sensitive information. For example, a bank can reveal the concentrations to a given category of clients through a co-efficient expressing whether a small number of clients accounts for a large share of credit exposure within the group. Using an index of dissimilarities can further refine the analysis.
- An independent risk aggregator builds, maintains, redistributes and supports the monographs under supervision of regulatory authorities.
- Financial institutions benchmark their own risk concentrations to those of the rest of their business environment and assess their potential liquidity requirements for worst case developments accordingly.
- Financial institutions disclose their distance to the benchmark to the regulators and shareholders with reports of alignment to risk and funding policies.

Measuring concentrations and dispersions for the major risk classes periodically and benchmarking them to an aggregated figure from the rest of the industry provides an accurate estimation of the potential effect on volatility and liquidity of tail events impacting concentrated portfolios. This will considerably improve the efficiency of stress tests and progressively drive towards the implementation of variable capital requirement rules.

24.1.2 Departure from the generalized assumption of normality

The shock of the crisis awoke the entire industry to the notions of systematic and systemic risks. It was also a stark reminder that tail events are generally repetitive. The issue is not so much to be unable to predict the future accurately but to turn a probability of occurrence into a frequency of occurrence. First, for each variable, the approach ignores the basic martingale every roulette player hopes for, according to which the conditional expectation of the next value is independent of its probability of occurrence (Poisson distributions). Second, the variables of the financial sector are far from independent, as the crisis painfully reminded all.

It would be beyond the purpose of this chapter to discuss in detail the very nature of the probability density functions of the financial market. Regardless of the findings, it is clear that the measures of risk, positions, performance and sensitivity should reflect the risk policies and risk appetite of each individual firm rather than the calibrations, methodologies and deficiencies of the sets of models used.

Risk measures for instruments, positions and portfolios should therefore be scenario based and focused on worst cases, as opposed to the current model-based probabilistic approach:

- Hedges, capital allocations and margining should be calculated for worst case scenarios, no longer for the most probable market developments.
- Stress tests do not necessarily reflect worst cases as the people of a firm understand them. The process merely stresses the financial models, bringing the algorithms to boundaries for which they might not have been calibrated.
- The assessment of risk sensitivity under scenarios is a key part of the risk culture, as it necessarily raises awareness across departments and constitutes a very important step towards making people responsible and accountable for their own risks.

To depart from the generalized assumption of normality and eliminate considerable model risks, regulators should no longer encourage modelling as the main methodology of quantitative risk assessments. Modelling VaR, conditional VaR, potential future exposure and implied credit ratings can still be used for benchmarking purposes, but it should not be pointed out as the most accurate and dynamic approach.

Worst case scenarios built out of consultation and cooperation bring a true reflection of the actual risk appetite of a firm. Not only is the outcome more relevant to a firm's shareholders and regulators than its modelling capabilities but the content of scenarios can also be recorded to benchmark how the perception of risk evolves within a firm and within a sector.

Figure 24.1 describes the process of obtaining worst case scenarios from within a firm, based on self-identified key risk factors and an internal perception of their interdependence. This type of framework is key to raising awareness and establishing a culture of risk management.

Both the outcome and content (factors, variables and stress) can be communicated to the regulators and aggregated by them to obtain a live picture of indiosyncratic risk assessments and areas of emotions within sectors and systems.

24.1.3 Benchmarks of risk exposure and liquidity concentrations

Gini index and Lorenz curves are commonly used to measure concentrations. The method provides a graphical representation of the cumulative distribution functions. It also allows for dispersion measures with an absolute mean difference, which represents tensions better within a portfolio than standard deviations, for example. Figure 24.2 exhibits the workflow.

The proposed framework consists of gathering each financial institution's exposure concentration periodically, expressed as a Gini index and mean difference, for the factors given below. A professional association, a third party aggregator or a regulator can aggregate the data periodically and produce a monograph of the industry's concentrations. Each firm will then be in a position to benchmark their own concentration to those of the market.

For the sell-side institutions, the key risk concentration factor categories are as follows:

248   The Handbook of Risk Management

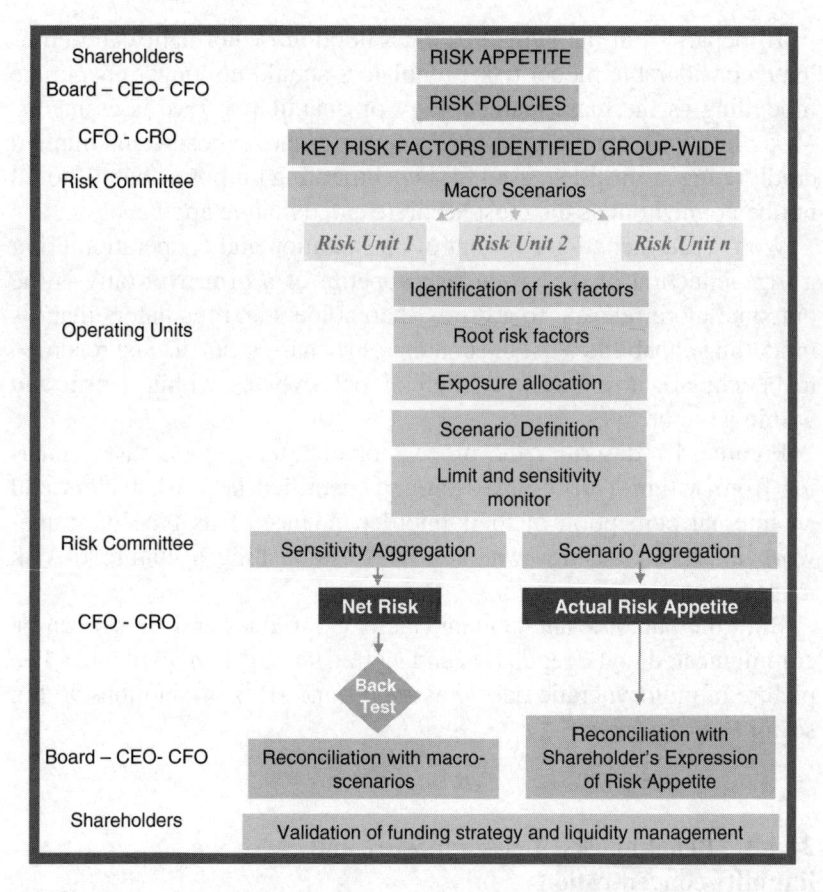

Figure 24.1 Dynamic reflections of a firm's appetite for risks through consensus-build firmwide scenarios

- Asset allocations by risk rating, counterparty type or rating, country, underlying group, mark-to-market frequency, time band, convertibility, optionality and vega time bucket.
- Liabilities by risk rating, time bucket, currency, country, funding channel, creditors' group, issuer, settlement type, collateral group, convertibility, optionality, vega bucket.
- Leverage ratios by client type, collateral, liquidity groups, derivative types.
- Cyclical factors such as inflation, energy and interest rates, for example.

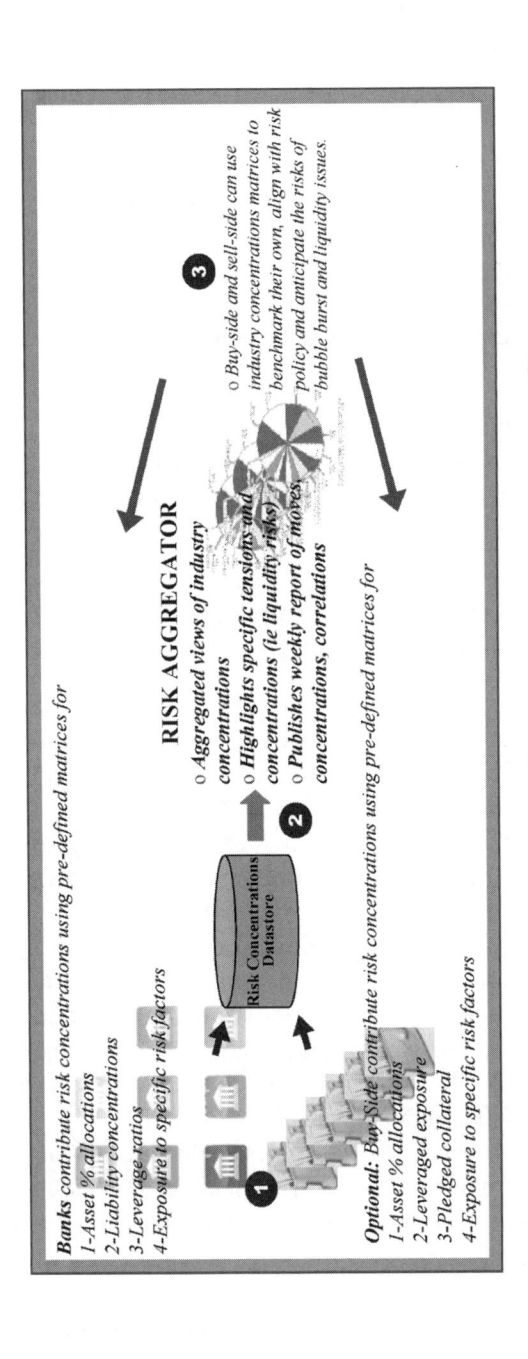

Banks *contribute risk concentrations using pre-defined matrices for*
1-Asset % allocations
2-Liability concentrations
3-Leverage ratios
4-Exposure to specific risk factors

Optional: *Buy-Side contribute risk concentrations using pre-defined matrices for*
1-Asset % allocations
2-Leveraged exposure
3-Pledged collateral
4-Exposure to specific risk factors

RISK AGGREGATOR
○ Aggregated views of industry concentrations
○ Highlights specific tensions and concentrations (ie liquidity risks)
○ Publishes weekly report of moves concentrations, correlations

○ Buy-side and sell-side can use industry concentrations matrices to benchmark their own, align with risk policy and anticipate the risks of bubble burst and liquidity issues.

❶ Each bank contributes exposure concentrations based on structural and cyclical factors decided by Committee:
1-Asset % allocations per asset class, instrument, time bucket,....
2-Liability concentrations per funding class, ratings, tenor,....
3-Option-based leverage ratios
4-Weekly changes in % of all of the above

❷ Regulators supported by risk aggregators compile and anonymize data, produce and publish an industry monograph (distribution of liquidity spikes)

❸ Regulators gets an aggregated view of risk concentrations (bubbles in the process)

Banks can benchmark their own concentrations against the industry (assess potential impact of burst)

Figure 24.2 Building risk and liquidity concentration benchmarks

The indicators proposed by the Committee on European Banking Supervisors (CEBS), London, 'Liquidity ID Card', 22 June 2009, can be used as templates.

For the buy-side institutions, the key risk concentration factor categories are as follows:

- Portfolio concentrations by sector, market, trading counterparties, issuers, underlying asset type, mark-to-market frequency.
- Leveraged exposure by derivative types, market, settlement type, volatility and sensitivity groups.
- Pledged collateral by instrument, sector, haircut ratio.
- Cyclical factors.

In line with banks, the templates should be defined in cooperation and consultation with prominent representatives of the insurance industry, the institutional asset management industry, hedge fund associations and their respective regulators.

24.2 PROPOSITIONS RELATING TO SYSTEMATIC RISKS

As previously explained, one source of systematic risks arising from the externalizations of idiosyncratic risks is due to the intricacies of financial systems and regulatory frameworks. A set of micro-prudential and macro-prudential supervisory structures are therefore being prepared to address those risks in the future, such as the creation of an European Systemic Risk Council (ESRC), as announced in a Communication from the European Commission, Brussels, dated 27 May 2009.

To create the correct mix of automatic stabilizers and discretionary measures recommended by Borio and Drehmann,[1] we suggest that the 'nervous system' should be equipped with a cross-system information workflow that would alert the respective regulators and prompt a course of action, such as temporarily closing some links to avoid spillover effects or supporting some of the funding channels.

Our analysis of externalities shows two main gates through which the contagion usually spreads out when one or several banks face a serious fall in asset value, either impacts on the interbank market and/or on the buy-side world.

---

[1] Claudio E. V. Borio and Mathias Drehmann, Towards an operational framework for financial stability: 'fuzzy' measurement and its consequences, BIS Working Paper 284, June 2009.

24.2.1 Required disclosure of term structures of assets and liabilities in foreign currencies

For the regulators, one way to anticipate the funding difficulties of a bank and its potential impact on the rest of the sector would be to obtain periodic information about the balance sheet structures and aggregate them, as previously suggested with regards to asset concentrations.

The FSA consultation paper 08/22[2] mentioned in paragraph 8.26 that the Bank of England and other stakeholders had pressed for greater transparency in foreign currency funding to highlight potential vulnerabilities and deteriorating funding conditions before they become critical. We suggest aggregating and redistributing term structures of currency mismatches through the information exchange workflow shown in Figure 24.3.

As with exposure concentrations, the aim is to produce a system-wide view of structural imbalances to alert the regulators in a timely manner and allow all market participants to benchmark their own structures relative to the rest of the market, thus assessing their own exposure to systematic risks.

24.2.2 Dynamic capital adequacy requirements

The deterioration of equity value mathematically impacts credit instruments whose valuations are based on default probability models. Rising default probabilities increase the funding costs of the issuer and the capital requirements of the funding entities. This leads to tighter credit and further depresses equities due to fire sales of assets in search of liquidity. In the case of large investment banks, which are known to fund as much as 50 % of their interbank positions through repos, the combined effects of the asset meltdown and the rise of haircut ratios have been devastating. This resulted in increasingly shorter liabilities funding assets that in principle remained of unchanged duration, though low liquidity may actually increase it.

The direct correlation between asset prices and credit spreads is illustrated by the chart on the left in Figure 24.4, which simultaneously exhibits the equity prices of UBS (lower line) and the 5 year credit protection cost of UBS as issuer (upper line) over the last 18 months. The subchart exhibits the correlation.

---

[2] FSA CP 08/22, *Strengthening Liquidity Standards*, Financial Services Authority, December 2008.

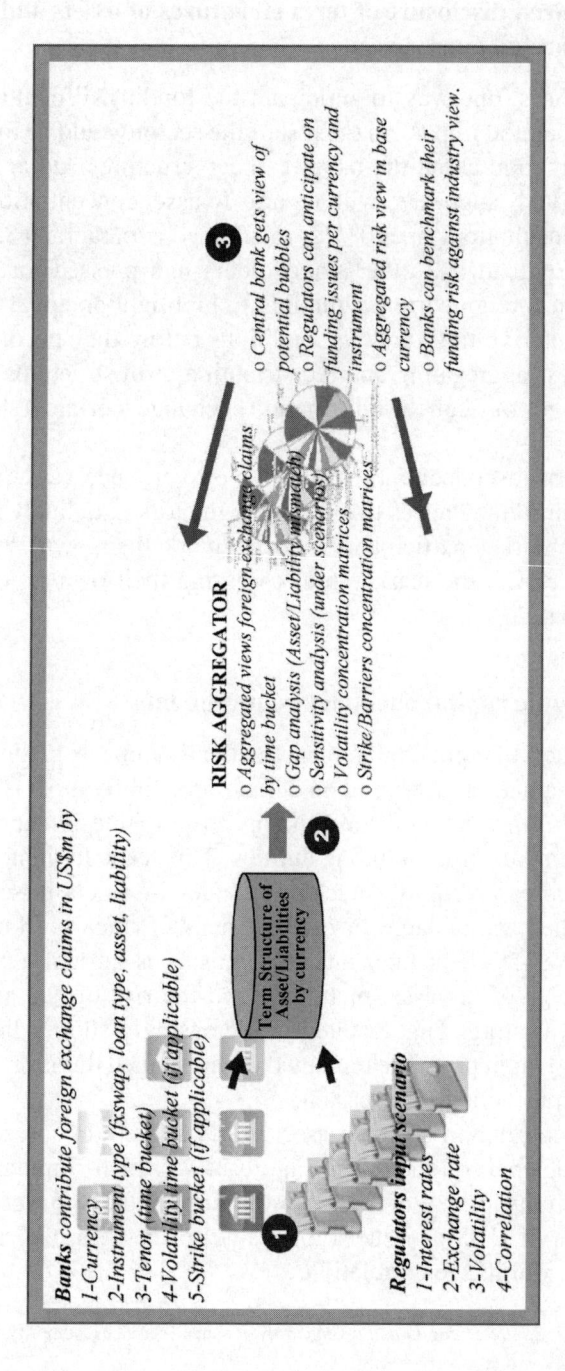

Figure 24.3 Information exchange workflow

Propositions for a Regulatory Upheaval 253

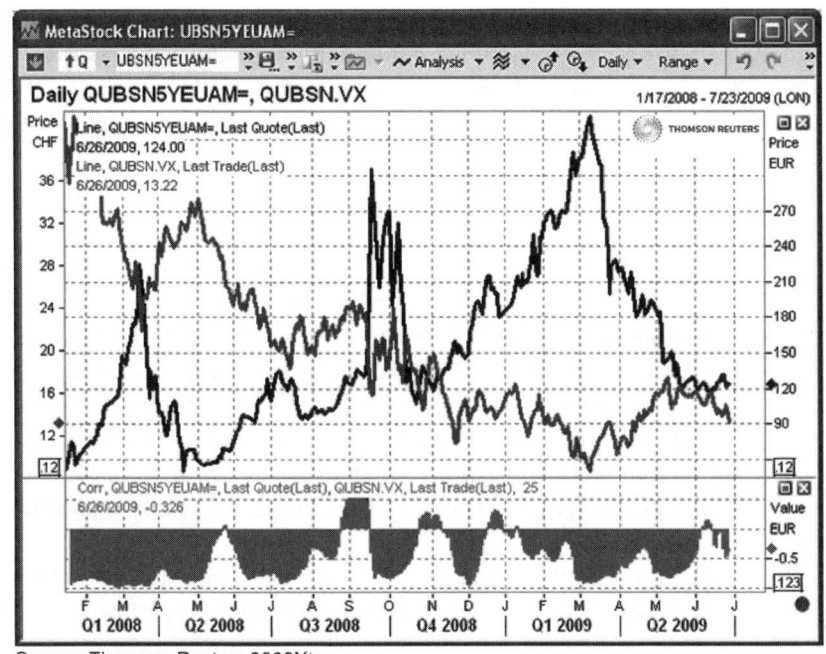

Figure 24.4 Charts showing the correlation between asset prices and credit spreads

The ongoing debate of whether the regulatory capital requirements should be procyclical (less capital in good times, more in bad times) or countercyclical (the opposite) is beyond the scope of this book. Irregardless of the regulators' decisions and evolution, there is a general consensus that capital requirements should become variable and linked as dynamically as possible to the external market conditions – liquidity risks in particular.

Using the periodic contributions and aggregated term structures described above, combining them with credit quality indices and other related data, the regulators will get the opportunity to:

- Adjust capital requirements in a procyclical or countercyclical fashion as required to accelerate or slow down the pace of credit (in the same spirit that central banks adjust interest rates).
- Influence the choices of funding channels and conduits to avoid saturation and liquidity holes.

Modifying capital adequacy ratios is a delicate task as it requires a timely response to factors that are continually evolving. This is critical since the weight of the variables changes when markets shift from fast to slow growth or fall into recession. Weights on maturity mismatch, credit spreads or market volatility need to be totally rethought when moving from one period to the other.

24.2.3 Preserving diversity

To manage risks is to diversify exposure. Uniform hedging tactics and regulatory-inspired uniformity of models have led to risk concentrations and systemic risks of unprecedented magnitude. Uniformity in strategies gave rise to risk concentrations. At the same time, uniform investment timeframes led to market illiquidity when everyone chose to be a long-term investor or to excessive volatility when there was a dominance of only short-term traders.

Reconnecting with the fundamental risk management principle that diversity mitigates risks while uniformity further concentrates them means that the regulators need to implement the same type of risk-based communication network that would keep the system as agile as an individual firm.

Risks cannot be hedged with a set of remedies uniformly imposed to patients not yet ill. It is a system-wide exchange of information and transparent communications that can keep the whole industry and the regulators aware of risks as they develop and better prepared to face the unexpected. Balance only comes from diversity.

We recommend in particular preserving diversity in the following areas:

- Independent and unbiased sources of information. While pricing transparency and better information flows ultimately address the challenges created by moral hazard, broadly available independent and unbiased sources of pricing and risk assessment instil significantly more confidence in the financial markets than regulatory rules.
- Innovation. There are many ways in which innovation in the financial markets has accelerated economic growth, created wealth and enhanced market stability, along with improving market efficiency. Without innovation, the financial markets will be challenged to support the needs of a dynamic and ever-changing economy.
- Risk management strategies. While cross-industry hedges and netting rules should be under tighter control, the diversity of hedging tools

and methodology within each system remains essential to ensuring that risks are properly diversified. Firms should be required to decide in agreement with their shareholders and in accordance with the risk policies what would be the most appropriate hedging techniques and derivative tools they will use and what would be the level of systematic risks they accept.
- Maintain structural flexibility. Markets face changing needs and many of those needs are impossible to predict today. Market structures change over time as buyers and sellers evolve with the complexity of the different securities. Blanket attempts to mandate specific market structures create unintended consequences, including impairing market health and providing incentives to move towards unregulated products, transactions and jurisdictions. Regulations should focus on healthy market functions and the markets need to determine the structures best suited to their needs.

24.3 PROPOSITIONS RELATING TO SYSTEMIC RISKS

Systemic risk was a name almost forgotten until it was once again revived in 2007 and became a daily headline, following the announcement by the EU Commission, the US Treasury and the UK Government on a course of action in application of the resolutions of the G20. Systemic risks, such as those linked to the transfer of credit derivatives from the banking industry to insurance companies, were exposed very early on,[3] but those warnings did not create any concern for the public and among regulators. It was perceived that the system would be able to sustain the risk of individual entities. What grounded the regulatory mechanism to a halt, spreading the liquidity crunch to the scale of a pandemic, was the inefficiency of the capital adequacy system applied to global institutions. As a result the various propositions to be implemented in 2010 will be focused on three particular issues:

- Systemic institutions (previously called too big to fail)
- Externalization of valuation and liquidity risks to other sectors
- Pro-cyclicality effects.

Although little discussion has been made in this book on the efficiency and adequacy of the measures announced, it is stressed that systemic

---

[3] Avinash Persaud Lecture at State Street, Boston, Massachusetts, November 2002.

risks can be prevented from happening, but once they occur the consequences can hardly be fixed. Reinforcing the structures that failed in the past will not entirely address the problem. Superimposing layers of macro-prudential regulatory structures overarching micro-prudential ones will certainly strengthen the system but is likely to make it more rigid and more complex, altogether decreasing its agility and responsiveness.

The proposition here is based on the spirit of creating an immune system that will evolve with the markets and adapt to the hazards of their environment. Again it relies on information interchange and intelligent data for the prevention of asset bubbles.

24.3.1 Establish controls for cross-industry transactions and exposure netting

The current crisis teaches that a set of toxic assets can contaminate entire industries across borders and systems when the hedging tools issued for a specific purpose are later repackaged and marketed for other purposes. The asset management and institutional investment industries, in particular, may be severely impacted by the leveraged exposure to hedging tools issued to hedge investment banking positions.

In the absence of strict boundaries rules such as the Glass–Steagall Act of 1932, one can avoid the potential spread of issues leading to unexpected falls in asset value with limits and caps triggered by high concentrations of potentially toxic assets. To reach this level of insight, it will be necessary to set up the following information workflow:

- Nomenclature of financial instruments with risk ratings as described in Section 24.1.
- Aggregation of sector exposures and concentrations as suggested in Section 24.2.
- Net exposure limits established at sector level by risk classes as described in Section 24.1.
- Change in regulatory rules to discourage further exposure beyond threshold.

For example, there could be a maximum possible exposure to structured products such as CDOs as a percentage of total assets held in portfolio. Once the threshold is hit, regulators can discourage further exposure through reserve requirements or even taxes.

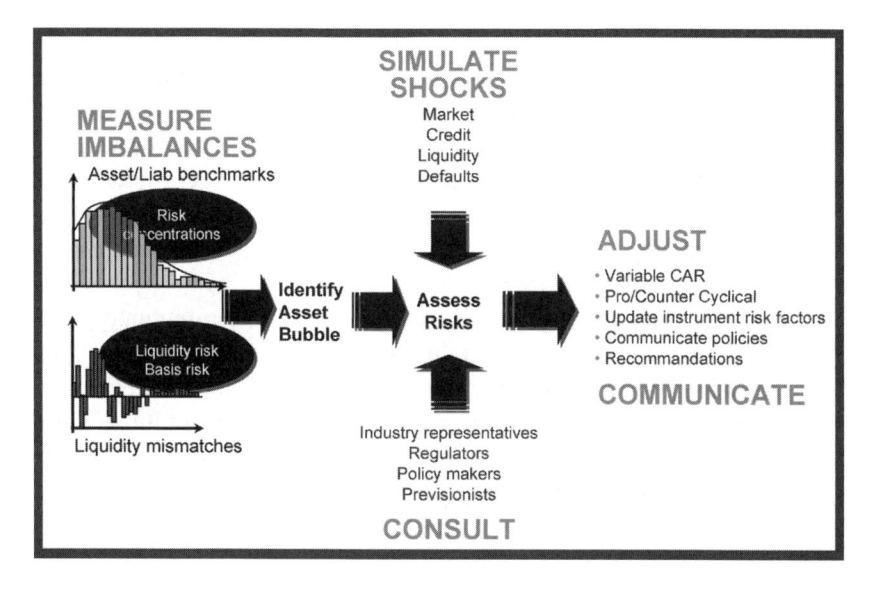

Figure 24.5 Consensus-based variable self-adjusting regulatory policies

24.3.2 Simulations involving multiple sectors and regulators

Stress-testing the main firms of a sector may reflect only one side of the banks' resilience to crises. Furthermore, the stress tests do not provide any view of potential domino effects, nor how thin liquidity could be stretched in addressing the issues. Finally, stress tests do not point towards any solution moving forward.

Leveraging the mapping and measurements proposed in this document, regulators can instead run cross-industry simulations as 'war games' and test their response. No simulation can reproduce the complexities and intricacies of modern finance, but the essential goal, which is to continuously to adapt supervisory structures to the evolution of the system, would be reached.

We propose a hybrid approach, leveraging the feedback on risk concentrations and liquidity mismatches obtained earlier, combining modelling with human judgement and involving all industry representatives to obtain a consensus-based regulatory policy, continuously adjusted to the observed and perceived tensions of the market.

Figure 24.5 describes the five-pronged framework: measure, simulate, consult, adjust and communicate.

Some models such as the risk assessment model for systemic institutions (RAMSI)[4] simulate crises of UK banks in an attempt to detect the risks of domino effects. The solution we propose reaches out to other sectors, in particular asset management, hedge funds and corporates, and adds to the RAMSI initiative a predominant layer of human judgement on top of modelling. We believe that it is important to involve the representatives of the various sectors physically or risk turning the whole endeavour into a pure theoretical exercise.

Eventually the simulation exercises might become a regulatory forum for the regulators and the industry to build appropriate levels of transparency based on the instruments themselves and on the interaction among sectors and systems. Immune systems and cultures alike are based on exchange of information, as a set of ever-adapting processes naturally involving and protecting each other.

---

[4] David Aikman, Piergiorgio Alessandri, Bruno Eklund, Prasanna Gai, Sujit Kapadia, Elizabeth Martin, Nada Mora, Gabriel Sterne and Matthew Willison, Funding liquidity risk in a quantitative model of systemic stability, Working Paper 372, Bank of England, June 2009.

Index

accountability
  achieving 14, 18, 33, 50, 84–5
  business units 66, 68–9
  importance of 54, 68
accounting methodologies, disclosure 204–5
actual risk appetite
  expression 48, 62, 86, 112
  reconciliation 48–9, 93, 131–2, 206, 208
aggregation of sensitivity 35, 36, 43, 45–7
  catastrophic scenarios 47–8, 62, 133–5
  cross-asset 115–7
  cross-division 117–22
  enterprise-wide 115–22
  qualitative assessments 135
agility
  communication and 85
  development 71
alerts 58, 128–9, 179, 181
  see also triggers
arbitrage pricing theory 155
arbitration 69, 74, 117
asset and liability management (ALM) 140, 149–50, 175–81
  business risk analysis 176–8
  convexity gaps 179–81
  duration gap sensitivity 178–9, 180
  margin analysis 176–8
asset liability risk 159–60
audit and control department
  as referees 33–4, 69, 73, 74, 117
  risk concentration monitoring 172
  role 43, 73–4, 111, 113
  transparency and 87
awareness 13, 18, 45

back-testing 38–9, 103, 139
balance sheet structure, disclosure 209–10
baseline scenarios 41, 62
Basle Accords
  concentrations 163
  disclosure policy 194–5
  modelling 4, 89, 90, 173
  regulatory entanglements 231
  risk aggregation 51, 52
  securitization 167, 240
  standardization 144
benchmarking
  regulatory capital reports 204
  risk concentrations 163–5, 175, 201, 231–2, 245–6, 247–50
bottom-up activity feedback 96, 97–8
  certification 110–1
  continuous efficiency monitoring 110
  monitoring exposures 109–10
  scenario feedback 111–2
business managers
  accountability 66, 68–9
  as risk managers 68–70, 71, 72
business resilience
  dynamic risk-weightings and 93
  as performance criterion 90
business risk analysis 176–8
business units
  control of risk data 114
  empowerment 66
  hedging strategies 75–7, 110
  mitigation 66, 68–9, 70, 75–7
  monitoring risk exposure 109–10
  risk appetite of 48
  risk factor identification 33, 34–5

Index

business units (*cont.*)
  risk management role 41
  scenario definition 43, 45, 56, 111
  sensitivity estimation 42, 53–4, 115–6, 117

capital adequacy
  dynamic 252, 254–5
  variable ratio 90
catastrophic scenarios 41–2
  aggregation 47–8, 62, 133–5
  definition and ownership 43, 45, 56, 247
  modelling 132–5
certification 110–1
Chief Executive Officers 1, 6, 7, 79, 80
Chief Financial Officers 6–7
Chief Risk Officers 71, 80
clearing houses, risk-free 217–8
communications
  agility and 85
  corporate culture 9, 200
  external 197–8, 221–2
  funding partners 193–4, 207–10
  industry representatives 193, 199–207
  information workflow 97
  market data availability 22–3
  with public 194, 210–2
  regulators 193, 199–207
  risk management 198–9
  shareholders 193–4, 207–10
  as strategic corporate goal 195
concentration risk 161–8
  analysis within portfolio 173
  benchmarking 163–5, 175, 201, 231–2, 245–6, 247–50
  categories 164–5, 249, 251
  counterparty interdependence 166–7
  disclosure 200–2
  dynamic concentrations 163–5
  enterprise view 174
  information workflow 247, 248–9
  managing 174–5
  measuring 163–4, 165–6, 249
  monitoring 172
  portfolio effects 201–2
  regulatory-driven 167–8, 218
  reporting 201
  risk policy reconciliation 173
  visualisation 172
confidentiality 207, 223, 224
continuous efficiency monitoring 110
control and reporting hierarchy 85–8

convexity gaps 179–81
corporate culture
  communications 9, 200
  creation 11–2
  definition 11
  requirement for change 8
  risk exposure and 17–8
  risk management 15
  root-risk factors and 37
corporate governance 184, 221–2
correlations
  cross-market effects and 118
  disclosure 202
  liquidity risk and 118–9, 120, 186–90
  monitoring 29–31
cost of risk management 197
countercyclical measures 90, 93
counterparty risk 78, 152, 166–7, 183–4
Crédit Agricole (CA) 18
credit risk 23, 24, 25, 52
credit spreads 37–8
cross-currency term structures 202–3, 251–2, 253
cumulative distribution functions 165

data aggregators 225, 226
data analysis 54–6
data enrichment 57–8
disaster recovery centres 110
disclosure 87
  accounting methodologies 204–5
  balance sheet structure 209–10
  Basle Accord 194–5
  capital adequacy 209–10
  confidentiality 207, 223, 224
  corporate governance 221–2
  cross-currency term structures 202–3, 251–2, 253
  economic capital reports 203–4, 209
  liquidity risk management 210
  macro-scenarios 205–6
  policies 199–213
  public relations and 212–3
  regulatory capital reports 203, 204, 209
  risk appetite 208–9
  risk concentrations 200–2
  risk management framework 199–200, 201, 204
  side effects 206–7
  stress test capital adequacy 210
  see also transparency

diversity
　from innovation 216
　as mitigation strategy 28, 37, 62, 168, 232, 243
　preserving 255–6
　vs standardization 37
duration gap sensitivity 178–9, 180
dynamic sensitivity control 76–7

economic capital, reporting 203–4, 209
education 33, 54, 62
efficient market hypothesis (EMH) 21–2, 23
emergency procedures 104–5
enterprise-wide aggregation
　cross-asset 115–7
　cross-division 117–22
　valuation risk 119–21
European Systemic Risk Council (ESRC) 251
executive management team 1, 65, 79, 84–5
Executive Risk Committee
　feedback 109
　mitigation strategies 76
　risk aggregation 35
　role 71–2, 80
　scenario preparation 43, 45
external auditors 83
external risks 28–9, 141–2, 143

FAS 157, 'fair-value' accounting 167, 240
feedback
　methodologies 98
　root-risk factor assessment 38–9
　see also bottom-up activity feedback
finance sector
　importance of 2
　risk management culture 9–10
forward volatility 92–3
fraud prevention 72
fund transfer pricing (FTP) process 177
funding partners, communications with 193–4, 207–10
funding risk 152, 159–68
　see also liquidity risk
funding strategy 147
　liquidity risk management 176
　as risk profile 190–2
　risk reconciliation 139–41
　see also liquidity

Gini index 163–4, 249
Glass-Steagall Act 1933 7, 144, 167, 231, 257

global credit/collateral exposure surveillance scheme 223–5, 226
globalization of financial activities 2, 235–6
governance scoring 222
government involvement 235–6
Greenspan, A. 168, 241
'Greenspan conundrum' 23

hedging strategies and tools
　business unit level 75–7, 110
　certification 110–1
　data requirements 66
　distribution 75
　dynamic nature 76–7
　example 75–6
　monitoring efficiency 110
　operational units 77–8
　stress testing 78
　traditional model 76
hierarchical decision models 127–9
high-severity scenarios 41
　aggregation 47–8, 62
　definition and ownership 43, 45, 56

idiosyncratic risk 17–27
　externalising 141–2, 143, 251
　identifying 18–20
　nature of 26
　reform proposals 231–2, 244–51
industry, communications with 193, 199–207
information
　exchange 223–5, 226, 245–6
　impact of technology 22–3
information systems
　alerts 58
　challenges 57–8
　data enrichment 57–8
　evolution 59–61
　multiple systems 57, 59
　risk monitoring 54–6
　scenario storage 58
　users' needs paramount 59
　see also IT infrastructure
information workflow
　design 58
　dynamic nature 100–1
　efficiency 104, 113
　evolution 59–61
　frameworks compared 59–60
　importance of 9–10
　IT requirements 57–8

information workflow (*cont.*)
  pre-emptive action rules 101–2
  pricing 119–22
  risk-based 95–8, 112–3
  technology risk 122
  triggers and responses 96–7, 101–2, 105–6, 110, 126–7
  see also bottom-up activity feedback; top-down information workflow
innovation 215–6, 255
instruments, classification 212, 216–7, 225, 257
interbank markets 160–1
international regulation 241
investments, long- and short-term 91–2
IT department 78, 113, 122, 172
IT infrastructure
  addition of new business 61
  challenges 57–8
  risk information bus 113–4
  see also information systems

Jorion, Prof P. 3
JP Morgan Investment Bank 3, 18

legal department, role 70, 73
legal risk, taxonomy 227
liquidation value 155
liquidity
  correlation and 118–9, 120
  cost of 155, 160
  as market efficiency driver 23–4
liquidity risk 160–1
  asset liability risk 159–60
  correlations 186–90
  counterparty-related 152, 166–7, 183–4
  external sources 152–3
  identifying 26–7
  internal balances 149–50
  internal sources 150–2
  management of *see* liquidity risk management
  market depth and 151, 156–7, 158, 182–3
  over-the-counter markets 152, 157–8
  regulatory-driven 152–3, 167–8, 184–6
  risk concentrations 161–3, 172–5
  see also concentration risk
  sources 148
  valuation-driven 151–2, 155–6, 159–60, 181–4

liquidity risk management 147–8, 149
  ALM analyses and 175–81
  corporate governance and 184
  disclosure 210
  framework 169, 170, 187
  FSA call for revision 185
  regulatory risk 184–6
  risk concentrations 172–5
  risk profile and 190–2
  risk reconciliation process 139–41
  root-risk factor identification 170–1
  valuation risk and 181–4
Long-Term Capital Management 4, 69
long-term investments 91–2
Lorenz curves 163–4, 165, 249

macro-scenarios 44
  aggregation 35, 43
  individual perspectives 35
  preparation 43
  see also scenarios
margin analysis 176–8
marginal supply-demand curves 155
mark to time-weighted volatility 91–3
market capital charge 90
market data 22–3
  see also information
market depth 151, 156–7, 158, 182–3
market efficiency
  efficient market hypothesis (EMH) 21–2, 23
  liquidity driven 23–4
  market efficiency hypothesis (MEH) 103
  selective 21–3
  volatility and 66
market risk 24, 25, 52, 227
Markets in Financial Instruments Directive (MIFID) 167, 212, 240
media, impact on information flow 22–3
MIFID *see* Markets in Financial Instruments Directive
mitigation
  audit of strategy 74, 110
  business unit level 66, 68–9, 70, 75–7
  certification of techniques 110–1
  choice of tools 43
  data requirements 66
  disclosure 207
  diversification 28, 37, 62, 168, 232, 243
  dynamic tactics 106–8
  liquidity risk 149

Index

management level 78–9
operational unit level 77–8
responsibility for 67–8
sensitivity assessment 18
model risk 52, 60
modelling
  for benchmarking 247
  development 3–4
  limitations 21, 54, 124, 241, 246–7
  reliance on 239
  risk exposure by business line 51–3, 59
  uses 42

new business, impact of addition 59–61
nonexecutive directors
  representation of shareholders 81, 83–4
  transparency and 87

operational capital charge 90
operational units, mitigation and hedging strategies 77–8
over-the-counter markets
  liquidity risk 152, 157–8
  risk-free clearing 217–8
  transparency 211–2
  valuation 120–1

performance
  objectives 10–1
  risk-weighted 65–6, 89–93
Peters, E. 91, 156
prediction errors 23
price quality ratings 244
pricing
  frequency 228–30
  methodologies 119–22
  transparency 216–7
  see also valuation
processes, transparency of 218–9
products
  information 206–7
  taxonomy 225–7, 230, 244
  transparency 216–7
public, communications with 194, 210–2
public relations 212–3

Rabobank 18
regulators
  challenges 233
  communications with 193, 199–207
  dynamic capital adequacy 254

global surveillance schemes and 224
indifference to risk 85
information workflow 10
international 168, 241
liquidity risk and 148
methodologies and 54
modelling 247
reform proposals 233, 236, 237, 238, 243
regulatory entanglements 153, 231, 240
rewarding diversity 85
role 233, 237
simulations and 259
as source of risk *see* regulatory-driven risk
source of systemic risk 135
standardization 5, 241
transparency and 87–8
regulatory capital reports 203, 204, 209
regulatory-driven risk
  introduction of 237–41
  as liquidity risk 152–3, 167–8, 184–6
  regulatory entanglement 153, 231, 240
  risk policy reconciliation 144–5
reporting
  hierarchy 85–6
  methodologies 87–8
  proposed frameworks 70, 244
  risk concentrations 201
  to shareholders 80–1, 84, 131
  traditional framework 70
  transparency 87–8
  see also communications; disclosure
reputational risk 25–6, 109
return on securities 21–2
risk
  balance with value generation 1–2, 4
  as essence of capitalism 1–2
  evolution of 234–6
  recategorization 234
risk appetite
  actual *see* actual risk appetite
  business units 48
  disclosure 208–9
  from worst case scenarios 247, 248
  live information 58
  reconciliation *see* risk reconciliation process
  shareholders *see* risk policies
risk assessment model for systemic institutions (RAMSI) 258–9

risk committees
  aggregation of sensitivities 43, 45–8
  role 33, 43, 71, 125
  sensitivity estimation 117
risk dashboards 123–5
risk exposure
  awareness 13, 18
  corporate roots and 17–8
  detachment of assessment 53
  distribution of 13, 15
  estimation 34–5, 62
  exchanges of information 194
  information workflow 14
  liquidity risk and 27
  modelling by business lines 51–3, 59
  monitoring by business units 109–10
  reporting 84
  translation to sensitivity 41
  understanding 99
  valuation risk and 24, 27
risk factors
  addition of new business 59, 60
  appropriateness 103–4
  distribution 15, 33–4, 36, 61
  granularity 34–5, 43
  identifying 15, 17–31, 33, 34–5
  idiosyncratic *see* idiosyncratic risk
  information workflow 58
  liquidity and 24
  risk reconciliation 135, 136–8
  sensitivity source *see* sensitivity subdivision 33
  systematic *see* systematic risk
  systemic *see* systemic risk
  see also root-risk factors
risk information bus 112–4, 220, 221
risk intelligence
  ratings 227–30
  requirement for 9–10, 199
  Risk Bus 220–1
  see also information workflow
risk management
  'Chinese Wall' 65, 68
  as communications media 198–9
  cost 197
  delegation 42, 45, 50
  development 6–7
  disclosure of framework 199–200, 201, 204
  dynamic nature 2, 126–7
  efficiency 109

establishing new culture 8, 11, 53–4, 56, 61–2
evolution 3–6, 72, 89
fundamental principles 243
hierarchy 127–9
human dimension 10–2
impact of VaR 4
isolation from business 4, 52, 65, 68, 85
proposed methodology 8, 12, 61–3
responsibility for 14–5, 18, 84–5
traditional approach 51–3, 59–60, 76
Risk Management Departments
  communication 85
  methodology responsibilities 70, 74
  mitigation strategies 75, 76
  risk aggregation 35
  role 33, 62, 65, 69
  scenario preparation 43, 45
  transparency responsibilities 70, 87
risk managers
  adaptation to culture 85
  aggregation of scenarios 62
  indifference to risk 85
  role 54, 56, 62, 71
risk methodologies
  auditing 73–4, 81–2, 83, 86–7
  feedback 98
  reporting 87–8
risk monitoring, data analysis 54–6
risk policies
  compliance 89
  concentrations and 173
  contents 99
  disclosure 199–200, 201
  diversity vs standardization 37
  elements 86
  reconciliation 112, 135–45, 208
  regulatory-driven risk 144–5
  tail event reconciliation 142, 144
  valuation methodologies 142, 205
risk profile
  balance sheet structure and 209
  cyclical factors 100
  disclosure 206
  exceptional factors 100
  funding strategy as 190–2
  liquidity risk management and 190–2
  reconciliation with risk appetite 93, 99–100, 208
  structural factors 100
risk ratings 257

risk reconciliation process 135–45
  funding strategy 139–41
  information repository 58
  liquidity management 139–41
  qualitative factors 138–9
  quantitative elements 136–8
  regulatory risk 144–5
  shareholders with company risk profile 99–100
  systematic risk 141–4
  transparency 208
risk targets
  distribution 97
  expression 78
  management level 78–9
  operational unit level 77–8
  overriding limits 102
  responsibility for compliance 69–70
  setting 76, 86, 97
  triggers and alerts 58
  use 41
risk units *see* business units
risk-adjusted return on capital (RAROC) 84, 89
risk-adjusted return on risk-adjusted capital (RARORAC) 89
risk-free clearing houses 217–8
risk-weighted capital 90
risk-weighted performance 89
  business resilience and 93
  mark to time-weighted volatility 91–3
  measurement 90–3
  proposed methodology 65–6
RiskMetrics 3
rogue traders 68, 72, 208
root-risk factors 20–4
  back-testing 38–9
  changing nature 21, 37–8
  identification 35–7, 61, 162
  liquidity risk management and 170–1
  maintaining 37–9
  monitoring 20, 21

Sarbanes Oxley Act 2002 221
scenario-based aggregations of sensitivity (SBAS) 45–6, 47
scenarios
  certification 110–1
  definition and ownership 43, 45
  disclosure 205–6
  feedback 111–2

  purpose 41–2
  refinement 43, 44
  as reflection of risk appetite 247, 248
  risk reconciliation 136–8
  sensitivity estimation 35, 36, 45, 62
  storage 58
  stress-testing 43, 47–8
  see also catastrophic scenarios
selective market efficiency 21–3
sensitivity
  aggregation 43, 45–7, 62
  appropriateness 103–4
  at management level 79
  cross-asset aggregation 115–7
  cross-division aggregation 117–22
  dynamic assessment 102–4
  dynamic control 76–7
  liquidity risk and 27
  measurement 91
  risk reconciliation 136–8
  root-risk factors *see* root-risk factors
  scenario estimations 35, 36, 45, 62
  thresholds 105–6, 128
  valuation risk and 24, 27
shareholders
  appetite for risk *see* risk policies
  communications 193–4, 207–10
  reporting to 80–1, 84, 131
  risk control role 83–4
short-term investments 91–2
side effects, disclosure 206–7
simulations, cross-industry 257–9
specific risk factors *see* idiosyncratic risk
Standard Chartered Bank 18
standardization *see* uniformity
stochastic supply curves 155
stress testing
  disclosure 210
  hedge performance 78
  importance 105
  limitations 132–3, 257–9
  scenarios 43, 47–8
surveillance systems 223–5, 226
systematic risk 17, 27–31
  correlation monitoring 29–31
  definition 28, 141
  external risks 28–9
  liquidity 160–1
  reform proposals 232, 251–6
  risk reconciliation 141–4
  sources 141, 143, 241

systemic risk 17
  causes 135, 239–41
  cross-industry simulations 257–9
  cross-industry transaction control 257
  exposure netting 257
  reform proposals 232, 256–9
  standardization and 37, 144, 168, 232, 239–40, 241

tail events
  effect 133
  risk policy reconciliation 142, 144–5
  successful management 104, 107
  unwilling exposure 144–5
tail risks 42, 62, 234, 243
  see also catastrophic scenarios
Taleb, N. 3–4
taxonomy of products 225–7, 230, 244
technology
  impact on information flow 22–3
  as operational risk 122
thresholds 105–6, 128
top-down information workflow 95–6, 97
  dynamic nature 126–7
  example 126–7
  hierarchical decision model 127–9
  pre-emptive decision frameworks 124–6
  risk dashboards 123–4
  triggers and responses 126–7
transparency
  achieving 18
  asset management 211
  audits 74, 87
  corporate governance rules 221–2
  counterparty risk 167
  enhancing 194
  external communications 221–2
  importance of 215
  information workflow 126
  internal process and procedures 218–21
  meaning 41, 215
  prices and valuations 215–8
  reporting 87–8
  responsibility for 70, 87
  as strategic corporate goal 195
triggers 58, 96–7, 101–2, 105–6, 110, 126–7

UCITS III 167, 211–2, 240
uniformity
  regulatory role 5, 241

as risk concentrator 62, 241, 243
as systemic risk source 37, 144, 168, 232, 239–40, 241

valuation
  accuracy 104
  frequency 229–30
  non-linear 151–2
  over-the-counter markets 120–1
  reconciliation with risk policy 142, 205
  transparency 215–8
valuation risk
  audit 87
  control 96
  corporate governance and 184
  counterparty-related risk 183–4
  enterprise-wide 119–21
  identifying 24–6
  impact 25
  importance 26
  as a liquidity risk 155–6, 171
  liquidity risk management and 159–60, 181–4
  as liquidity risk source 151–2
  market depth and 151, 156–7, 158, 182–3
  proposed methodology 62
  risk classes 228
  risk ratings 227–8
value-at-risk (VaR) 46–7
  convexity and 180
  correlations 118
  development 3–4
  limitations 52, 103, 115, 139
  uses 53, 117, 123, 126
variable capital adequacy ratio 90
volatility
  dynamic risk management 107–8
  effect on markets 22
  impact of timeframe 92–3
  mark to time-weighted 91–3
  market efficiency and 66
  measurement 91–3
  systematic risk and 28
volatility surfaces 134

worst case scenarios see catastrophic scenarios

yield curves 134